Berichte aus der Mathematik

Ulrich Horst

Asymptotics of Locally and Globally Interacting Markov Chains Arising in Microstructure Models of Financial Markets

Shaker Verlag
Aachen 2001

Die Deutsche Bibliothek - CIP-Einheitsaufnahme

Horst, Ulrich:
Asymptotics of Locally and Globally Interacting Markov Chains Arising in Microstructure Models of Financial Markets / Ulrich Horst.
Aachen : Shaker, 2001
(Berichte aus der Mathematik)
Zugl.: Berlin, Humboldt-Univ., Diss., 2000
ISBN 3-8265-8534-8

1. Gutachter: Prof. Dr. Hans Föllmer (Humboldt-Universität zu Berlin)
2. Gutachter: Prof. Dr. Hans-Otto Georgii (Ludwig-Maximilians-Universität München)
3. Gutachter: Prof. José-Alexander Scheinkman, Ph.D. (Princeton University)
4. Gutachter: Prof. Dr. Martin Schweizer (Technische Universität Berlin)

Tag der mündlichen Prüfung: 20. November 2000

Printed in Germany.

ISBN 3-8265-8534-8
ISSN 0945-0882

Shaker Verlag GmbH • P.O. BOX 1290 • D-52013 Aachen
Phone: 0049/2407/9596-0 • Telefax: 0049/2407/9596-9
Internet: www.shaker.de • eMail: info@shaker.de

To my parents

Preface

In mathematical finance, the price process of a risky assert is usually modeled as the trajectory of a stochastic process on some underlying probability space $(\Omega, \mathcal{F}, \mathbb{P})$. Such a probabilistic approach was first initiated by Bachelier (1900) who introduced Brownian motion as a model for price fluctuations on the Paris stock exchange. Since asset prices should stay positive, Samuelson (1964) suggested to use instead geometric Brownian motion. This financial market model has become a canonical reference model in the analysis of financial price fluctuations. In particular, Black and Scholes (1973) developed their celebrated approach to price and hedge option in the context of this model. Kreps (1982) showed that such a diffusion model can be justified as the rational expectation equilibrium in a market with highly rational and sophisticated agents who all believe in this kind of price dynamics.

Traders, by contrast, consider financial markets as being much less rational. Many practitioners believe that herd effects unrelated to economic fundamentals can cause bubbles or crashes. In particular, they are typically aware of the fact that asset prices may be driven by sudden shifts in the sentiment of investors. In view of such market realities, it seems natural to regard price processes as the result of an interaction between many agents with bounded rationality. When the number of agents involved in the formation of stock prices becomes large, such an approach allows to bring in techniques from Markov random field theory or from the theory of interacting Markov processes. In models motivated by statistical mechanics, one typically has in mind local forms of interaction. For applications in economics, however, it makes immediate sense to introduce at time an additional dependence on macroscopic quantities into the interaction as agents are directly affected by signals about aggregate quantities. This information is carried by, e.g., the empirical distribution of individual agents' characteristics.

In this thesis, we study some aspects of the asymptotic behaviour of interactive Markov chains on infinite product spaces. We consider Markov chains with an interactive dynamics where the interaction has both a local and a global component. The asymptotic behaviour of such Markov chains is analyzed on the microscopic level and on the macroscopic level of empirical fields.

We use Markov chains with an interactive dynamics as a mathematical framework for analyzing the asymptotic behaviour of asset prices in a financial market model where the demand results from the interaction of a large number of traders. Assuming a simple log-linear structure for individual excess demand leads to a class of log-linear asset price processes in a random environment where the environment is generated by an underlying Markov chain with an interactive dynamics. In the context of such a model, we study the long run behaviour of stock prices. In particular, we state conditions which guarantee that the price process converges to a stationary regime. Nonetheless, simulations show that asset prices may be subject to large and sudden fluctuations. These fluctuations do not necessarily reflect rational adjustments to new economic fundamentals but may be due to a sudden shift in the "mood" of the market.

The present book is a revised version of my doctoral thesis submitted to the Humboldt–University of Berlin. It is a pleasure to express my deep gratitude to my supervisor Hans Föllmer who accompanied me in my fascinating journey into mathematical finance and Markov random field theory and who generously shared with me his knowledge and his general view of probability theory. Especially, I would like to thank him for his patience, for numerous suggestions and for many motivating inputs.

I am grateful to Hans-Otto Georgii, José-Alexander Scheinkman and Martin Schweizer for readily accepting to task of being co-examiners. Furthermore, I am deeply indebted to my colleagues and friends Dirk Becherer, Felix Esche, Peter Leukert, Alexander Schied and Ching-Tang Wu for all their help and support on my thesis. Special merit goes to Peter Bank for innumerable and fruitful discussions.

A final thanks must of course got to my parents for all their love and generous support.

Financial support by the Deutsche Forschungsgemeinschaft through SFB 373 ("Quantification and Simulation of Economic Processes") is gratefully acknowledged.

Berlin, December 2000 Ulrich Horst

Contents

Introduction **1**

1 The Microeconomic Setup **9**

1.1 Asset Prices as Temporary Equilibria . . . 9

1.2 The Dynamics of Individual States . . . 15

1.2.1 Interaction in a Deterministic Environment . . . 16

1.2.2 Interaction in a Random Environment . . . 23

2 Local and Global Interaction in a Deterministic Environment **25**

2.1 Macroscopic Interaction . . . 26

2.2 A strong Law of large Numbers for Ergodic Empirical Fields . . . 31

2.3 Convergence Theorems . . . 37

2.3.1 Macroscopic Convergence . . . 43

2.3.2 Microscopic Convergence . . . 56

2.3.3 Asymptotic Dynamics in Mean-Field-Models . . . 61

2.4 Some Comments on the Induced Driving Sequence of the Asset Price Process . . . 63

3 Local and Global Interaction in a Random Environment **69**

3.1 Constant External Conditions . . . 71

3.1.1 Dynamics of the Macroscopic Process . . . 74

3.1.2 Dynamics of the Microscopic Process . . . 85

3.1.3 Some Comments on the Induced Driving Sequence of the Asset Price Process . . . 102

3.2 Random External Conditions . . . 107

4 Dynamics of Equilibrium Prices 111

4.1 Discrete-Time Models 113

4.1.1 Equilibrium Prices in a Stationary Environment 113

4.1.2 The Stochastic Equation $P_{t+1} = A_t P_t + B_t$ in a Non-Stationary Environment 115

4.1.3 Equilibrium Prices in a Non-Stationary Environment 138

4.2 Continuous-Time Models 143

4.2.1 Continuous-Time Models in a Stationary Environment 144

4.2.2 Continuous-Time Models in a Non-stationary Environment . 150

4.2.3 Diffusion Approximation of the Price Process in a Financial Market Model with Interacting Agents – Some Case Studies . 154

4.3 Numerical Simulations 156

A Random Systems with Complete Connections 159

Bibliography 165

Index of Notation 169

Introduction

In this book, we analyze some aspects of the long run behaviour of Markov chains on an infinite product space of the form $S = C^{\mathbb{A}}$, where C is a finite state space and $\mathbb{A}$ is a countably infinite set. We will interpret $\mathbb{A}$ as a set of agents who are active on a financial market and C as a set of individual states. We consider Markov chains with an interactive dynamics describing the stochastic evolution of the individual states of all the agents. The behaviour of an agent $a \in \mathbb{A}$ is influenced both by the local situation in some neighborhood $N(a)$ and by the average situation throughout the whole population. If the agents are located on the d-dimensional integer lattice the average situation in the whole system can be described by the empirical distribution of individual agents' states $\varrho(x)$ associated with the configuration $x = (x^a)_{a \in \mathbb{A}}$ or, more completely, by the empirical field $R(x)$ viewed as an ergodic probability measure on the configuration space S. In such a framework, we analyze the long run behaviour of the Markov chain $\{x_t\}_{t \in \mathbb{N}}$, both on a microscopic level and on the macroscopic level of empirical fields.

In Chapter 2, we consider situations where the empirical fields evolve in a deterministic manner, due to a spatial law of large numbers. We use a variant of the Dobrushin-Vasserstein contraction technique in order to analyze the interplay between macroscopic and microscopic convergence. In Chapter 3, we assume that individual agents do not observe directly the aggregate behaviour. Instead, they receive some signal whose law depends on the empirical field In this context, we use results from the theory of random systems with complete connections in order to study the asymptotics of the Markov chain $\{x_t\}_{t \in \mathbb{N}}$.

We are going to use such Markov chains, where the interaction has both a local and a global component, as a mathematical framework for analyzing the log run behaviour of asset prices in a microeconomic model where demand results from the interaction of a large number of traders. Under simplifying assumptions on the preferences of the agents the market clearing condition generates a logarithmic price dynamics of the form

$$P_{t+1} = A_t P_t + B_t \qquad (t \in \mathbb{N}) \tag{1}$$

where the stochastic process $\{(A_t, B_t)\}_{t\in\mathbb{N}}$ is generated by the sequence of empirical fields $\{R(x_t)\}_{t\in\mathbb{N}}$. Thus, logarithmic prices may be viewed as a linear recursive sequence in a random environment.

The asymptotic behaviour of solutions of a recursive linear equation $\{P_t\}_{t\in\mathbb{N}}$ of the form (1) in a random environment $\{(A_t, B_t)\}_{t\in\mathbb{N}}$ has been extensively investigated in the literature; see Borovkov (1998). For example, Brandt (1986) discusses convergence of the sequence $\{P_t\}_{t\in\mathbb{N}}$ governed by (1) under the assumption that the environment is stationary and ergodic. For our purposes, however, such a stationarity assumption is rather restrictive. Instead, we will only assume that the environment becomes stationary in the long run. Under this assumption, we prove in Chapter 4 that the sequence $\{P_t\}_{t\in\mathbb{N}}$ converges to a stationary regime, given that the destabilizing effects of the random environment are on average not too strong.

Before we describe our mathematical results in greater detail, let us first explain the economic motivation for this thesis. In mathematical finance, the price process of a risky assert is usually modeled as the trajectory of a stochastic process on some underlying probability space $(\Omega, \mathcal{F}, \mathbb{P})$. Such a probabilistic approach was first initiated by Bachelier (1900) who introduced Brownian motion as a model for price fluctuations on the Paris stock exchange. Since asset prices should stay positive, Samuelson (1964) suggested to use instead geometric Brownian motion. This model has become a canonical reference model in the analysis of financial price fluctuations.

However, since prices are generated by the demand of agents who are active on the financial market, such an approach should be supported by a microeconomic model of interacting agents. One possibility is to justify geometric Brownian motion as an rational expectation equilibrium in a market with highly sophisticated agents; see, e.g., Kreps (1982) or Bick (1987). Such models assume identical investors who share the same expectations about a future asset price, and who instantaneously and rationally discount all market information into the present price. From this theoretic point of view, large and sudden price fluctuations reflect rational changes in the valuation of an asset rather than irrational shifts in sentiment of investors.

Traders, by contrast, consider financial markets as being much less rational. Many practitioners believe that technical trading is possible, that some kind of "market psychology" exists and that herd effects unrelated to economic fundamentals can cause bubbles or crashes. In particular, traders are typically aware of the fact that asset prices may be driven by sudden shifts in the "mood" of the market. In view of such market realities, it seems natural to regard price processes as the result of an interaction between many agents with bounded rationality. In particular, one should admit imitation and contagion effects in the formation of agents' expectations. When the number of agents involved in the formation of stock prices becomes large, such an approach allows to bring in techniques from the theory of interacting Markov processes or from Markov random field theory. An early attempt into this direction has been made by Föllmer (1974) who considers a static model of endogenous preference formation. Other examples of applications of statistical mechanics models in economics include production and inventory dynamics (Bak, Chen, Scheinkman, and Woodford (1993)), business cycles (Durlauf (1993)) and game theory (Blume (1993)).

In this thesis, we introduce a mathematical framework which allows us to analyze the long run behaviour of an asset price process in a financial market model where many agents interact both locally and globally. Our idea is to view the price process of a risky asset as a sequence of temporary price equilibria. More precisely, we shall assume that the excess demand of agent a in period t depends on his individual state x_t^a at that date. Economically, different individual states may reflect different expectations about the future evolution of the price process of a risky asset. For example, there may be optimistic and pessimistic fundamental traders involved in the formation of equilibrium prices. The expectation of a fundamental trader typically is based on the idea that the next price will move closer to his current subjective perception of the fundamental value of the asset. In addition, there is usually a certain fraction of "chartists" active on the market who believe that technical trading is possible and who try to forecast the future evolution of the price process by a simple extrapolation of previous asset prices.

Such a distinction between different individual states describing, for example, different expectations about the future evolution of asset prices, has been a major topic in the recent literature on financial markets and on dynamic microeconomic models; see, e.g., Black (1986), Brock (1991), Durlauf (1993), Ioannides (1995), Kirman (1993), Kirman (1998), Lux (1998) or Lux and Marchesi (1999). It makes economic sense to assume that the price expectation of an agent $a \in \mathbb{A}$ for the following period depends both on the average expectation in the whole population and on the expectations of the agents in his neighborhood $N(a)$. More precisely, for a given configuration of individual states $x = (x^a)_{a \in \mathbb{A}}$ we shall assume that the law of the state of an agent $a \in \mathbb{A}$ in the following period depends on the current states $(x^b)_{b \in N(a)}$ of his neighbors and on the average situation in the whole system described by the empirical field $R(x)$.

The dynamics of the price process $\{p_t\}_{t \in \mathbb{N}}$ will then be induced by the sequence $\{x_t\}_{t \in \mathbb{N}} = \{(x_t^a)_{a \in \mathbb{A}}\}_{t \in \mathbb{N}}$ which describes the stochastic evolution of all the individual states. If the evolution of the empirical distribution of the agents' states is the only component affecting the formation of temporary price equilibria, then the market clearing condition of zero total excess demand yields a recursive relation of the form

$$p_{t+1} = F(\varrho(x_{t+1}), p_t) \qquad (t \in \mathbb{N}) \tag{2}$$

for the evolution of the price process. If the transformation F takes a log-linear form, then the logarithmic price process $\{P_t\}_{t \in \mathbb{N}} = \{\log p_t\}_{t \in \mathbb{N}}$ is defined recursively by the linear relation

$$P_{t+1} = f(\varrho(x_{t+1}))P_t + g(\varrho(x_{t+1})) \qquad (t \in \mathbb{N}). \tag{3}$$

Thus, logarithmic prices satisfy the recursive linear equation (1) in a random environment generated by the sequence $\{\varrho(x_t)\}_{t \in \mathbb{N}}$ of empirical distributions, i.e., by the evolution of the "mood of the market".

We are now going to describe our mathematical results in greater detail. In Chapter 2, we consider a model with locally and globally interacting agents where the dynamics on the macroscopic level of empirical fields proceeds in a deterministic manner. The dynamics of the microscopic process $\{x_t\}_{t \in \mathbb{N}}$ will be described by a Markov chain with transition probability $\Pi(x; dy)$ on the set S_0 of configurations x which admit an ergodic empirical field $R(x)$. We assume that the transition to a new configuration itself is interactive. This idea is captured by a model where the measure $\Pi(x; \cdot)$ is a Gibbs measure with respect to a local specification $\gamma^x = (\gamma_a^x)_{a \in \mathbb{A}}$. A local specification $\gamma = (\gamma_a)_{a \in \mathbb{A}}$ specifies, for any agent $a \in \mathbb{A}$, the conditional distribution of his next state, given the states of all the other agents in the following period.

The local specifications $(\gamma^x)_{x \in S_0}$ may depend on x both in a local and in a global manner. Thus, an agent $a \in \mathbb{A}$ reacts to the local situation $(x^b)_{b \in N(a)}$ of the present configuration x in a neighborhood of a and to the average situation in the whole population described by the empirical field $R(x)$. The specifications are spatially homogeneous and satisfy a Markov property of order $l \in \mathbb{N}$, both in their local dependence on the present configuration x and in their dependence on the boundary condition.

We formulate a uniform Dobrushin-type condition on the local specifications $(\gamma^x)_{x \in S_0}$ which guarantees that each random field $\Pi(x;\cdot)$ is uniquely determined by γ^x. In this case, we show that the microscopic process $\{x_t\}_{t\in\mathbb{N}}$ induces almost surely a sequence of ergodic empirical fields $\{R(x_t)\}_{t\in\mathbb{N}}$. More precisely, in Proposition 2.8 we establish a spatial law of large numbers which yields the deterministic equation

$$R(x_{t+1}) = \int_{S_0} \Pi(y;\cdot)R(x_t)(dy) =: \hat{G}(R(x_t)) \qquad \Pi(x_t;\cdot)\text{-a.s.} \tag{4}$$

for the evolution of the macroscopic process $\{R(x_t)\}_{t\in\mathbb{N}}$. Thus, the dynamics of the macroscopic process is almost surely determined by the deterministic iteration of the function $\hat{G}$ acting on empirical fields. This allows us to regard the underlying microscopic process $\{x_t\}_{t\in\mathbb{N}}$ as a Markov chain in a time-inhomogeneous but deterministic environment.

We analyze the asymptotic dynamics of the sequence $\{x_t\}_{t\in\mathbb{N}}$ both on the microscopic level and on the macroscopic level of empirical fields. In our case the kernel Π typically does not have the Feller property, due to the macroscopic dependence on the configuration x via the empirical field $R(x)$. Thus, we cannot apply the method of Vasserstein (1969) in order to establish the existence of stationary measures for the transition kernel Π. Instead, we analyze the macroscopic and the underlying microscopic process separately. Under suitable contraction conditions on the specifications, we prove in Theorem 2.24 that the macroscopic process $\{R(x_t)\}_{t\in\mathbb{N}}$ converges almost surely in the weak topology to a random field μ on S. Using a perturbation of the Dobrushin-Vasserstein contraction technique, we show in Theorem 2.29 that convergence of the macroscopic process implies local convergence of the underlying microscopic process, and that we have convergence to μ also on the microscopic level. This allows us to characterize the class of all possible limiting distributions for the Markov chain $\{x_t\}_{t\in\mathbb{N}}$ by a fixed-point property. With these results, we fill a gap in the convergence proof of Föllmer (1979a), and at the same time we extend the approach to the case of interactive transitions.

In Chapter 3, we consider a model with locally and globally interacting agents in a situation where the dynamics on the macroscopic level of empirical fields is described by a stochastic process. Given the present configuration x, individual agents do not observe directly the average situation over the whole infinite system of all agents. Instead, they receive some signal $e \in E$ whose law $Q(R(x); de)$ depends on the empirical field. The dynamics of the microscopic process $\{x_t\}_{t\in\mathbb{N}}$ will again be described by a Markov chain on the state space S_0. In Theorem 3.1, we verify that the macroscopic process is a Markov chain on the set of all ergodic probability measures on S. Under the assumption that the local interaction is not too strong, Theorem 3.10 states conditions on the stochastic kernel Q which guarantee that the macroscopic process converges in law to a unique equilibrium as $t \to \infty$. The proof uses results from the theory of random systems with complete connections. In Theorem 3.16, we show that the underlying microscopic process has local asymptotic loss of memory. Here, we use again a variant of the Dobrushin-Vasserstein contraction technique. If the macroscopic process converges to some random absorbing point, then the microscopic process converges weakly to a probability measure on S which will typically depend on the initial configuration. In a pure mean-field setting, we show that the microscopic process converges locally in the sense of a strong coupling to a stationary process if the macroscopic process is already in equilibrium. In Section 3.2, we extend our model by introducing an additional dependence of individual behaviour on random external conditions. Again, we can apply results from the theory of random systems with complete connections in order to provide conditions which guarantee that the sequence of empirical fields converges in distribution.

Chapter 4 is devoted to the analysis of the long run behaviour of solutions of stochastic recursive sequences of the form (1). In Section 4.1.1, we consider a stationary reference model, i.e, we assume that the sequence $\{\varrho(x_t)\}_{t \in \mathbb{N}}$ is stationary. In economic terms, we analyze the asymptotic dynamics of the asset price process in a financial market model with many agents in a situation where the mood of the market is already in equilibrium. In this case, we apply results provided in Borovkov (1998) in order to formulate conditions which ensure that the sequence of temporary price equilibria converges pathwise to a stationary process as $t \to \infty$. In a second step, we concentrate on log-linear dynamics in a non-stationary environment.

To this end, we analyze in Section 4.1.2 the long run behaviour of the linear stochastic sequence $\{P_t\}_{t \in \mathbb{N}}$ governed by (1) in a non-stationary random environment specified by a stochastic process $\{(A_t, B_t)\}_{t \in \mathbb{N}}$. The asymptotic dynamics of $\{P_t\}_{t \in \mathbb{N}}$ has been extensively investigated under a mean contraction condition and under the assumption that the environment is stationary. For example, Vervaat (1979) considers the case where the driving sequence consists of independent and identically distributed random variables. Brandt (1986) and Borovkov (1998) assume that the environment is stationary and ergodic, and that the destabilizing effects of the random environment are on average not too strong. In this case, one can prove pathwise convergence of the sequence $\{P_t\}_{t \in \mathbb{N}}$ to a uniquely determined stationary process.

For non-stationary driving sequences, ergodic theorems can be proved if the driving sequence converges in the sense of a strong coupling to a stationary process; see Borovkov (1998), Chapter 3.11. However, for our purposes this condition is too strong or too hard to verify. Instead, we replace the stationarity assumption by an asymptotic stability condition on the driving sequence $\{(A_t, B_t)\}_{t\in\mathbb{N}}$. We formulate conditions on the non-stationary environment which guarantee that the solution of (1) converges to a stationary regime as $t \to \infty$. In a first step, we analyze the dynamics of the process $\{P_t\}_{t\in\mathbb{N}}$ governed by (1) under the assumption that the driving sequence $\{(A_t, B_t)\}_{t\in\mathbb{N}}$ has a "nice" tail structure. In this case, we establish in Theorem 4.9 a global convergence result under a mean contraction condition on the environment as in Brandt (1986). More precisely, we prove convergence in law of the sequence $\{P_t\}_{t\in\mathbb{N}}$ governed by (1) to a uniquely determined stationary process. In a second step, we weaken the regularity condition that the driving sequence $\{(A_t, B_t)\}_{t\in\mathbb{N}}$ becomes stationary in the long run. Instead, we shall assume that the environment can be approximated in law by a sequence of "nice" processes. In this case, we establish in Theorem 4.12 a "local" version of the convergence result.

We will use this result in order to analyze the long run behaviour of the asset price process in a financial market model with many agents when the excess demand functions take a log-linear form. In such a situation the logarithmic price process $\{P_t\}_{t\in\mathbb{N}}$ is governed by the linear stochastic equation (3). Here, we combine our results about the long run behaviour of the macroscopic process $\{R(x_t)\}_{t\in\mathbb{N}}$ and about the asymptotics of the linear recursive equation $\{P_t\}_{t\in\mathbb{N}}$ governed by (1). In Theorem 4.28, we state conditions on the functions f and g which guarantee that the finite dimensional distributions of the logarithmic price process converge to the finite dimensional distributions of a uniquely determined stationary process.

A large part of mathematical finance is based on models with continuous-time security trading. Thus, it seems natural to study a diffusion approximation of our discrete-time price process $\{p_t\}_{t\in\mathbb{N}}$. In Chapter 4.2, we show how the price dynamics described by (3) converges to a Black-Scholes type diffusion with deterministic volatility. Under the assumption that the microscopic process induces a stationary mood of the market, we follow the approach taken by Föllmer and Schweizer (1993). In Section 4.2.2, we consider the general linear stochastic equation (1) and obtain a diffusion approximation in a non-stationary environment which has a "nice" asymptotic behaviour. Thus, a price dynamics of the log-linear form (3) can be approximated by a diffusion process with deterministic volatility if the driving sequence has a "nice" asymptotic behaviour.

Chapter 1

The Microeconomic Setup

1.1 Asset Prices as Temporary Equilibria

Let us describe a temporary equilibrium model for the price evolution of a speculative asset. We consider a financial market model with a countably infinite set $\mathbb{A}$ of economic agents trading a single risky asset. In reaction to a proposed stock price p in period t, each agent $a \in \mathbb{A}$ forms an excess demand $z_t^a(p)$. Individual excess demand at time t is to be thought of as the difference between individual demand and individual initial endowment in period t. The actual stock price p_t at date t will be determined by the equilibrium condition of zero total excess demand, and so the price process will be given by a sequence of temporary price equilibria $\{p_t\}_{t \in \mathbb{N}}$. We assume that the **excess demand** of an individual agent $a \in \mathbb{A}$ takes the form

$$z_t^a(p) = z(p, p_t^a). \tag{1.1}$$

Here, p_t^a denotes an **individual reference level** of an agent a at date t, e.g., his price expectation for the following period $t+1$. We shall assume that agents are heterogeneous in their individual reference levels. More precisely, at any given date $t \in \mathbb{N}$, the value p_t^a depends on the present **individual state** x_t^a of agent $a \in \mathbb{A}$, on the previous equilibrium price p_{t-1} and on the proposed stock price p. Thus, it takes the form

$$p_t^a(p) = g(x_t^a, p_{t-1}, p) \tag{1.2}$$

for some measurable function $g : C \times \mathbb{R}^2 \to \mathbb{R}$. Here, we denote by

$$C := \{c_1, \ldots, c_N\} \tag{1.3}$$

a fixed **set of individual states**.

Example 1.1 *("Fundamentalists and Chartists") Let us consider a financial market model where the individual excess demand function takes the log-linear form*

$$z(p, p_t^a) = \log p_t^a - \log p \tag{1.4}$$

as in Föllmer and Schweizer (1993). We put $C = \{-1, 0, +1\}$ *and consider a model with optimistic* ($x_t^a = +1$) *and pessimistic* ($x_t^a = -1$) *information traders ("fundamentalists") and with chartists* ($x_t^a = 0$).

Independent of the proposed stock price p*, the individual reference level of an information trader takes the form*

$$\log p_t^a(p) = \log p_{t-1} + c_f(\log L + x_t^a - \log p_{t-1}) \qquad (c_f > 0). \tag{1.5}$$

Thus, the expectation of an information trader is based on the idea that the next price will move closer to his current subjective perception $\log L + x_t^a$ *of the fundamental value of the asset at time* t.

The chartist, on the other hand, takes the proposed price as a serious signal about the future evolution of the security price and replaces L *in (1.5) by* p*. Thus, his price expectation takes the form*

$$\log p_t^a(p) = \log p_{t-1} + c_c(\log p - \log p_{t-1}) \qquad (c_c > 0). \tag{1.6}$$

In our model, the dynamics of the price process will be induced by an underlying **microscopic process** $\{x_t\}_{t\in\mathbb{N}} = \{(x_t^a)_{a\in\mathbb{A}}\}_{t\in\mathbb{N}}$ which describes the stochastic evolution of all the individual states. The process $\{x_t\}_{t\in\mathbb{N}}$ takes values in the **configuration space**

$$S := C^{\mathbb{A}} = \{x = (x^a)_{a\in\mathbb{A}} : x^a \in C\}. \tag{1.7}$$

We shall view S as a compact metric space which is equipped with the product topology. We let $\mathcal{S}$ be the product-σ-field on S, and denote by $\mathcal{M}(S)$ the class of all probability measures on $(S, \mathcal{S})$.

Let us now concentrate on the resulting stock price process $\{p_t\}_{t\in\mathbb{N}}$. To start with, we consider a situation where only finitely many investors are active on the market. To this end, we fix a sequence $\{\mathbb{A}_n\}_{n\in\mathbb{N}}$ of finite subsets of $\mathbb{A}$ which satisfies $\mathbb{A}_n \uparrow \mathbb{A}$ as $n \uparrow \infty$. If only the traders in $\mathbb{A}_n$ are active on the market, the equilibrium stock price p_t^n at date t is determined by the market clearing condition of zero total excess demand, i.e., p_t^n is given by an implicit solution of the equation

$$\sum_{a\in\mathbb{A}_n} z_t^a(p_t^n) = 0. \tag{1.8}$$

In view of (1.1) and (1.2), and in terms of per capita excess demand, we can rewrite (1.8) as

$$\int_C z(p_t^n, g(c, p_{t-1}^n, p_t^n))\varrho^n(x_t)(dc) = 0. \tag{1.9}$$

Here,

$$\varrho^n(x_t) := \frac{1}{|\mathbb{A}_n|} \sum_{a \in \mathbb{A}_n} \delta_{x_t^a}(\cdot) \in \mathcal{M}(C) \tag{1.10}$$

denotes the empirical distribution of the states assumed by the traders $a \in \mathbb{A}_n$ in period t, and $\mathcal{M}(C)$ is the class of all probability measures on C.

For any $n \in \mathbb{N}$, the implicit equation (1.9) defines the sequence of temporary equilibrium prices $\{p_t^n\}_{t\in\mathbb{N}}$ in the case of a finite set $\mathbb{A}_n$ of traders who are involved in the formation of equilibrium prices. In order to extend the construction of equilibrium prices to the infinite system of all agents, we are going to restrict our state space S to a class S_0 of "regular" configurations $x = (x^a)_{a\in\mathbb{A}} \in S$ such that, for all $x \in S_0$, the **empirical distribution**

$$\varrho(x) := \lim_{n\to\infty} \varrho^n(x) \tag{1.11}$$

exists; the precise definition of the set S_0 is given in (1.30) below. We will call $\varrho(x_t)$ the **mood of the market** at time t.

We are now ready to define the equilibrium price p_t at date t. In the limit of an infinite set of agents, p_t will be given as an implicit solution of the equation

$$\int_C z(p_t, g(c, p_{t-1}, p_t))\varrho(x_t)(dc) = 0 \tag{1.12}$$

which is the limiting form of (1.9). In order to obtain a uniquely defined stock price process, we impose the following condition on the excess demand function z:

Assumption 1.2 *There exists a measurable function $F : \mathcal{M}(C) \times \mathbb{R} \to \mathbb{R}$ such that the implicit equation*

$$\int_C z(p^*, g(c, p, p^*))\varrho(dc) = 0 \tag{1.13}$$

admits a unique solution

$$p^* = F(\varrho, p) \tag{1.14}$$

for any pair $(\varrho, p) \in \mathcal{M}(C) \times \mathbb{R}$.

Example 1.3 *Let us return to the log-linear demand structure described by (1.4) together with (1.5) and (1.6). For a given configuration $x_t \in S_0$, the empirical* *distribution $\varrho(x_t)$ is described by the proportions ϱ_t^+, ϱ_t^- and ϱ_t^0 of optimistic and pessimistic fundamentalists and of chartists. In the limit of an infinite set of agents the market clearing condition (1.12) implies the following linear structure for the evolution of the logarithmic stock price process:*

$$\log p_{t+1} = f(\varrho(x_{t+1})) \log p_t + g(\varrho(x_{t+1})), \tag{1.15}$$

where

$$f(\varrho(x_t)) := \frac{1 - c_f(\varrho_t^+ - \varrho_t^-) - c_c\varrho_t^0}{1 - c_c\varrho_t^0}, \quad g(\varrho(x_t)) := \frac{c_f(\log L + \varrho_t^+ - \varrho_t^-)}{1 - c_c\varrho_t^0}. \tag{1.16}$$

Thus, at any given date t, the equilibrium price p_t depends continuously on the mood of the market $\varrho(x_t)$ if the fraction of chartist who are active in the market always exceeds or always remains below the value $\frac{1}{c_c}$. In this case, we will prove in Section 4.1 that the sequence $\{\log p_t\}_{t\in\mathbb{N}}$ becomes stationary in the long run if the mood of the market settles down as $t \to \infty$.

Given that our Assumption 1.2 holds true, the stock price process $\{p_t\}_{t\in\mathbb{N}}$ is defined by the recursive relation

$$p_{t+1} = F(\varrho(x_{t+1}), p_t) \qquad (t = 0, 1, 2, \ldots). \tag{1.17}$$

In our present setting, the evolution of the empirical distribution of agents' states is the only component affecting the formation of temporary price equilibria. Thus, the process $\{x_t\}_{t\in\mathbb{N}}$ generates – via the aggregate quantities $\{\varrho(x_t)\}_{t\in\mathbb{N}}$ – an **endogenous environment** for the evolution of the stock price process.

Example 1.4 *Let us illustrate how our approach fits into the utility maximization setting analyzed in, e.g., Brock and Hommes (1995) or in Kirman (1998).*

We consider a binary choice model, i.e., $C = \{0, +1\}$ and choose a special (excess) demand function z derived from a standard mean-variance utility maximization problem. For each agent $a \in \mathbb{A}$ and a for any given price process $\{p_t\}_{t\in\mathbb{N}}$, the dynamics of his wealth process $\{W_t^a\}_{t=0,1,2,\ldots}$ takes the form

$$W_{t+1}^a = (1+r)W_t^a + (p_{t+1} - (1+r)p_t)z_t^a.$$

Here, z_t^a is the number of shares purchased at date t and r denotes the risk-free interest rate. If all investors are myopic mean variance maximizers, then the utility function of an agent $a \in \mathbb{A}$ takes the form

$$U^a(z_t^a) = \mathbb{E}_t^a(W_{t+1}^a) - \frac{\eta^a}{2}\mathbb{V}_t^a(W_{t+1}^a),$$

where $\mathbb{E}_t^a$ and $\mathbb{V}_t^a$ denote the conditional expectation and the conditional variance based on the information available to this agent at time t. Thus,

$$\mathbb{V}_t^a = \mathbb{E}_t^a[(W_{t+1}^a)^2 - (\mathbb{E}_t^a W_{t+1}^a)^2].$$

The parameter η^a describes the risk aversion of the agent $a \in \mathbb{A}$. For analytical tractability, we assume that the risk aversion and the beliefs about the conditional variance of excess returns per share are the same for all investors, i.e.,

$$\eta^a = \eta, \qquad \mathbb{V}_t^a(W_{t+1}^a) = \sigma_t^2(z_t^a)^2 \qquad (a \in \mathbb{A}).$$

However, we assume that investors are heterogeneous in their expected value about the future asset price. For a proposed stock price p at time t, each agent $a \in \mathbb{A}$ forms an individual expectation $p_t^a(p)$ about the equilibrium price in the next period $t+1$. Given that the proposed stock price clears the market, i.e., in equilibrium, any agent forms an opinion about the future evolution of the asset price process and tries to maximize his expected utility. His optimal demand $\tilde{z}_t^a$ for shares at time t solves

$$\max_{z_t^a}\{\mathbb{E}_t^a(W_{t+1}^a) - \frac{\eta}{2}\mathbb{V}_t^a(W_{t+1}^a)\}.$$

Thus,

$$\tilde{z}_t^a(p) = \frac{p_t^a(p) - (1+r)p}{\eta\sigma_t^2}.$$

We assume that the individual price expectation p_t^a in period t depends on the proposed stock price p, on the previous equilibrium price p_{t-1} and on the individual state x_t^a and that it takes the form

$$p_t^a(p) = p + g(x_t^a, p_{t-1}). \tag{1.18}$$

Here, $g : [0,+1] \times \mathbb{R}^+ \to \mathbb{R}^+$ is a measurable function which is linear in the first argument.

If the total supply of the risky asset is equal to zero, then the dynamics of equilibrium prices is described as follows. In a situation where only the traders in $\mathbb{A}_n$ are active on the market, the market clearing condition (1.9) yields

$$p_t^n = \frac{1}{r}\frac{1}{|\mathbb{A}_n|}\sum_{a\in\mathbb{A}} g(x_t^a, p_{t-1}^n) = \frac{1}{r}g\left(\frac{1}{|\mathbb{A}_n|}\sum_{a\in\mathbb{A}_n} x_t^a, p_{t-1}^n\right).$$

In the limit of an infinite set of agents, the equilibrium price process takes the form

$$p_t = \frac{1}{r}g(m(x_t), p_{t-1}) =: F(\varrho(x_t), p_{t-1}),$$

due to the market clearing condition (1.12). Here, $m(x_t)$ *denotes the empirical average induced by the configuration* $x_t \in S_0$*, i.e.,* $\varrho(x_t) = (1 - m(x_t), m(x_t))$.

In a large system with a countably infinite set of traders we have a law of large numbers when the interaction between traders is not too strong and if the traders have complete information about the mood of the market at any given date t. This means that the dynamics of the mood of the market, i.e., the dynamics of the sequence of empirical distributions $\{\varrho(x_t)\}_{t \in \mathbb{N}}$ becomes deterministic; cf. (1.25) or (1.34) below. The asset price process $\{p_t\}_{t \in \mathbb{N}}$ is then uniquely determined by the transformation F, by the initial price p_0 and by the initial empirical distribution $\varrho(x_0) \in \mathcal{M}(C)$. Such a model will be analyzed in Chapter 2. If the agents do not have complete information about aggregate behaviour, i.e., about the mood of the market, then the sequence $\{\varrho(x_t)\}_{t \in \mathbb{N}}$ becomes a stochastic process. We will study such situations in Chapter 3.

Even if the microscopic process $\{x_t\}_{t \in \mathbb{N}}$ induces a deterministic sequence of empirical distributions $\{\varrho(x_t)\}_{t \in \mathbb{N}}$, it may make economic sense to model the sequence of temporary price equilibria $\{p_t\}_{t \in \mathbb{N}}$ as a stochastic process. For example, we might view the subsystem $A_t \subset \mathbb{A}$ of agents who are directly involved in the formation of price equilibria at date t as a randomly drawn large but finite set of representative agents in $\mathbb{A}$. By saying that A_t is a set of representative agents we mean that the empirical distribution $\tilde{\varrho}_t$ of the states assumed by the traders in A_t is a random variable whose law depends on the current mood of the market. Though randomness on the level of empirical distributions may disappear in the infinite system of all traders, it is still present in the smaller set A_t of agents who are active on the market. Thus, we shall admit an additional source of randomness in the formation of stock prices. We will assume that the sequence $\{p_t\}_{t \in \mathbb{N}}$ is driven by a stochastic process $\{\tilde{\varrho}_t\}_{t \in \mathbb{N}}$ taking values in $\mathcal{M}(C)$. The conditional law

$$\tilde{Q}(\varrho(x_t); \cdot) \tag{1.19}$$

of the random variable $\tilde{\varrho}_t$ given the present mood of the market $\varrho(x_t)$, is described by a stochastic kernel $\tilde{Q}$ on $\mathcal{M}(C)$. In this case, the price process obeys a recursive relation of the form

$$p_{t+1} = F(\tilde{\varrho}_{t+1}, p_t) \qquad (t = 0, 1, 2, \ldots). \tag{1.20}$$

Of course, the dynamical model (1.17) corresponds to the case $\tilde{Q}(\varrho; \cdot) = \delta_\varrho(\cdot)$.

Our goal is to analyze the long run behaviour of the price process. To this end, we have to analyze the asymptotics of the driving sequence $\{\tilde{\varrho}_t\}_{t\in\mathbb{N}}$. In the next section, we begin by describing the dynamics of the microscopic process $\{x_t\}_{t\in\mathbb{N}}$.

Suppose that our microscopic process is such that the mood of the market is already in equilibrium, i.e., assume that the sequence $\{x_t\}_{t\in\mathbb{N}}$ induces a stationary process $\{\varrho(x_t)\}_{t\in\mathbb{N}}$. Then the environment for the evolution of the price process $\{\tilde{\varrho}_t\}_{t\in\mathbb{N}}$ is also stationary. In this case, we will show in Section 4.1.1 that the price process itself becomes stationary in the long run whenever the random environment is on average not too destabilizing. However, a stationarity assumption on the process $\{\varrho(x_t)\}_{t\in\mathbb{N}}$ is rather restrictive. In Chapters 2 and 3 we will formulate conditions which guarantee that the sequence of empirical distributions $\{\varrho(x_t)\}_{t\in\mathbb{N}}$ settles down in the long run as $t \to \infty$. In this case, and for a price dynamics of the log-linear form (1.15), we prove in Section 4.1.3 that the price process converges to a stationary regime if the destabilizing effects of the random environment are on average not too strong.

1.2 The Dynamics of Individual States

In this section, we describe the dynamics of our microscopic process. We assume that, in each period t, any agent $a \in \mathbb{A}$ chooses his next state x^a_{t+1} at random according to some probability law which depends on the present configuration of individuals states $x_t = (x^a_t)_{a\in\mathbb{A}}$. This dependence can have both a local and a global component. Local dependence in the choice of an individual agent $a \in \mathbb{A}$ refers to dependence of the law on some set of **neighbors** $b \in N(a)$. Thus, introducing the notion of local interaction means to endow the countable set $\mathbb{A}$ with the structure of a graph, where the agents are the nodes and where interactive links between certain pairs of agents exist. Since we focus on the joint effect of local and global interaction, we will need to consider ergodic averages over the whole graph of agents. Therefore, we limit ourselves to the case best understood so far, where $\mathbb{A}$ carries a lattice structure. Thus, we assume that the agents are located on the d-dimensional integer lattice, i.e., $\mathbb{A} := \mathbb{Z}^d$.

The neighborhood $N(a)$ of an agent $a \in \mathbb{A}$ is given by the set

$$N(a) := \{b \in \mathbb{A} : |a - b| \leq l < \infty\}. \tag{1.21}$$

Here, $|\cdot|$ denotes the Euclidean distance on $\mathbb{R}^d$ and $l \in \mathbb{N}$ is a fixed "interaction radius". In terms of such neighborhoods we can now model situations where the current reference level p^a_{t+1} of agent a, e.g., his expectation about the future evolution of the stock price, is influenced by the previous states $(x^b_t)_{b\in N(a)}$ of his neighbors. For example, this allows agents to imitate the behaviour of their friends. Observe that in our model any agent affects the next state of just 2^{dl} other persons, and so no individual trader is able to influence the mood of the whole market in one single period. In this sense, we consider a financial market model with many small investors.

In contrast to models in statistical physics where the emphasis is on dynamics with local interaction, for applications in economics it makes immediate sense to introduce at the same time an additional dependence on macroeconomic information into the interaction. Below, this will be specified in terms of, e.g., the empirical distribution $\varrho(x)$ of individual agents' states.

1.2.1 Interaction in a Deterministic Environment

We are now going to describe the dynamics of the microscopic process $\{x_t\}_{t\in\mathbb{N}}$ in a financial market model with locally and globally interacting agents in a deterministic environment. In a first step, we shall assume, as in Föllmer (1994), that different agents make their transitions to a new state independently of each other, given the present configuration $x \in S$. In this case, it is enough to observe the individual agents and to determine, separately for any trader $a \in \mathbb{A}$, his probability law $\pi^a(x;\cdot)$ on C. The individual distributions $(\pi^a(x;\cdot))_{a\in\mathbb{A}}$ specify the law of the configuration in the following period. More precisely, our microscopic process will be described by a Markov chain with transition kernel

$$\Pi(x; dy) = \prod_{a\in\mathbb{A}} \pi^a(x; dy^a) \tag{1.22}$$

on the product space $S = C^{\mathbb{A}}$. Later, we will concentrate on models with interactive transition probabilities which include (1.22) as a special case. In such a setting, it is not enough to specify, separately for any trader $a \in \mathbb{A}$, his distribution $\pi^a(x;\cdot)$ on C. In addition, one has to have information about the joint behaviour of any coalition $A \subset \mathbb{A}$ in order to describe the transition to a new configuration.

In the next subsection, we shall illustrate our main idea by concentrating on the special case where the dynamics of the microscopic process is of mean-field type. In such a setting, we derive a macroscopic equation for the evolution of the sequence of empirical distributions $\{\varrho(x_t)\}_{t\in\mathbb{N}}$. The mood of the market at a given time $t \in \mathbb{N}$ is then almost surely determined by the initial empirical distribution $\varrho(x_0)$. This will allow us to formulate conditions which ensure that the mood of the market converges as $t \to \infty$. Later, we shall extend this model by introducing a local dependence into the interaction. In this more general case, we will typically not have a simple macroscopic equation which describes the dynamics of the mood of the market. Instead, the dynamics on an aggregate level will be described by a sequence of empirical fields $\{R(x_t)\}_{t \in \mathbb{N}}$ generated by the underlying microscopic process $\{x_t\}_{t \in \mathbb{N}}$. The empirical field $R(x)$ induced by a configuration $x \in S_0$ may be viewed as a probability measure on our configuration space $(S, \mathcal{S})$ which carries all macroeconomic information about x. The precise definition of the empirical field $R(x)$ is given in (1.30) below. In Chapter 2, we establish a macroscopic equation for the evolution of the sequence $\{R(x_t)\}_{t \in \mathbb{N}}$ and formulate conditions which guarantee that the mood of the market converges as $t \to \infty$.

Mean-Field Interaction

Let us now describe the dynamics of individual behaviour in a simple mean-field type model. In this case, the transition law π^a of an individual agent $a \in \mathbb{A}$ depends on the agent's own state x_t^a. The interactive influence of the whole configuration $x_t = (x_t^a)_{a \in \mathbb{A}}$ is felt only through the empirical distribution of individual states $\varrho(x_t)$.

In order to describe the dynamics of the microscopic process, we fix a stochastic kernel π from $C \times \mathcal{M}(C)$ to C. If the present configuration x belongs to the space S_0 of "regular" configurations given by (1.30) below, then the configuration x admits the empirical distribution $\varrho(x)$ introduced in (1.11). Thus, we can define the probability $\pi^a(x; c)$ for the state of an agent $a \in \mathbb{A}$ being $c \in C$ in the next period as

$$\pi^a(x; c) = \pi(x^a, \varrho(x); c). \tag{1.23}$$

In such a situation, the interaction is spatially homogeneous in the sense that any agent reacts in the same manner to his present state x_t^a. In Chapter 2, we will show that the measure $\Pi(x; \cdot)$ on the product space $S = C^{\mathbb{A}}$ defined by

$$\Pi(x; dy) = \prod_{a \in \mathbb{A}} \pi(x^a, \varrho(x); dy^a) \tag{1.24}$$

is concentrated on the set S_0. The microscopic process will therefore be described by a Markov chain on the state space S_0 with transition kernel Π – viewed as a stochastic kernel on S_0. In particular, the sequence $\{x_t\}_{t \in \mathbb{N}}$ induces almost surely the sequence of empirical distributions $\{\varrho(x_t)\}_{t\in\mathbb{N}}$. Using the strong law of large numbers for independent bounded random variables, the dynamics of the empirical distribution of agents' states is easily calculated.

Proposition 1.5 *For any fixed initial configuration $x \in S_0$, we have*

$$\varrho(x_{t+1})(\cdot) = \int_S \pi(y, \varrho(x_t); \cdot)\varrho(x_t)(dy) =: G(\varrho(x_t)) \qquad \Pi(x_t; \cdot)\text{-}a.s. \tag{1.25}$$

Proof: Given $x_t = (x_t^a)_{a\in\mathbb{A}} \in S_0$, the random variables $(x_{t+1}^a)_{a\in\mathbb{A}}$ are independent with distribution $\pi(x^a, \varrho(x); \cdot)$. For each $c \in C$, the law of large numbers for independent bounded entered random variables implies

$$\lim_{n\to\infty} \frac{1}{|\mathbb{A}_n|} \sum_{a\in\mathbb{A}_n} \left(\mathbf{1}_c(x_{t+1}^a) - \pi(x_t^a, \varrho(x_t); c)\right) = 0 \qquad \Pi(x_t; \cdot)\text{-a.s.}$$

along a sequence of finite subsets $\mathbb{A}_n \uparrow \mathbb{A}$. This shows that, for $\Pi(x_t; \cdot)$-almost all $x_{t+1} \in S$, the empirical distribution $\varrho(x_{t+1})$ exists and that the identification (1.25) holds true. □

As a result of Proposition 1.5, the dynamics of the mood of the market is almost surely specified by the deterministic iteration of the function G acting on empirical distributions. Thus, we can easily formulate conditions on G which guarantee that the mood of the market settles down in the long run as $t \to \infty$.

Example 1.6 *Let us put $C = \{-1, +1\}$ and assume that the conditional choice probabilities take the form of an Ising model of statistical mechanics. For a given configuration $x_t \in S_0$, the individual transition law $\pi^a(x_t; \cdot)$ of agent $a \in \mathbb{A}$ in period t takes the form*

$$\pi^a(x_t; c) = \frac{\exp\{c\beta\,(m(x_t) + x_t^a)\}}{\exp\{c\beta\,(m(x_t) + x_t^a)\} + \exp\{-c\beta\,(m(x_t) + x_t^a)\}} \qquad (\beta > 0). \tag{1.26}$$

Here, $m(x_t)$ denotes the average situation at date t, i.e.,

$$m(x_t) := \lim_{n\to\infty} \frac{1}{|\mathbb{A}_n|} \sum_{a\in\mathbb{A}_n} x_t^a, \tag{1.27}$$

and so $\varrho(x_t) = \left(\frac{1-m(x_t)}{2}, \frac{m(x_t)+1}{2}\right)$. It follows from Proposition 1.5 that the evolution of the sequence of empirical averages $\{m(x_t)\}_{t\in\mathbb{N}}$ proceeds almost surely in a deterministic manner. We have that

$$m(x_{t+1}) = \frac{m(x_t)+1}{2} g_+(m(x_t)) + \frac{1-m(x_t)}{2} g_-(m(x_t)) \qquad \Pi(x_t, \cdot)\text{-}a.s. \tag{1.28}$$

where

$$g_{\pm}(m) \quad := \quad \tanh\{\beta(m \pm 1)\}.$$

Local and Global Interaction with Independent Transition Probabilities

We are now going to introduce an additional local interaction into the individual transition dynamics. In the presence of both local and global interaction we assume that, for a given configuration $x \in S_0$, the transition law of an individual agent $a \in \mathbb{A}$ depends on

- the states $(x^b)_{b \in N(a)}$ of his neighbors
- macroscopic properties of the present configuration x, e.g., the induced empirical distribution of individual states $\varrho(x)$.

In order to specify what we mean by "macroscopic properties of the configuration x_t" we introduce the family of shift maps $\theta_a : S \to S$ $(a \in \mathbb{A})$ on the configuration space S defined by $(\theta_a x)(b) = x^{a+b}$.

Definition 1.7 *(i) A probability measure $\mu \in \mathcal{M}(S)$ is called* ***stationary****, if μ is invariant under the shift maps $(\theta_a)_{a \in \mathbb{A}}$. The class of all stationary probability measures μ on $(S, \mathcal{S})$ is denoted by $\mathcal{M}_s(S)$, i.e.,*

$$\mathcal{M}_s(S) := \{\mu \in \mathcal{M}(S) \ : \ \mu = \mu \circ \theta_a \textit{ for all } a \in \mathbb{A}\}.$$

(ii) A stationary probability measure $\mu \in \mathcal{M}_s(S)$ is called ***ergodic****, if μ satisfies a 0-1-law on the σ-field $\mathcal{J}$ of all shift invariant events. The class of all ergodic probability measures μ on $(S, \mathcal{S})$ is denoted by $\mathcal{M}_0(S)$, i.e.,*

$$\mathcal{M}_0(S) := \{\mu \in \mathcal{M}_s(S) \ : \ \mu(B) \in \{0, 1\} \textit{ for all } B \in \mathcal{J}\}.$$

For a given $n \in \mathbb{N}$, let us put

$$\mathbb{A}_n := [-n, n]^d \cap \mathbb{A}, \tag{1.29}$$

and define the set

$$S_0 := \left\{ x \in S : \exists\ R(x) := \lim_{n \to \infty} \frac{1}{|\mathbb{A}_n|} \sum_{a \in \mathbb{A}_n} \delta_{\theta_a x}(\cdot) \ \in \mathcal{M}_0(S) \right\}. \tag{1.30}$$

Thus, for any $x \in S_0$, the **empirical field** $R(x)$ associated with the configuration x exists and is ergodic. The probability measure $R(x)$ on $(S, \mathcal{S})$ carries all macroscopic information about the configuration $x = (x^a)_{a \in \mathbb{A}} \in S_0$.

Remark 1.8 *For any* $x \in S_0$, *we have* $\Pr(R(x)) = \varrho(x)$, *where*

$$\Pr : \mathcal{M}_s(S) \to \mathcal{M}(C), \qquad \mu \mapsto \mu^0 \tag{1.31}$$

denotes the projection mapping which assigns to any stationary random field μ *on* $(S, \mathcal{S})$ *its marginal distribution* μ^0 *at site* 0.

In a model with locally and globally interacting agents we could fix a stochastic kernel π from $C^{2^{dl}+1} \times \mathcal{M}_0(S)$ to C and assume that, for a given configuration $x_t \in S_0$ at date t, the law $\pi^a(x_t; \cdot)$ of the random variable x^a_{t+1} takes the form

$$\pi^a(x_t; \cdot) := \pi((x^b_t)_{b \in N(a)}, R(x_t); \cdot). \tag{1.32}$$

Later, we will concentrate on models with an interactive transition dynamics which include individual transition laws of the form (1.32) as a special case. For any agent $a \in \mathbb{A}$, the interactive influence of the whole configuration $x_t = (x^a_t)_{a \in \mathbb{A}}$ is now felt through the local situation $(x^b_t)_{b \in N(a)}$ in a neighborhood of a and through the empirical field $R(x_t)$.

In Chapter 2, we shall prove that the measure $\Pi(x_t; \cdot)$ on $(S, \mathcal{S})$ defined by

$$\Pi(x_t; dx_{t+1}) := \prod_{a \in \mathbb{A}} \pi((x^b_t)_{b \in N(a)}, R(x_t); dx^a_{t+1}) \tag{1.33}$$

is concentrated on the set S_0. Thus, our microscopic process will be described by a Markov chain on the state space S_0 with transition kernel Π – viewed as a stochastic kernel on S_0. In particular, any configuration x_t induces the ergodic empirical field $R(x_t)$, and so the microscopic process $\{x_t\}_{t \in \mathbb{N}}$ will almost surely generate the **macroscopic process** $\{R(x_t)\}_{t \in \mathbb{N}}$.

Due to the additional local interaction in the transition laws, we will typically not obtain a simple equation for the evolution of the empirical distribution of individual states. However, in Proposition 2.8 we establish a spatial law of large numbers which yields the deterministic equation

$$R(x_{t+1}) = \int_{S_0} \Pi(y; \cdot) R(x_t)(dy) =: \hat{G}(R(x_t)) \qquad \Pi(x_t; \cdot)\text{-a.s.} \tag{1.34}$$

for the evolution of the sequence of ergodic empirical fields $\{R(x_t)\}_{t \in \mathbb{N}}$. In particular, the dynamics of the macroscopic process $\{R(x_t)\}_{t \in \mathbb{N}}$ is almost surely specified by the deterministic iteration of the function $\hat{G}$ acting on empirical fields. This will allow us to formulate conditions on the individual transition laws which ensure that the sequence $\{R(x_t)\}_{t\in\mathbb{N}}$ converges in the weak topology. Due to (1.31), this implies that the mood of the market settles down as $t \to \infty$.

Local and Global Interaction with Interactive Transition Probabilities

In the dynamical model (1.33), the individual transition probabilities $(\pi^a)_{a\in\mathbb{A}}$ are interactive, but the transition itself is not since the measures $\Pi(x;\cdot)$ $(x \in S_0)$ were assumed to have a product form. Now, we want to introduce an interactive structure into the transition itself. This idea is captured by a model where the measure $\Pi(x;\cdot)$ is a Gibbs measure with respect to a local specification $\gamma^{x,R(x)}$. A local specification $\gamma = (\gamma_a)_{a\in\mathbb{A}}$ specifies, for any agent $a \in \mathbb{A}$, the conditional distribution of his state, given his microscopic environment, i.e., given the present states of all the other agents $b \neq a$.

Definition 1.9 *(i) The* ***microscopic environment*** *of an agent $a \in \mathbb{A}$ is a map $v : \mathbb{A}\backslash\{a\} \to C$ which specifies the states of all the other agents.*

(ii) The ***characteristics*** *of an agent $a \in \mathbb{A}$ is given by a probability kernel γ_a which assigns to each microscopic environment $v : \mathbb{A}\backslash\{a\} \to C$ a probability measure $\gamma_a(\cdot;v)$ on C.*

(iii) Following Föllmer (1974), we say that a probability measure μ on the configuration space $(S, \mathcal{S})$ is a ***global phase*** *of the economy, if μ is consistent with the system of characteristics $(\gamma_a)_{a\in\mathbb{A}}$ in the sense that*

$$\mu(x^a = c|v) = \gamma_a(c;v) \qquad \mu\text{-}a.s. \qquad (a \in \mathbb{A}).$$

We say that the characteristics $(\gamma_a)_{a\in\mathbb{A}}$ are consistent, if they admit at least one global phase.

Economically, a local specification describes how the current price expectation of any individual trader is affected by his microscopic environment, that is, by the actual expectations of all the other agents. In such a setting, it is not enough to determine, separately for any $a \in \mathbb{A}$, his transition law π^a. In addition, we have to know the joint behaviour of any coalition $A \subset \mathbb{A}$ in order to describe the transition to a new configuration. Observe, however, that knowledge of the characteristics γ_a of agent $a \in \mathbb{A}$ does not presume any information on the dynamics which governs his environment. In this sense, no a-priori information about aggregate behaviour is needed.

Let us now illustrate our general setting by introducing the concept of an interaction potential.

Definition 1.10 *An* ***interaction potential*** *is a family of mappings*

$$\Phi = \{\Phi_A : S \to \mathbb{R} : A \subset \mathbb{A}, |A| < \infty\}. \tag{1.35}$$

Here, the mapping Φ_A ($|A| < \infty$) is measurable with respect to the σ-field generated by the projections $x \mapsto x^a$ ($a \in A$).

Suppose that, for each configuration $x \in S_0$, we are given an interaction potential $\Phi^{x,R(x)}$. In this case, we specify the probability for the next state of an agent $a \in \mathbb{A}$ being $c \in C$, given that the previous configuration was x and given his microscopic environment v, as

$$\gamma_a^{x,R(x)}(c; v) = \frac{\exp\left(\sum_{A \ni a} \Phi_A^{x,R(x)}(v_{a,c})\right)}{\sum_{\hat{c} \in C} \exp\left(\sum_{A \ni a} \Phi_A^{x,R(x)}(v_{a,\hat{c}})\right)} \qquad (c \in C). \tag{1.36}$$

Here, the configuration $v_{a,c} = (v^b_{a,c})_{b \in \mathbb{A}}$ is given by $v^b_{a,c} = v^b$ for $b \neq a$ and $v^b_{a,c} = c$ if $b = a$.

Example 1.11 *Suppose that agents interact only with their nearest neighbors, i.e., let $l = 1$. We assume that the conditional probabilities characterizing the individual transition laws take the form of an Ising model of statistical mechanics. For a given configuration $x \in S_0$, the interaction potential $\Phi^{x,,R(x)}$ is of the form*

$$\Phi_A^{x,,R(x)}(v) = \begin{cases} \beta(x) v^a v^b & A = \{a, b\}, |a - b| = 1 \\ \beta(x) v^a (\psi_a(x) + h) & A = \{a\} \\ 0 & \textit{otherwise}, \end{cases} \tag{1.37}$$

where $h \in \mathbb{R}$ denotes some fixed external condition, $\psi_a(x) = \psi((x_b)_{b \in N(a)}, R(x))$ for a bounded measurable function $\psi : C^{2^d+1} \times \mathcal{M}_0(S) \to \mathbb{R}$, and $\beta : S \to \mathbb{R}$ is a measurable mapping which determines the strength of interaction between different agents.

If the additional interaction in the transition itself is not too strong, then any local specification $\gamma^{x,R(x)}$ ($x \in S_0$) determines a unique global phase $\Pi(x; \cdot)$ on

S_0. The microscopic process will therefore be described by a Markov chain on the state space S_0 with transition kernel Π – again viewed as a stochastic kernel on S_0. In particular, any configuration x_t induces the ergodic empirical field $R(x_t)$. The dynamics of the macroscopic process $\{R(x_t)\}_{t\in\mathbb{N}}$ will be given by the deterministic iteration of the function $\hat{G}$ acting on empirical fields defined in (1.34). If the local interaction in the kernel Π is weak enough, and under suitable contraction conditions on the specifications, the macroscopic process converges almost surely in the weak topology. In particular, this implies convergence of the mood of the market as $t \to \infty$, due to (1.31). These results will be explained in Chapter 2.

1.2.2 Interaction in a Random Environment

We are now going to describe a financial market model with locally and globally interacting agents in a random environment. From an economic point of view it makes sense to assume that individual agents' reference levels do not only depend on the mood of the market and on the opinions of their neighbors in the previous period, but also on some exogenous economic fundamentals like interest rates or government spending. Moreover, investors typically do not have complete information about the empirical distribution of individual agents' states $\varrho(x_t)$ in a given period t. Instead, it might be appropriate to assume that they just receive a common noisy signal e_t about aggregate behaviour at date t. For example, e_t could be a signal about the fraction of chartists or optimistic information traders who are active on the market in period t and may be revealed via some stock market index, by newspaper articles or by an opinion poll.

More precisely, we assume that, given configuration $x \in S_0$, an individual agent $a \in \mathbb{A}$ reacts to

- the states $(x_t^b)_{b\in N(a)}$ of his neighbors
- a random signal e_t about the induced empirical field $R(x_t)$,
- some random (exogenous) economic fundamentals in period t summarized by a parameter h_t.

Mathematically, such an approach provides an additional smoothing effect. In many situations, this smoothing effect allows us to establish convergence in law of the macroscopic process $\{R(x_t)\}_{t\in\mathbb{N}}$ without any condition which controls the dependence of individual behaviour on the signal about the present empirical field.

In our model, the dynamics of the external conditions is described by a Markov chain $\{h_t\}_{t\in\mathbb{N}}$ on a compact metric state space (H, d_H). The signal sequence $\{e_t\}_{t\in\mathbb{N}}$ is modeled by a stochastic process taking values in an arbitrary measurable space $(E, \mathcal{E})$; the "signal space". The conditional law

$$Q(R(x);\cdot) \tag{1.38}$$

of the signal $e \in E$, given the present empirical field $R(x) \in \mathcal{M}_0(S)$, is specified by a stochastic kernel Q from $\mathcal{M}_s(S)$ to $\mathcal{E}$.

We consider a situation where the transition to a new configuration itself is interactive. Given a configuration $x \in S_0$, an economic fundamental value $h \in H$ and a signal $e \in E$ about the average situation throughout the entire system of all traders, the transition to a new configuration is described by a Gibbs measure $\Pi_{e,h}(x,\cdot)$ on S_0 with respect to a local specification $\gamma^{x,e,h} = (\gamma_a^{x,e,h})_{a\in\mathbb{A}}$. If we are given an interaction potential $\Phi^{x,e,h}$, then we may specify the probability for the next state of agent $a \in \mathbb{A}$ being $c \in C$, given his microscopic environment v, as

$$\gamma_a^{x,e,h}(c;v) = \frac{\exp\left(\sum_{A\ni a}\Phi_A^{x,e,h}(v_{a,c})\right)}{\sum_{\hat{c}\in C}\exp\left(\sum_{A\ni a}\Phi_A^{x,e,h}(v_{a,\hat{c}})\right)} \qquad (c \in C). \tag{1.39}$$

For any fixed pair (e,h), the probability measure $\Pi_{e,h}(x;\cdot)$ is concentrated on the set S_0 whenever $x \in S_0$. Thus, given a sequence $\{(e_t,h_t)\}_{t\in\mathbb{N}}$ of signals about aggregate behaviour and of economic fundamentals, the microscopic process $\{x_t\}_{t\in\mathbb{N}}$ may be viewed as a time-inhomogeneous Markov process on the state space S_0 with transition kernels $\{\Pi_{e_t,h_t}\}_{t\in\mathbb{N}}$. In this sense, the dynamics of the microscopic process $\{x_t\}_{t\in\mathbb{N}}$ is described by a Markov chain on the state space S_0 in the random environment which is specified by the process $\{(e_t,h_t)\}_{t\in\mathbb{N}}$.

Of course, in our present setting the dynamics of the macroscopic process will typically not be deterministic. However, by analogy with (1.34), we will see that any fixed environment $\{(e_t,h_t)\}_{t\in\mathbb{N}}$ induces a sequence of mapping $\{\hat{G}_t\}_{t\in\mathbb{N}}$ acting on empirical fields, such that

$$R(x_{t+1}) = \int_{S_0}\Pi_{e_t,h_t}(y;\cdot)R(x_t)(dy) =: \hat{G}_t(R(x_t)) \qquad \Pi_{e_t,h_t}(x_t;\cdot)\text{-a.s.} \tag{1.40}$$

Thus, the sequence of empirical fields $\{R(x_t)\}_{t\in\mathbb{N}}$ follows almost surely a conditionally deterministic dynamics. In Chapter 3, we shall prove that the process $\{(R(x_t),h_t)\}_{t\in\mathbb{N}}$ is a Markov chain on the state space $\mathcal{M}_0(S)\times H$. We will establish convergence in law of the macroscopic process under the assumption that the local interaction in the transition kernels $\Pi_{e,h}$ is not too strong.

Chapter 2

Local and Global Interaction in a Deterministic Environment

In this chapter, we analyze the asymptotic behaviour of both the *macroscopic* and the *microscopic* process in a financial market model with interacting agents in a deterministic environment, i.e., in a situation where the dynamics on the macroscopic level of empirical fields proceeds almost surely in a deterministic manner. Given a configuration x, an individual agent $a \in \mathbb{A}$ reacts to the local situation $(x^b)_{b \in N(a)}$ in his neighborhood and to the empirical field $R(x)$. The dynamics of the microscopic process $\{x_t\}_{t \in \mathbb{N}}$ will be described by a Markov chain on the state space S_0 with transition probability $\Pi(x; dy)$. We give for each configuration x a local specification γ^x, i.e., a system of conditional probabilities and formulate a uniform Dobrushin-type condition on the specifications $(\gamma^x)_{x \in S}$ which guarantees that each γ^x admits a unique global phase $\Pi(x; \cdot)$. This means that $\Pi(x; \cdot)$ is a Gibbs measure, and so the transition to a new configuration itself is interactive. Since γ^x may depend on x both in a local and in a global manner, the stochastic kernel Π typically does not have the Feller property. Thus, we can not apply the method of Vasserstein (1969) in order to analyze the long run behaviour of the Markov chain $\{x_t\}_{t \in \mathbb{N}}$.

In Section 2.2, we prove that the microscopic process $\{x_t\}_{t \in \mathbb{N}}$ induces almost surely a sequence of ergodic empirical fields $\{R(x_t)\}_{t \in \mathbb{N}}$. More precisely, Proposition 2.8 establishes a spatial law of large numbers for ergodic empirical fields which yields a deterministic equation for the evolution of the macroscopic process $\{R(x_t)\}_{t \in \mathbb{N}}$. This allows us to regard the underlying microscopic process as a Markov chain in a time-inhomogeneous but *deterministic* environment. The environment is generated by the macroscopic process, and we are going to analyze the microscopic and the macroscopic process separately.

If the local interaction in the transition kernel Π is not too strong and given that the dependence of γ^x on $R(x)$ satisfies a suitable contraction condition, we show in Theorem 2.24 that the sequence of ergodic empirical fields $\{R(x_t)\}_{t\in\mathbb{N}}$ converges almost surely to a unique random field on $(S, \mathcal{S})$. In this case, the asset price process evolves asymptotically in an environment which is generated by a sequence of i.i.d. random variables. For price dynamics of a log-linear form, this allows us to analyze the long run behaviour of the induced sequence of temporary price equilibria.

Theorem 2.29 shows that convergence of the macroscopic process $\{R(x_t)\}_{t\in\mathbb{N}}$ implies local convergence of the underlying microscopic process $\{x_t\}_{t\in\mathbb{N}}$. We state conditions which guarantee that the macroscopic and the microscopic limit coincide. In this case, we have at the same time macroscopic and microscopic convergence to the same probability measure on S, and so we are able to characterize the class of all possible limiting distributions for the microscopic process by a fixed-point property.

2.1 Macroscopic Interaction

Let us first introduce the concept of a random field as a probability measure on a configuration space. We define a metric d_S on the configuration space

$$S = C^{\mathbb{A}} = \{x = (x^a)_{a\in\mathbb{A}} : x^a \in C\}$$

by the relation

$$d_S(x, y) := \sum_{a\in\mathbb{A}} 2^{-\eta|a|}\mathbf{1}_{\{x^a\neq y^a\}} \tag{2.1}$$

for some $\eta > 0$ which will be specified later. Here, $|a| := \sqrt{\sum_{i=1}^d a_i^2}$ is the Euclidean norm of the vector $a = (a_1, a_2, \dots, a_d) \in \mathbb{R}^d$. In particular, (S, d_S) is a compact metric space with respect to the product topology.

We denote by $\mathcal{S}$ the product σ-field on S. A **random field** μ is a probability measure on $(S, \mathcal{S})$, and the set of random fields will be denoted $\mathcal{M}(S)$. For $A \subset \mathbb{A}$, we introduce the σ-field $\mathcal{S}_A$ generated by the projections $x \mapsto x^a$ $(a \in A)$ and denote by

$$\mathcal{A} := \{A \subset \mathbb{A} : |A| < \infty\} \tag{2.2}$$

the system of all finite ("local") subsets of $\mathbb{A}$.

Definition 2.1 *(i) A* ***local specification*** *is a system* $\gamma = \{\gamma_A\}_{A \in \mathcal{A}}$ *of probability kernels* γ_A *from* $\mathcal{S}_{A^c}$ *to* S *such that*

$$\gamma_A(\cdot; v) = \delta_v(\cdot) \quad on \quad \mathcal{S}_{A^C}$$

and such that, for any $A_1 \subset A_2 \in \mathcal{A}$, *the consistency condition*

$$\gamma_{A_2}\gamma_{A_1}(\cdot; v) := \int \gamma_{A_2}(\cdot; w)\gamma_{A_1}(dw; v) = \gamma_{A_2}(\cdot; v)$$

is satisfied.

(ii) We say that $\mu \in \mathcal{M}(S)$ *is specified by a local specification* $\gamma = \{\gamma_A\}_{A \in \mathcal{A}}$ *if*

$$\mu(B|\mathcal{S}_{A^c})(\cdot) = \gamma_A(B; \cdot) \quad \mu\text{-}a.s. \qquad (A \in \mathcal{A}, B \in \mathcal{S}_A).$$

Remark 2.2 *Let* μ *be a random field on* $(S, \mathcal{S})$. *Since the set of possible individual states* C *is finite, we can choose, for all* $A \in \mathcal{A}$, *a regular conditional distribution of* μ *with respect to* $\mathcal{S}_{A^c}$, *i.e., a stochastic kernel* γ_A^μ *from* $\mathcal{S}_{A^c}$ *to* $\mathcal{S}$. *Since the induced family of probability measures* $\gamma^\mu := \{\gamma_A^\mu\}_{A \in \mathcal{A}}$ *is consistent, every random field* μ *defines a local specification* γ^μ. *However, a random field* μ *is not necessarily uniquely determined by* γ^μ. *There may occur a "phase transition", i.e., there may exist a measure* $\nu \neq \mu$ *which is also specified by* γ^μ *in the sense described above.*

On the set $\mathcal{M}(S)$ we introduce the topology of **weak convergence**. We say that a sequence of random fields $\{\mu_t\}_{t \in \mathbb{N}}$ converges weakly to $\mu \in \mathcal{M}(S)$ and write $\mu_t \xrightarrow{w} \mu$, if

$$\mu_t(f) := \int f d\mu_t \overset{t \to \infty}{\longrightarrow} \mu(f) \qquad (f \in \mathcal{C}(S)) \tag{2.3}$$

Since the state space C is finite, any continuous function $f \in \mathcal{C}(S)$ can be uniformly approximated by local functions. A real-valued function f on S is called **local**, if it depends only on finitely many coordinates. The set of all local functions is denoted $\mathcal{L}(S)$. Thus, in order to establish weak convergence of a sequence of probability measures $\{\mu_t\}_{t \in \mathbb{N}}$ on $(S, \mathcal{S})$, it is enough to verify **local convergence**, i.e., to verify (2.3) with $f \in \mathcal{L}(S)$.

Below, we are going to introduce a Markov chain $\{x_t\}_{t \in \mathbb{N}}$ on the configuration space given by a transition probability $\Pi(x; dy)$ on $(S, \mathcal{S})$. Instead of defining the transition kernel Π itself, we give for each configuration $x \in S$ the local specification $\{\gamma_A^x\}_{A \in \mathcal{A}}$ of $\Pi(x; \cdot)$ and state conditions on γ^x which guarantee that the random field $\Pi(x; \cdot)$ is uniquely determined by its conditional probabilities. We consider the case where the conditional distribution of the states of a finite set of agents $A \in \mathcal{A}$, given the present configuration $x \in S$, does not only depend on the local behaviour of $x \in S$ in a neighborhood of A, but also on "macroscopic properties" of x carried in the empirical field $R(x)$.

To this end, we fix, for any configuration $x \in S$ and for all $\mu \in \mathcal{M}_s(S)$, a local specification $\gamma^{x,\mu} = \{\gamma_A^{x,\mu}\}_{A \in \mathcal{A}}$ and assume that the mapping

$$(x, \mu) \mapsto \gamma_A^{x,\mu}(B; v) \qquad (A \in \mathcal{A}, B \in \mathcal{S}_A) \tag{2.4}$$

from $S \times \mathcal{M}_s(S)$ to $[0, 1]$ is measurable for each boundary condition v on A^c. For any *given* random field $\mu \in \mathcal{M}_s(S)$, we impose the following conditions on the family of local specifications $(\gamma^{x,\mu})_{x \in S}$.

First, we specify what we mean by saying that an agent interacts locally with his neighbors in terms of a Markov property of his characteristics. For this, we define the neighborhood of a given set of agents $A \subset \mathbb{A}$ as

$$N(A) := \{b \in \mathbb{A} : \exists\; a \in A \text{ such that } |b - a| \leq l\}.$$

Assumption 2.3 *The local specifications $(\gamma^{x,\mu})_{x \in S}$ satisfy a* ***Markov property of order*** *l both in their dependence on the boundary condition v and on the present configuration x:*

(i) For any fixed $x \in S$, we have

$$\gamma_A^{x,\mu}(\cdot; v) = \gamma_A^{x,\mu}(\cdot; w) \quad \textit{if } v = w \textit{ on } N(A) \backslash A \qquad (A \in \mathcal{A}). \tag{2.5}$$

(ii) For any fixed boundary condition v on A^c, we have

$$\gamma_A^{x,\mu}(\cdot; v) = \gamma_A^{y,\mu}(\cdot; v) \quad \textit{if } x = y \textit{ on } N(A) \qquad (A \in \mathcal{A}). \tag{2.6}$$

Second, we assume that all agents react in the same manner to their environment. Mathematically, this means that our local specifications are spatially homogeneous.

Assumption 2.4 *The local specifications $(\gamma^{x,\mu})_{x \in S}$ are* ***spatially homogeneous*** *in the sense that*

$$\gamma_A^{\theta_a x,\mu}(\cdot; \theta_a v) = \gamma_{-a+A}^{x,\mu}(\cdot; v) \circ \theta_a \qquad (A \in \mathcal{A}),$$

respectively,

$$\gamma_A^{\theta_a x,\mu}(f, \theta_a v) := \int f(y) \gamma_A^{\theta_a x,\mu}(dy; \theta_a v) = \gamma_{-a+A}^{x,\mu}(f \circ \theta_a, v) \qquad (f \in C(S)).$$

Finally, we assume that the interaction between different agents is not too strong. We specify this by means of a uniform Dobrushin-type condition on the family of conditional probabilities $(\gamma^{x,\mu})_{x\in S}$.

Assumption 2.5 *The local specifications $(\gamma^{x,\mu})_{x\in S}$ satisfy the following* ***uniform Dobrushin condition****. If $C(x,\mu) = (c_{i,j}(x,\mu))_{i,j\in\mathbb{A}}$ denotes the Dobrushin interaction matrix for $\gamma^{x,\mu}$, i.e., if*

$$c_{i,j}(x,\mu) := \sup\left\{\frac{1}{2}\|\gamma_j^{x,\mu}(\cdot;v) - \gamma_j^{x,\mu}(\cdot;w)\| : v = w \text{ off } i\right\} \tag{2.7}$$

then

$$\hat{c} := \sup_{x,\mu}\sup_j \sum_i c_{i,j}(x,\mu) < 1. \tag{2.8}$$

Here,

$$\|\gamma_j^{x,\mu}(\cdot;v) - \gamma_j^{x,\mu}(\cdot;w)\|$$

denotes the total variation of the signed measure $\gamma_j^{x,\mu}(\cdot;v) - \gamma_j^{x,\mu}(\cdot;w)$ on C.

Observe that our Assumption 2.4 implies

$$c_{i,j}(x,\mu) = c_{i-j,0}(\theta_{-j}x,\mu)$$

for all $i,j\in\mathbb{A}$, for each $x\in S$ and for any $\mu\in\mathcal{M}_s(S)$. Thus, (2.8) is equivalent to

$$\sup_{x,\mu}\sum_{i\in\mathbb{A}} c_{i,0}(x,\mu) < 1.$$

For a given specification $\gamma^{x,\mu}$, the quantity $c_{i,0}(x,\mu)$ measures the dependence of the state of agent $0\in\mathbb{A}$ on the present state of agent $i\in\mathbb{A}$, and so $\sum_i c_{i,0}(x,\mu)$ measures the dependence of the state of an individual agent on his microscopic environment, given the previous configuration $x\in S$ and the random field μ. Thus, (2.8) states that, uniformly in $x\in S$ and in $\mu\in\mathcal{M}_s(S)$, the dependence of the state of an agent on his environment is weak enough.

Remark 2.6 *(i) Due to our Assumption 2.4, we have that*

$$\sup_{x,\mu} c_{i,k}(x,\mu) = \sup_{x,\mu} c_{i-k,0}(x,\mu) = 0 \text{ for } |i-k| > l.$$

Thus, we may choose a small enough $\lambda > 0$ in order to obtain

$$c(\lambda) := \sup_{x,\mu}\sum_i c_{i,0}(x,\mu)e^{\lambda|i|} < 1, \tag{2.9}$$

due to the uniform Dobrushin condition (2.8).

(ii) *It follows from the Markov property of order l that the configuration $\gamma^{x,\mu}$ is continuous for any fixed $\mu \in \mathcal{M}_s(S)$ in the sense that the mapping*

$$x \mapsto \gamma_A^{x,\mu}(f, v) \qquad (A \in \mathcal{A})$$

is continuous for all $f \in \mathcal{C}(S)$ and for any given boundary condition v on A^c.

Due to a fundamental uniqueness theorem by Dobrushin, our Assumption 2.5 excludes phase transitions. The random field specified by $\gamma^{x,\mu}$ is uniquely determined; see, e.g., Dobrushin (1968) or Georgii (1989), Theorem 8.7. Let us denote this random field by

$$\Pi_\mu(x; \cdot) \qquad (x \in S). \tag{2.10}$$

It follows from our measurability assumption (2.4) on the family $(\gamma^{x,\mu})_{x \in S}$ that (2.10) defines a stochastic kernel Π_μ on $(S, \mathcal{S})$.

Let us now introduce some notation. By $\Delta(f)$ we mean the oscillation of the function f on S, i.e.,

$$\Delta(f) := \sup_{x,y} |f(x) - f(y)| \tag{2.11}$$

and, for any two sets $A_0, A_1 \subset \mathbb{A}$, we denote by $s(A_0, A_1)$ the distance of A_0 and A_1:

$$s(A_0, A_1) := \min_{i \in A_0, j \in A_1} |i - j|. \tag{2.12}$$

For a given random field $\mu \in \mathcal{M}_s(S)$, the following lemma establishes two basic properties of the transition kernel Π_μ specified by the specifications $(\gamma^{x,\mu})_{x \in S}$.

Lemma 2.7 *Under the above Assumptions the following holds true.*

(i) *For any fixed $\mu \in \mathcal{M}_s(S)$, the kernel Π_μ has the Feller property.*

(ii) *For any fixed $\mu \in \mathcal{M}_s(S)$, the kernel Π_μ satisfies the "homogeneity equation"*

$$\Pi_\mu f \circ \theta_a = \Pi_\mu(f \circ \theta_a) \qquad (a \in \mathbb{A}, f \in \mathcal{C}(S)). \tag{2.13}$$

Proof: Let $\{A_n\}_{n \in \mathbb{N}}$ be a cofinal sequence of finite sets satisfying $A_n \uparrow \mathbb{A}$ and let $f \in \mathcal{L}(S)$ be any $\mathcal{S}_A$-measurable function $(A \in \mathcal{A})$. By Assumption 2.5 and due to Proposition 7.11 in Georgii (1989), we have that

$$\Pi_\mu f(x) = \lim_{n \to \infty} \gamma_{A_n}^{x,\mu}(f, v) \quad \text{uniformly in } v \in S. \tag{2.14}$$

Due to Remark 2.6 (i) and because of Theorem 8.23 (ii) and Remark 8.26 in Georgii (1989), we also have

$$\sup_{v\in S} |\Pi_\mu f(x) - \gamma_{A_n}^{x,\mu}(f,v)| \leq \Delta(f)|A|\frac{1}{1-c(\lambda)}e^{-\lambda s(A,A_n^c)}. \tag{2.15}$$

Observe that the right hand side in (2.15) is independent of $x \in S$. Therefore

$$\lim_{n\to\infty} \gamma_{A_n}^{x,\mu}(f,v) = \Pi_\mu f(x) \quad \text{uniformly in } x \in S.$$

Thus, (i) follows from Remark 2.6 (ii).

Our second assertion follows immediately from (2.14) together with the homogeneity Assumption 2.4. Indeed, we have that

$$\begin{aligned} \Pi_\mu f(\theta_a x) &= \lim_{n\to\infty} \gamma_{A_n}^{\theta_a x,\mu}(f,\theta_a v) \\ &= \lim_{n\to\infty} \gamma_{-a+A_n}^{x,\mu}(f\circ\theta_a, v) \\ &= \Pi_\mu(f\circ\theta_a)(x). \end{aligned}$$

□

For any $x \in S_0$, the specification $\gamma^{x,R(x)}$ determines a unique Markov random field $\Pi_{R(x)}(x;\cdot)$ on $(S,\mathcal{S})$, due to our Assumption 2.5. Since the mapping $x \mapsto R(x)$ from S_0 to $\mathcal{M}_0(S)$ is measurable, it follows form (2.4) that $x \mapsto \Pi_{R(x)}(x;\cdot)$ defines a measurable mapping, and so we can define a stochastic kernel $\Pi : S_0 \times \mathcal{S} \to [0,1]$ by the relation

$$\Pi(x;B) := \Pi_{R(x)}(x;B). \tag{2.16}$$

In fact, Proposition 2.8 below will show that the probability measures $\Pi(x;\cdot)$ ($x \in S_0$) are concentrated on S_0, and so Π can be viewed as a transition kernel on the configuration space S_0. Moreover, it follows from Lemma 2.7 that Π is spatially homogeneous. Indeed, we have that

$$\Pi\mathbf{1}_B(\theta_a x) = \Pi_{R(x)}\mathbf{1}_B(\theta_a x) = \Pi_{R(x)}(\mathbf{1}_B\circ\theta_a)(x) = \Pi(\mathbf{1}_B\circ\theta_a)(x) \tag{2.17}$$

for all $a \in \mathbb{A}$ and for any $B \in \mathcal{S}$. Our aim is now to study the asymptotics of the Markov chain with state space S_0 which is defined by Π.

2.2 A strong Law of large Numbers for Ergodic Empirical Fields

This section is devoted to the proof of a spatial law of large numbers for ergodic empirical fields which will be the basis for our subsequent analysis.

Proposition 2.8 *("Law of large numbers").*

(i) For all configurations $x \in S_0$ and for $\Pi(x;\cdot)$-a.e. $y \in S$, the empirical field $R(y)$ exists, is ergodic and takes the from

$$R(y)(\cdot) = \int_S \Pi_{R(z)}(z;\cdot)R(x)(dz) = \int_S \Pi_{R(x)}(z;\cdot)R(x)(dz). \tag{2.18}$$

(ii) For any ergodic random field μ on $(S, \mathcal{S})$, we have $\mu\Pi \in \mathcal{M}_0(S)$.

Proof: Our proof is a modification an argument given in Föllmer (1979a), where the result is verified for the case of product measures instead of Gibbs measures. In order to establish our assertion, we proceed in several steps.

1. Let us first show that, for any $x \in S_0$ and for $\Pi(x;\cdot)$-a.e. $y \in S$, the empirical field $R(y)$ exists and that the identification (2.18) holds true.

   For any $x \in S_0$, we have $R(x)(S_0) = 1$ because $R(x)$ is an ergodic probability measure on $(S, \mathcal{S})$, and so the first integral in (2.18) is well-defined. The ergodic theorem implies that $R(x) = \mu$ for μ-a.e. $x \in S$ whenever $\mu \in \mathcal{M}_0(S)$ and this yields

$$R(z)(\cdot) = R(x)(\cdot) \quad \text{for} \quad R(x)(\cdot)\text{-a.e. } z \in S \qquad (x \in S_0). \tag{2.19}$$

   Thus, the second equality in (2.18) holds true, and so it remains to establish the existence of $R(y)$.

   Let $A \in \mathcal{A}$ and $f \in \mathcal{L}(S)$ be any $\mathcal{S}_A$-measurable function. Since the stochastic kernels $(\Pi_\mu)_{\mu \in \mathcal{M}_s(S)}$ on $(S, \mathcal{S})$ have the Feller property and satisfy the homogeneity equation (2.13), we have

$$\begin{aligned} \int_S \int_S f(y)\Pi_{R(z)}(z;dy)R(x)(dz) &= \int_S (\Pi_{R(x)}f)(z)R(x)(dz) \\ &= \lim_{n\to\infty} \frac{1}{|\mathbb{A}_n|} \sum_{a\in\mathbb{A}_n} \Pi_{R(x)}(f \circ \theta_a)(x) \end{aligned}$$

   by definition of the empirical field $R(x)$ given in (1.30).

   We denote by $\mathbb{E}_{\Pi(x;\cdot)}$ the expectation with respect to the measure $\Pi(x;\cdot) = \Pi_{R(x)}(x;\cdot)$, introduce the sets

$$L_n := \{a = (a_1, \ldots, a_d) \in \mathbb{A} : \max_i |a_i| = n\} \qquad (n \in \mathbb{N}) \tag{2.20}$$

and put

$$Y_i := \sum_{a \in L_i} f \circ \theta_a \qquad (i \in \mathbb{N}). \tag{2.21}$$

Thus, for $x \in S_0$, we have

$$\lim_{n \to \infty} \frac{1}{|\mathbb{A}_n|} \sum_{i=0}^{n} \mathbb{E}_{\Pi(x;\cdot)} Y_i = \int_S \Pi f(y) R(x)(dy).$$

In order to establish the existence of $R(y)$ and the identification (2.18), it is therefore enough to show that

$$\lim_{n \to \infty} \frac{1}{|\mathbb{A}_n|} \sum_{i=0}^{n} \{Y_i - \mathbb{E}_{\Pi(x;\cdot)} Y_i\} = 0 \qquad \Pi(x;\cdot)\text{-a.s.} \tag{2.22}$$

2. We shall not prove (2.22) directly. Instead, we will first show that (2.22) holds true if we replace the expectation $\mathbb{E}_{\Pi(x;\cdot)} Y_i$ by a suitable conditional expectation. It will then be verify that this conditional expectation can be chosen such that it is almost surely close enough to $\mathbb{E}_{\Pi(x;\cdot)} Y_i$.

To this end, let us introduce, for any $n \in \mathbb{N}$, the random variable

$$M_n := \sum_{i=0}^{n} \left\{ Y_i - \mathbb{E}_{\Pi(x;\cdot)} [Y_i | Y_0, \ldots, Y_{i-1}] \right\},$$

where $\mathbb{E}_{\Pi(x;\cdot)}[Y_0|Y_0, Y_{-1}] := \mathbb{E}_{\Pi(x;\cdot)}[Y_0]$. Since the function $f : S \to S$ is bounded, the sequence $\{M_n\}_{n \in \mathbb{N}}$ is a square integrable martingale with respect to the measure $\Pi(x;\cdot)$ and the filtration

$$\{\mathcal{S}_{n,0}\}_{n \in \mathbb{N}} = \{\sigma(Y_0, Y_1, \ldots, Y_n)\}_{n \in \mathbb{N}}.$$

Note that $|L_n| \leq 2d(2n+1)^{d-1}$ and that $|\mathbb{A}_n| = (2n+1)^d$. Thus, there exists a constant $c < \infty$ such that

$$\sum_{n \geq 1} \frac{\mathbb{E}_{\Pi(x;\cdot)}[(M_n - M_{n-1})^2 | \mathcal{F}_{n-1}]}{|\mathbb{A}_n|^2} \leq \sum_{n \geq 1} \frac{c}{(2n+1)^2} < \infty \qquad \Pi(x;\cdot)\text{-a.s.}$$

It follows from the strong law of large numbers for square integrable martingales provided in, e.g., Shiryaev (1989), Chapter VII, §5, Theorem 4, that

$$\lim_{n \to \infty} \frac{1}{|\mathbb{A}_n|} \sum_{i=0}^{n} \{Y_i - \mathbb{E}_{\Pi(x;\cdot)}[Y_i | Y_0, \ldots, Y_{i-1}]\} = 0 \qquad \Pi(x;\cdot)\text{-a.s.} \tag{2.23}$$

For $n, k \in \mathbb{N}$, let us put

$$Y_{n,0} := Y_n, \quad Y_{n,k} := \mathbb{E}_{\Pi(x;\cdot)}[Y_n|\mathcal{S}_{n-1,k-1}], \quad \mathcal{S}_{n,k} := \sigma(Y_{0,k}, \dots, Y_{n,k}),$$

where $\mathcal{S}_{-1,k} := \{\emptyset, \Omega\}$. Iterating (2.23) we obtain for any $k \in \mathbb{N}$ that

$$\begin{aligned}&\lim_{n\to\infty} \frac{1}{|\mathbb{A}_n|} \sum_{i=0}^{n} \{Y_{i,k} - \mathbb{E}_{\Pi(x;\cdot)}[Y_i|\mathcal{S}_{i-1,k}]\} \\ = &\lim_{n\to\infty} \frac{1}{|\mathbb{A}_n|} \sum_{i=0}^{n} \{Y_{i,k} - Y_{i,k+1}\} = 0 \qquad \Pi(x;\cdot)\text{-a.s.}\end{aligned} \tag{2.24}$$

Observe that $\mathcal{S}_{n,k} \subset \mathcal{S}_{n+1,k}$ for all $k, n \in \mathbb{N}$. Thus, the random variable $Y_{i,k}$ is $\mathcal{S}_{n-1,k-1}$-measurable if $i \leq n$. This yields

$$\mathcal{S}_{n,k} \subset \mathcal{S}_{n-1,k-1} \subset \cdots \subset \mathcal{S}_{n-k,0} \qquad (n \geq k). \tag{2.25}$$

Due to (2.24), we have $\Pi(x;\cdot)$-a.s. that

$$\lim_{n\to\infty} \frac{1}{|\mathbb{A}_n|} \sum_{i=0}^{n} \{Y_i - \mathbb{E}_{\Pi(x;\cdot)}[Y_i|\mathcal{S}_{i-1,k-1}]\} = \lim_{n\to\infty} \frac{1}{|\mathbb{A}_n|} \sum_{i=0}^{n} \{Y_i - Y_{i,k}\} = 0.$$

Hence, (2.22) holds true with $\mathbb{E}_{\Pi(x;\cdot)} Y_i$ replaced by $\mathbb{E}_{\Pi(x;\cdot)}[Y_i|\mathcal{S}_{i-1,k-1}]$. Our objective is now to show that we can find a large enough $k \in \mathbb{N}$ such that

$$\lim_{n\to\infty} \frac{1}{|\mathbb{A}_n|} \sum_{i=0}^{n} \{\mathbb{E}_{\Pi(x;\cdot)}[Y_i|\mathcal{S}_{i-1,k-1}] - \mathbb{E}_{\Pi(x;\cdot)} Y_i\} < \epsilon \qquad \Pi(x;\cdot)\text{-a.s.} \tag{2.26}$$

3. Let us fix $\epsilon > 0$. In order to achieve our goal, we are first going to verify that we can choose a constant $k_0 = k_0(\epsilon)$ such that, for all $n \geq k \geq k_0$, we have

$$\left|\mathbb{E}_{\Pi(x;\cdot)}[f \circ \theta_a|\mathcal{S}_{n-1,k-1}] - \mathbb{E}_{\Pi(x;\cdot)}[f \circ \theta_a]\right| < \epsilon \qquad \Pi(x;\cdot)\text{-a.s.} \tag{2.27}$$

This will then allow us to establish (2.26).

To this end, we introduce, for $n \geq k$, the set

$$A^{n,k} := \bigcup_{i=0}^{n-k} \bigcup_{j \in L_i} \{j + A\}.$$

Since the mapping $f : S \to \mathbb{R}$ is $\mathcal{S}_A$-measurable, the random variable Y_i is $\mathcal{S}_{A^{n,k}}$-measurable whenever $i \leq n - k$, and so

$$\mathcal{S}_{n,k} \subset \mathcal{S}_{n-1,k-1} \subset \cdots \subset \mathcal{S}_{n-k,0} \subset \mathcal{S}_{A^{n,k}} \qquad (n \geq k). \tag{2.28}$$

Let us now denote by

$$\Pi^{v,A^{n,k}}(x;\cdot)$$

the conditional joint distribution of the random variables y^a $(a \in (A^{n,k})^c)$ with respect to $\mathcal{S}_{A^{n,k}}$ and $\Pi(x;\cdot)$, given the boundary condition v on $A^{n,k}$. Since the local specification $\gamma^x = \{\gamma_A^x\}_{A\in\mathcal{A}}$ satisfies our Assumption 2.5, we can apply Theorem 8.23 in Georgii (1989). The random field $\Pi^{v,A^{n,k}}(x;\cdot)$ is Markov of order l and is uniquely determined by its conditional distributions $\{\gamma_A^{v,x}\}_{A\in\mathcal{A}}$ which take the form

$$\gamma_A^{v,x}(\cdot;w) = \gamma_{A\backslash A^{n,k}}(\cdot;w^v). \tag{2.29}$$

Here, w^v is the boundary condition on $(A\backslash A^{n,k})^c$ which is equal to v on $A^{n,k}$ and equal to w on $A^c\backslash A^{n,k}$.

For any $a \in \mathbb{A}$, (2.28) implies that

$$\begin{aligned} \mathbb{E}_{\Pi(x;\cdot)}[f\circ\theta_a|\mathcal{S}_{n-1,k-1}] &= \mathbb{E}_{\Pi(x;\cdot)}\left[\mathbb{E}_{\Pi(x;\cdot)}[f\circ\theta_a|\mathcal{S}_{A^{n,k}}]|\mathcal{S}_{n-1,k-1}\right] \\ &\le \sup_v \int f\circ\theta_a(y)\Pi^{v,A^{n,k}}(x;dy) \qquad \Pi(x;\cdot)\text{-a.s.} \end{aligned}$$

In particular, we have $\Pi(x;\cdot)$-a.s. that

$$\begin{aligned} &\left|\mathbb{E}_{\Pi(x;\cdot)}[f\circ\theta_a|\mathcal{S}_{n-1,k-1}] - \mathbb{E}_{\Pi(x;\cdot)}[f\circ\theta_a]\right| \\ \le\ &\sup_v \left|\int f\circ\theta_a(y)\Pi^{v,A^{n,k}}(x;dy) - \int f\circ\theta_a(y)\Pi(x;dy)\right|. \end{aligned} \tag{2.30}$$

For any $n \in \mathbb{N}$ and for all $a \in L_n$, the distance $s(a+A, A^{n,k})$ of the sets $a+A$ and $A^{n,k}$ does only depend on k. We can therefore choose a small enough $\lambda \in \mathbb{R}$ and a sufficiently large $k_0 = k_0(\epsilon) \in \mathbb{N}$ satisfying (2.9) and

$$\exp(-\lambda s((a+A), A^{n,k})) < \frac{\epsilon}{2} \qquad (n \ge k \ge k_0,\ a \in L_n). \tag{2.31}$$

For $n \ge k \ge k_0$, let us now choose a set $V \in \mathcal{A}$ such that, for all $a \in L_n$, the following holds true:

$$V \cap A^{n,k} = \emptyset, \quad a + A \subset V, \quad \exp(-\lambda s((a+A), V^c)) < \epsilon.$$

Thus, our uniform Dobrushin condition (2.8) together with Theorem 8.23 and with Remark 8.26 in Georgii (1989) yields the following estimate:

$$
\begin{aligned}
& \sup_v \left| \int f \circ \theta_a(y) \Pi^{v,A^{n,k}}(x;dy) - \int f \circ \theta_a(y)\Pi(x;dy) \right| && (2.32) \\
= & \sup_v \left| \int f \circ \theta_a(y) (\Pi^{v,A^{n,k}}(x;\cdot)\gamma_V^{v,x})(dy) - \int f \circ \theta_a(y)\Pi(x;dy) \right| \\
\leq & \sup_w \left| \int f \circ \theta_a(y) (\gamma_V^x(dy;w) - \Pi(x;dy)) \right| && (2.33) \\
\leq & \Delta(f)|A| \frac{1}{1-c(\lambda)} \exp(-\lambda s((a+A), V^c)) && (2.34) \\
\leq & c\epsilon
\end{aligned}
$$

for some constant $c < \infty$ depending on f. Here, (2.33) follows from (2.29).

4. We can now apply the preceding estimates in order to establish (2.26) and (2.22). Since $|L_n| \leq 2d(2n+1)^{d-1}$ it follows from (2.27) that there exists $c < \infty$ such that

$$
|\mathbb{E}_{\Pi(x;\cdot)}[Y_n|\mathcal{S}_{n-1,k-1}] - \mathbb{E}_{\Pi(x;\cdot)}Y_n| \leq \epsilon c(2n+1)^{d-1} \qquad \Pi(x;\cdot)\text{-a.s.} \qquad (2.35)
$$

for all $n \geq k \geq k_0$. Thus, as $|\mathbb{A}_n| = (2n+1)^d$, we deduce from (2.24) and from (2.35) that there exists a large enough $k \in \mathbb{N}$ which satisfies

$$
\begin{aligned}
& \lim_{n\to\infty} \frac{1}{|\mathbb{A}_n|} \left| \sum_{i=0}^n \{Y_i - \mathbb{E}_{\Pi(x;\cdot)}Y_i\} \right| \\
\leq & \lim_{n\to\infty} \frac{1}{|\mathbb{A}_n|} \left| \sum_{i=0}^n \{Y_i - \mathbb{E}_{\Pi(x;\cdot)}[Y_i|\mathcal{S}_{i-1,k-1}]\} \right| \\
& + \lim_{n\to\infty} \frac{1}{|\mathbb{A}_n|} \left| \sum_{i=0}^n \{\mathbb{E}_{\Pi(x;\cdot)}[Y_i|\mathcal{S}_{i-1,k-1}] - \mathbb{E}_{\Pi(x;\cdot)}Y_i\} \right| \\
\leq & c\epsilon \qquad \Pi(x;\cdot)\text{-a.s.}
\end{aligned}
$$

This shows (2.22) and, therefore, establishes the existence of the empirical field $R(y)$ for $\Pi(x;\cdot)$-a.e. $y \in S$ and the identification (2.18) as $\epsilon > 0$ is arbitrary.

5. Before we show that $R(y) \in \mathcal{M}_0(S)$, let us first establish (ii).

   To this end, we fix $\mu \in \mathcal{M}_0(S)$ and verify that $\mu\Pi$ is an ergodic random field on $(S, \mathcal{S})$. Due to (2.17), the probability measure $\mu\Pi$ is spatially homogeneous:

$$
(\mu\Pi)(\mathbf{1}_B \circ \theta_a) = \mu(\Pi(\mathbf{1}_B \circ \theta_a)) = \mu(\Pi(\mathbf{1}_B) \circ \theta_a) = \mu\Pi(\mathbf{1}_B) \qquad (a \in \mathbb{A}, B \in \mathcal{S}).
$$

Thus, Birkhoff's ergodic theorem implies that $\mu\Pi \in \mathcal{M}_0(S)$ whenever

$$R(y) = \mu\Pi \qquad \mu\Pi\text{-a.s.} \tag{2.36}$$

Since $\mu = R(x)$ for μ-a.e. $x \in S$ it follows from (2.18) that

$$\mu\Pi(\{y : R(y) = \mu\Pi\}) = \int_S \Pi(x; \{y : R(y) = R(x)\Pi\})\mu(dx) = 1,$$

and so $\mu\Pi \in \mathcal{M}_0(S)$. This shows (ii).

6. We can now easily show that $\Pi(x; S_0) = 1$ whenever $x \in S_0$. Indeed, for any $x \in S_0$, we have $R(x) \in \mathcal{M}_0(S)$, and so it follows from (ii) that $R(x)\Pi \in \mathcal{M}_0(S)$. Thus, $R(y) = R(x)\Pi \in \mathcal{M}_0(S)$ for $\Pi(x; \cdot)$-a.e. $y \in S$, due to (2.18) and therefore $\Pi(x; S_0) = 1$. This completes the proof.

□

Corollary 2.9 *(i) Let $\mu \in \mathcal{M}_s(S)$ and $x \in S_0$ be given. It follows from the proof of Proposition 2.8 that $\Pi_\mu(x; S_0) = 1$ and that $\nu\Pi_\mu \in \mathcal{M}_0(S)$ whenever $\nu \in \mathcal{M}_0(S)$.*

(ii) For any $x \in S_0$, we can define a sequence of ergodic empirical fields $\{R_t^x\}_{t\in\mathbb{N}}$ by the relation

$$R_0^x(\cdot) := R(x)(\cdot) \qquad \text{and} \qquad R_{t+1}^x(\cdot) := R_0^x\Pi^t(\cdot) \qquad (t = 0, 1, 2, \ldots). \tag{2.37}$$

Due to Proposition 2.8, this sequence satisfies the following recurrence relation:

$$R_{t+1}^x = R_t^x\Pi_{R_t^x} = R_0^x\Pi_{R_0^x}\cdots\Pi_{R_t^x} \qquad (t = 0, 1, 2, \ldots). \tag{2.38}$$

2.3 Convergence Theorems

We are now ready to study the dynamics of the Markov chain $\{x_t\}_{t\in\mathbb{N}}$ on the state space S_0 defined by the transition kernel

$$\Pi(x; \cdot) = \Pi_{R(x)}(x; \cdot) \tag{2.39}$$

on S_0. For any $x \in S_0$, we denote by $\mathbb{P}_x$ the distribution of the Markov chain $\{x_t\}_{t\in\mathbb{N}}$ with transition kernel Π and initial state x and introduce, for a random field μ which is concentrated on the set S_0, the law

$$\mathbb{P}_\mu(\cdot) := \int_S \mathbb{P}_x(\cdot)\mu(dx). \tag{2.40}$$

For every $t \in \mathbb{N}$, the configuration $x_t \in S_0$ induces an ergodic empirical field $R(x_t)$. We shall call $\{x_t\}_{t\in\mathbb{N}}$ and $\{R(x_t)\}_{t\in\mathbb{N}}$ the **microscopic** and the **macroscopic process**, respectively. Observe that, given the present configuration x_t, the transition to a new state x_{t+1} has

- a *local interactive structure* through the dependence on the microscopic configuration x_t, and
- a *global component* through the dependence on the present configuration x_t via the induced empirical field $R(x_t)$.

Moreover, we admit an additional local interaction in the transition itself.

Let us first show that the strong law of large numbers for ergodic empirical fields yields a decoupling result which allows us to analyze the microscopic and the macroscopic process separately. To this end, we consider, for each starting point $x \in S_0$ of the microscopic process, the sequence of empirical fields $\{R_t^x\}_{t\in\mathbb{N}}$ defined by (2.38) and verify that this sequence coincides $\mathbb{P}_x$-a.s. with our macroscopic process. Indeed, due to Proposition 2.8, the empirical field $R(x_t)$ at time t does not depend on the whole microscopic configuration x_{t-1} in the previous period. Instead, $R(x_t)$ is $\mathbb{P}_x$-a.s. determined by the empirical field $R(x_{t-1})$. By induction we see that the random field $R(x_t)$ is almost surely determined by the initial empirical field $R_0^x := R(x)$ and that

$$R_t^x = R(x_t) \qquad \mathbb{P}_x\text{-a.s.} \qquad (t = 0, 1, 2, \ldots).$$

In this sense, for any initial state $x \in S_0$, the microscopic process may be viewed as a Markov chain evolving in a time-inhomogeneous but deterministic environment $\{R_t^x\}_{t\in\mathbb{N}}$ which is generated by the macroscopic process. In particular, the law of the random variable x_{t+1} takes the form

$$\Pi^{t+1}(x;\cdot) = (\Pi_{R_0^x} \cdots \Pi_{R_t^x})(x;\cdot). \tag{2.41}$$

Our aim is now to study the asymptotics of the Markov chain $\{x_t\}_{t\in\mathbb{N}}$ both on the microscopic level and on the macroscopic level of empirical fields. Suppose that the microscopic process **converges locally** to some equilibrium in the sense that $\delta_x \Pi^t \xrightarrow{w} \nu_x$ as $t \to \infty$ $(x \in S_0)$. In this case, the sequence of empirical fields $\{R_t^x\}_{t\in\mathbb{N}} = \{R(x)\Pi^t\}_{t\in\mathbb{N}}$ converges weakly to the measure

$$\bar{\nu}_x(\cdot) := \int \nu_z(\cdot) R(x)(dz).$$

Thus, Proposition 2.8 implies that we have at the same time convergence of macroscopic quantities of the form

$$\int f(z)R(x_t)(dz) = \lim_{n\to\infty} \frac{1}{|\mathbb{A}_n|} \sum_{a\in\mathbb{A}_n} f(\theta_a x_t) \qquad (f \in \mathcal{C}(S))$$

along $\mathbb{P}_x$-almost all paths of the microscopic process to their "equilibrium averages"

$$\int f(z)\bar{\nu}_x(dz).$$

Hence, microscopic convergence implies macroscopic convergence. Sections 2.3.1 and 2.3.2 may be viewed as a converse construction: Section 2.3.1 provides a direct proof of macroscopic convergence. We shall formulate conditions on the specifications $(\gamma^x)_{x\in S}$ which guarantee that the process of empirical fields $\{R_t^x\}_{t\in\mathbb{N}}$ converges in the weak topology. In Section 2.3.2, we will show that, conversely, macroscopic convergence implies microscopic convergence.

Remark 2.10 *For purely locally interacting systems, Vasserstein (1969) gives sufficient conditions which ensure local convergence of the associated Markov chain to some equilibrium. In our setting, this amounts to local convergence of Markov chain associated with the stochastic kernel Π_μ to some measure ν_μ, i.e.,*

$$\Pi_\mu^t(x; B) \stackrel{t\to\infty}{\longrightarrow} \nu_\mu(B) \qquad (x \in S, \mu \in \mathcal{M}_s(S), B \in \mathcal{S}_A, A \in \mathcal{A}).$$

Vasserstein's approach uses the Feller property of Π_μ. In our case, however, the kernel Π typically does not have the Feller property, due to the macroscopic dependence on the configuration x via the empirical field $R(x)$. Thus, we can not apply Vasserstein's result in order to establish the existence of stationary measures for Π. Instead, we will use the two-step procedure described above.

We start with some preliminaries and recall a comparison theorem for Gibbs measures established in Föllmer (1982). Let ν_1 be any random field on S with local specification γ and with Dobrushin-Vasserstein interaction matrix V defined as in (2.7). We introduce the matrix D as the sum of the non-negative powers of $V = (v_{i,j})_{i,j\in\mathbb{A}}$, i.e.,

$$D := \sum_{n\geq 0} V^n. \tag{2.42}$$

For any probability measure ν_2 on S with local specification $\tilde{\gamma}$ let us define a vector $b = (b_i)_{i\in\mathbb{A}}$ with components

$$b_i = \frac{1}{2}\int \|\gamma_i(\cdot; v) - \tilde{\gamma}_i(\cdot; v)\|\nu(dv). \tag{2.43}$$

In order to compare ν_1 and ν_2, we denote by $\Delta_a(f)$ the oscillation of a function f on S at site $a \in \mathbb{A}$, i.e.,

$$\Delta_a(f) := \sup\{|f(x) - f(y)| \ : \ x = y \text{ off } a\},$$

and say that a vector $r = (r_i)_{i\in\mathbb{A}}$ is an **estimate** for the measures ν_1 and ν_2 on the product space $(S, \mathcal{S})$ if

$$|\nu(f) - \mu(f)| \leq \sum_{i\in\mathbb{A}} r_i \Delta_i(f) \qquad (f \in \mathcal{C}(S)).$$

If the interaction matrix $V = (v_{i,a})_{i,a\in\mathbb{A}}$ satisfies the condition

$$\sup_a \sum_i v_{i,a} < 1, \tag{2.44}$$

then the following variant of Dobrushin's comparison theorem holds true; see, e.g., Föllmer (1982), Theorem 2.4.

Theorem 2.11 *Under condition (2.44) we have*

$$\left| \int f d\mu - \int f d\nu \right| \leq \sum_i (bD)_i \Delta_i(f) \qquad (f \in \mathcal{C}(S)).$$

In particular, under assumption (2.44) the random field μ is uniquely determined by its local specification. Moreover, the vector $r = (r_i)_{i\in\mathbb{A}}$ with components

$$r_i = \sum_j D_{j,i} b_j \tag{2.45}$$

is an estimate for the measures ν_1 and ν_2.

Let us now apply Theorem 2.11 to the random fields $\nu_1 := \Pi_\mu(x;\cdot)$ and $\nu_2 := \Pi_\mu(y;\cdot)$, where $x = y$ off a. By analogy with (2.42), we introduce for $x \in S$ and $\mu \in \mathcal{M}_s(S)$, the matrix $D(x,\mu) = (D(x,\mu)_{i,j})_{i,j\in\mathbb{A}}$ as the sum of the non-negative powers of the Dobrushin interaction matrix $C(x,\mu)$ defined in (2.7), i.e.,

$$D(x,\mu) := \sum_{n\geq 0} C^n(x,\mu).$$

Due to our homogeneity assumption, we see by induction that

$$c^n_{j,i}(x,\mu) = c^n_{j-i,0}(\theta_{-i}x,\mu),$$

where $c^n_{j,i}(x,\mu)$ denotes the (j,i)-th entry of the matrix $C^n(x,\mu)$. This yields

$$D_{j,i}(x,\mu) = D_{j-i,0}(\theta_{-i}x,\mu). \tag{2.46}$$

For all $i \in \mathbb{A}$, for any $x \in S$ and for each $\mu \in \mathcal{M}_s(S)$, we have

$$\sum_j c^2_{j,i}(x,\mu) = \sum_{j,k} c_{j,k}(x,\mu)c_{k,i}(x,\mu) \leq \left(\sup_k \sum_j c_{j,k}(x,\mu)\right) \sum_k c_{k,j}(x,\mu) \leq \hat{c}^2,$$

where the uniform Dobrushin constant $\hat{c}$ is defined in (2.8). By induction we obtain that $\sum_j c^n_{j,i}(x,\mu) \leq \hat{c}^n$, and so

$$\sup_{i,x,\mu} \sum D_{j,i}(x,\mu) = \sup_{x,\mu} \sum_j D_{j,0}(x,\mu) \leq \frac{1}{1-\hat{c}}. \tag{2.47}$$

For a given random field $\mu \in \mathcal{M}_s(S)$, we shall denote by $r^\mu_a(x,y) = (r^\mu_{a,i}(x,y))_{i\in\mathbb{A}}$ an estimate for the measures $\Pi_\mu(x;\cdot)$ and $\Pi_\mu(y;\cdot)$, where $x = y$ off a, and put

$$r^\mu_{a,i} := \sup_{x,y} r^\mu_{a,i}(x,y), \quad r^\mu_a := (r^\mu_{a,i})_{i\in\mathbb{A}}.$$

In terms of these quantities we have the following lemma.

Lemma 2.12 *For any $f \in C(S)$, the quantities $(r^\mu_{a,i})_{a,i\in\mathbb{A}}$ lead to the following inequality:*

$$\Delta_a(\Pi_\mu f) \leq \sum_{i\in\mathbb{A}} r^\mu_{a,i}\Delta_i(f) \qquad (a \in \mathbb{A}).$$

We are now going to introduce some specific estimates for the measures $\Pi_\mu(x;\cdot)$ and $\Pi_\mu(y;\cdot)$, where $x = y$ off a. Suppose first that the transition to a new configuration itself is made independently by different agents. Since the interaction is assumed to be spatially homogeneous, the random field $\Pi_\mu(x;\cdot)$ takes the product form

$$\Pi_\mu(x;\cdot) = \prod_{a\in\mathbb{A}} \pi_\mu(\theta_a x;\cdot) = \prod_{a\in\mathbb{A}} \pi_\mu((x^b)_{b\in N(a)};\cdot) \tag{2.48}$$

for some transition kernel π_μ from S to C. In this case, we define the vector $r^\mu_a = (r^\mu_{a,i})_{i\in\mathbb{A}}$ $(a \in \mathbb{A})$ by the relation

$$r^\mu_{a,i} := \sup\left\{\frac{1}{2}\|\pi_\mu(x;\cdot) - \pi_\mu(y;\cdot)\| : x = y \text{ off } a - i\right\} \tag{2.49}$$

as in, e.g., Vasserstein (1969), Section 3. Note that

$$r^{\mu}_{a,i} = r^{\mu}_{a-i,0} \qquad (a, i \in \mathbb{A})$$

by translation invariance.

Let us now consider a situation, where the transition to a new configuration itself is interactive. By analogy with (2.45), we introduce the vector $r^{\mu}_{a} = (r^{\mu}_{a,i})_{i \in \mathbb{N}}$ with components

$$r^{\mu}_{a,i} := \sup \left\{ \sum_{j \in \mathbb{A}} D_{j,i}(x, \mu) b_j(x, y, \mu) : x = y \text{ off } a \right\}, \tag{2.50}$$

where, by analogy with (2.43), we put

$$b_j(x, y, \mu) := \frac{1}{2} \int_S \| \gamma^{x,\mu}_j(\cdot; v) - \gamma^{y,\mu}_j(\cdot; v) \| \Pi_\mu(x; dv).$$

This defines an estimate for the measures $\Pi_\mu(x; \cdot)$ and $\Pi_\mu(y; \cdot)$ if $x = y$ off a, due to Theorem 2.11. By Lemma 2.7 (ii) and by translation invariance we have for $i, j \in \mathbb{A}$ that

$$\begin{aligned} b_j(x, y, \mu) &= \frac{1}{2} \int_S \| \gamma^{\theta_{-i}x,\mu}_{j-i}(\cdot; \theta_{-i}v) - \gamma^{\theta_{-i}y,\mu}_{j-i}(\cdot; \theta_{-i}v) \| \Pi_\mu(x; dv) \\ &= \frac{1}{2} \int_S \| \gamma^{\theta_{-i}x,\mu}_{j-i}(\cdot; v) - \gamma^{\theta_{-i}y,\mu}_{j-i}(\cdot; v) \| \Pi_\mu(\theta_{-i}x; dv) \\ &= b_{j-i}(\theta_{-i}x, \theta_{-i}y, \mu). \end{aligned}$$

Using (2.46) it is now easily seen that

$$r^{\mu}_{a,i} = r^{\mu}_{a-i,0} \qquad (a, i \in \mathbb{A}),$$

i.e., the vector r^{μ}_{a} defines an translation invariant estimate for the random fields $\Pi_\mu(x; \cdot)$ and $\Pi_\mu(y; \cdot)$ if $x = y$ off a.

Remark 2.13 *Suppose that we have translation invariant estimates* r^{μ}_{a} $(a \in \mathbb{A}, \mu \in \mathcal{M}_s(S))$ *such as (2.49) or (2.50) and that the following* ***uniform Dobrushin-Vasserstein-Condition*** *is satisfied:*

$$\alpha_0 := \sup_{\mu} \sum_{a} r^{\mu}_{a,0} < 1. \tag{2.51}$$

In this case, the following estimate holds true:

$$\Delta(\Pi_\mu f) \leq \sum_{a,i} r^\mu_{a,i}\Delta_i(f) \leq \left(\sup_i \sum_a r^\mu_{a-i,0}\right)\sum_i \Delta_i(f) \leq \alpha_0 \sum_i \Delta_i(f).$$

For any sequence $\{\mu_t\}_{t\in\mathbb{N}} \subset \mathcal{M}_0(S)$ *and for all* $t \geq 1$*, we obtain by induction that*

$$\Delta(\Pi_{\mu_0}\cdots\Pi_{\mu_t} f) \leq \sum_{a,i} r^{\mu_1}_{a,i}\Delta_i(\Pi_{\mu_1}\cdots\Pi_{\mu_t} f) \leq \alpha_0^{t+1}\sum_i \Delta_i(f). \tag{2.52}$$

Thus, in a fixed environment $\{\mu_t\}_{t\in\mathbb{N}}$*, we have*

$$\lim_{t\to\infty} \Delta(\Pi_{\mu_0}\cdots\Pi_{\mu_t} f) = 0$$

for any continuous function f *on* S*. In this sense, the microscopic process* $\{x_t\}_{t\in\mathbb{N}}$ *is weakly ergodic, i.e., has "local asymptotic loss of memory" as soon as (2.51) holds true. In particular, for any fixed random field* μ *on* $(S, \mathcal{S})$*, the Feller kernel* Π_μ *admits a unique equilibrium* ν_μ *and for any* $x \in S$ *we have that* $\Pi_\mu(x;\cdot) \xrightarrow{w} \nu_\mu$ *as* $t \to \infty$*. This is Vasserstein's fundamental convergence theorem. In our present setting, local asymptotic loss of memory is easy to establish. In Chapter 3, we will analyze a model with locally and globally interacting agents in a situation where the dynamics on the macroscopic level of empirical fields is described by a stochastic process. In such a situation, it becomes harder to verify weak ergodicity of the microscopic process.*

2.3.1 Macroscopic Convergence

This subsection is devoted to the analysis of the long run behaviour of the macroscopic process. Our purpose is to formulate conditions on the individual characteristics of agents which guarantee convergence of the processes of ergodic empirical fields $\{R^x_t\}_{t\in\mathbb{N}}$ $(x \in S_0)$ defined recursively by (2.38) in the weak topology. Since $R(x_t) = R^x_t$ for $\mathbb{P}_x$-a.e. $x_t \in S$, due to Proposition 2.8, this yields weak convergence of the macroscopic process $\{R(x_t)\}_{t\in\mathbb{N}}$ along almost all paths of the microscopic process $\{x_t\}_{t\in\mathbb{N}}$.

Our conditions will be twofold. On the one hand, we will use a weighted uniform Dobrushin-Vasserstein-Condition (Assumption 2.16) in order to control the local interaction in the kernels $(\Pi_\mu)_{\mu\in\mathcal{M}_s(S)}$. On the other hand, we need an additional contraction condition (Assumption 2.21) which controls the dependence of the specifications $(\gamma^{x,\mu})_{x\in S}$ on the parameter μ.

To this end, let us first introduce a metric $d(\cdot,\cdot)$ on the set $\mathcal{M}(S)$ of all probability measures on $(S, \mathcal{S})$ by the relation

$$d(\mu,\nu) := \sup_{f\in\mathcal{C}(S)} \frac{|\mu(f)-\nu(f)|}{\sum_a 2^{\eta|a|}\Delta_a(f)} \qquad (\mu,\nu\in\mathcal{M}(S)). \tag{2.53}$$

Remark 2.14 *(i) Observe that $d(\mu,\nu)=0$ implies $\mu(f)=\nu(f)$ for any local function $f: S\to\mathbb{R}$. Since each continuous function f can be uniformly approximated by local functions, it follows that $d(\mu,\nu)=0$ implies $\mu=\nu$, and so $d(\cdot,\cdot)$ is indeed a metric.*

(ii) Note that

$$d(\mu,\nu)\le \sup_{f\in\mathcal{C}(S)} \frac{|\mu(f)-\nu(f)|}{\sum_a \Delta_a(f)} \le \sup_{f\in\mathcal{C}(S)} \frac{|\mu(f)-\nu(f)|}{\Delta(f)} \le \|\mu-\nu\|.$$

The proof of the following proposition shows that

$$d(\mu,\nu)\le d_V(\mu,\nu).$$

Here, d_V denotes the Vasserstein distance on $\mathcal{M}(S)$, i.e.,

$$d_V(\mu,\nu) := \sup\left\{\frac{|\mu(f)-\nu(f)|}{m(f)} : f\in\mathcal{C}(S)\right\} \tag{2.54}$$

and

$$m(f) := \sup_{x\neq y}\left\{\frac{|f(x)-f(y)|}{d_S(x,y)}\right\}$$

is the Lipschitz coefficient of the function f.

Proposition 2.15 *The metric $d(\cdot,\cdot)$ defined by (2.53) induces the weak topology on $\mathcal{M}(S)$. In particular, $(\mathcal{M}(S), d)$ is a compact metric space.*

Proof: In a first step, we are going to show that the metric d is dominated by the Vasserstein distance, i.e., we will verify that

$$d(\mu,\nu)\le d_V(\mu,\nu) \qquad (\mu,\nu\in\mathcal{M}(S)). \tag{2.55}$$

To this end, let $f: S\to\mathbb{R}$ be a continuous function which satisfies $\sum_{a\in\mathbb{A}} 2^{\eta|a|}\Delta_a(f) < \infty$. In order to verify (2.55), it is enough to show that

$$m(f)\le \sum_{a\in\mathbb{A}} 2^{\eta|a|}\Delta_a(f).$$

Let $x, y \in S$ and put

$$J := \{a \in \mathbb{A} \; : \; x^a \neq y^a\}.$$

With no loss of generality, we may assume that $J = (j_n)_{n \in \mathbb{N}}$. Let $(x_n)_{n \in \mathbb{N}}$ be a sequence of configurations in S such that $x_0 = x$, such that $\lim_{n\to\infty} x_n = y$ and such that the following holds true for $n, m \in \mathbb{N}$:

$$x_n^{j_n} \neq x_{n+1}^{j_n}, \qquad x_n^b = x_{n+1}^b \;\; (b \neq j_n), \qquad x_{n+m+1}^{j_n} = y^{j_n}.$$

Thus, we have that

$$\begin{aligned} |f(x) - f(y)| &\leq \sum_{n \in \mathbb{N}} |f(x_n) - f(x_{n+1})| \\ &\leq \sum_{a \in J} \Delta_a(f) \\ &= \sum_{a \in \mathbb{A}} \Delta_a(f) 2^{\eta|a|} 2^{-\eta|a|} \mathbf{1}_{\{x^a \neq y^a\}} \\ &\leq \sum_{a \in \mathbb{A}} \left(\sum_{b \in \mathbb{A}} 2^{\eta|b|} \Delta_b(f) \right) 2^{-\eta|a|} \mathbf{1}_{\{x^a \neq y^a\}} \\ &= d_S(x, y) \sum_{a \in \mathbb{A}} 2^{\eta|a|} \Delta_a(f). \end{aligned}$$

Dividing both sides of this inequality by $d_S(x, y)$, we see that

$$m(f) \leq \sum_a 2^{\eta|a|} \Delta_a(f).$$

In particular, we have

$$d(\mu, \nu) = \sup_{f \in \mathcal{C}(S)} \frac{|\mu(f) - \nu(f)|}{\sum_a 2^{\eta|a} \Delta_a(f)} \leq d_V(\mu, \nu).$$

Suppose now that $\lim_{n\to\infty} d(\mu_n, \mu) = 0$. Hence, for any local function $f \in \mathcal{L}(S)$, we have that $\lim_{n\to\infty} \mu_n(f) = \mu(f)$. Since every continuous function f on S can be uniformly approximated by local functions, we see that $\lim_{n\to\infty} d(\mu_n, \mu) = 0$ implies $\lim_{n\to\infty} \mu_n(f) = \mu(f)$ for all $f \in \mathcal{C}(S)$ and therefore $\mu_n \to \mu$ weakly as $n \to \infty$.

Finally, recall that $(\mathcal{M}(S), d_V)$ is a compact metric space as S is compact. This yields our assertion. □

Let us now introduce a uniform **weighted Dobrushin-Vasserstein-Condition** in order to control the local interaction in the transition kernels Π_μ.

Assumption 2.16 *For $\mu \in \mathcal{M}_s(S)$ and for $a \in \mathbb{A}$, let r_a^μ be a translation invariant estimate for the random fields $\Pi_\mu(x;\cdot)$ and $\Pi_\mu(y;\cdot)$, where $x = y$ off a. For some $\eta > 0$, we have*

$$\alpha := \sup_\mu \sum_a 2^{\eta|a|} r_{a,0}^\mu < 1. \tag{2.56}$$

For any *given* empirical field μ, the quantity $r_{a,0}^\mu$ measures how the *present* state of agent 0 is affected by the *previous* state of agent a. Thus, the quantity $\sup_\mu \sum_a r_{a,0}^\mu$ measures the maximal dependence of the current state of agent 0 on the previous configuration. Our Assumption 2.16 is satisfied if this dependence is sufficiently weak, i.e., if the local interaction between different agents is not too strong. In the case of a pure mean-field interaction, i.e., for $\Pi(x;\cdot) = \prod_{a\in\mathbb{A}} \pi(x^a, \varrho(x);\cdot)$, this condition reduces to

$$\sup_{\varrho,c} \frac{1}{2} \|\pi(c,\varrho;\cdot) - \pi(c,\varrho;\cdot)\| \le \alpha < 1. \tag{2.57}$$

Let us now introduce quantitative bounds for the dependence of the local specifications $(\gamma^{x,\mu})_{x\in S,\mu\in\mathcal{M}_s(S)}$ on the configuration x which guarantee that Assumption 2.16 is satisfied.

Proposition 2.17 *(i) If the transition to a new configuration itself is made independently by different agents, i.e., if $\Pi(x;\cdot)$ is a product measure, then Assumption 2.16 is equivalent to the uniform Dobrushin-Vasserstein-Condition (2.51).*

(ii) In the case of interactive transition probabilities, the following two conditions imply Assumption 2.16:

a) The decay of the influence of agent a on agent 0 is sufficiently strong, i.e., there exists a sufficiently large constant $\xi > 0$ such that

$$\sup_{x,\mu} c_{a,0}(x,\mu) \le e^{-\xi|a|}. \tag{2.58}$$

b) The dependence of the local specification $\gamma^{x,\mu}$ on the configuration $x \in S$ is weak enough in the sense that there exists a constant $\tilde{c} < 1 - \hat{c}$ such that, for all $a \in \mathbb{A}$ and for any $\mu \in \mathcal{M}_s(S)$, we have

$$\sup \left\{ \frac{1}{2} \int_S \|\gamma_0^{\theta_{-j}x,\mu}(\cdot;v) - \gamma_0^{\theta_{-j}y,\mu}(\cdot;v)\| \Pi_\mu(\theta_{-j}x;dv) \right\} < \frac{\tilde{c}}{2^{ld}+1}. \tag{2.59}$$

Here, the supremum is taken over all $j \in \mathbb{A}$ and over all $x, y \in S$ with $y = x$ off a, and $\hat{c}$ is defined in (2.8).

Proof: For any $a \in \mathbb{A}$ and for all $\mu \in \mathcal{M}_s(S)$, let $r_a^\mu = (r_{a,i}^\mu)_{i \in \mathbb{A}}$ be the vector defined in (2.50). If the transition to a new configuration itself is made independently by different agents we have

$$r_{a,0}^\mu = 0 \tag{2.60}$$

if $|a| > l$, due to our Markov property of order l. Therefore, Assumption 2.16 reduces to condition (2.51). In fact, if (2.51) is satisfied, then there exists a small enough $\epsilon > 0$ such that $\sup_\mu (1+\epsilon) \sum_a r_{a,0}^\mu < 1$. Thus, we can take $\eta > 0$ such that $2^{l\eta} < 1+\epsilon$ in order to obtain our Assumption 2.16.

In the case of interactive transition probabilities, the analysis becomes more involved as (2.60) is no longer correct. For any $a \in \mathbb{A}$, let us define a vector $b^a = (b_j^a)_{j \in \mathbb{A}}$ with components

$$b_j^a := \sup_\mu \sup \left\{ \frac{1}{2} \int_S \|\gamma_0^{\theta_{-j}x,\mu}(\cdot;v) - \gamma_0^{\theta_{-j}y,\mu}(\cdot;v)\| \Pi_\mu(\theta_{-j}x; dv) : x = y \text{ off a} \right\}.$$

Due to the Markov property of order l, we have $b_j^a = 0$ for $|a - j| > l$, and so

$$r_{a,0}^\mu \leq \sup_{x,\mu} \sum_{|j-a| \leq l} b_j^a D_{j,0}(x,\mu). \tag{2.61}$$

Due to (2.58), and because of (2.47) we can estimate $D_{j,0}(x,\mu)$ by

$$D_{j,0}(x,\mu) \leq \frac{1}{1-\hat{c}} e^{-\xi|j|}.$$

It follows from (2.61) that

$$r_{a,0}^\mu \leq \frac{1}{1-\hat{c}} \sum_{|j-a| \leq l} b_j^a e^{-\xi|j|}.$$

Due to (2.59), the uniform Dobrushin-Vasserstein-Condition (2.51) is met whenever

$$\frac{1}{1-\hat{c}} \sum_{a \in \mathbb{A}} \sum_{|a-j| \leq l} \frac{\tilde{c}}{2^{ld}+1} e^{-\xi|j|} = \frac{\tilde{c}}{1-\hat{c}} \sum_{a \in \mathbb{A}} e^{-\xi|a|} < 1,$$

or, equivalently, if

$$\tilde{c} \sum_{a \in \mathbb{A}} e^{-\xi|a|} < 1 - \hat{c}.$$

This inequality, however, holds true for all ξ sufficiently large as $\tilde{c} < 1 - \hat{c}$. Hence, choosing $\eta > 0$ sufficiently small, we see that

$$\sup_\mu \sum_{a \in \mathbb{A}} 2^{\eta|a|} r_{a,0}^\mu \leq \frac{\tilde{c}}{1-\hat{c}} \sum_{a \in \mathbb{A}} e^{-(\xi - \eta \log 2)|a|} < 1$$

holds true whenever (2.58) and (2.59) are satisfied. □

Remark 2.18 *(i) In terms of the quantities b^a and $D(x,\mu)$ $(a \in \mathbb{A}, x \in S, \mu \in \mathcal{M}_s(S))$, our Assumption 2.16 amounts to*

$$\sup_{x,\mu} \sum_{a,j} 2^{\eta|a|} b_j^a D_{j,0}(x,\mu) < 1$$

for some $\eta > 0$.

(ii) Recall that, under (2.51), we have local convergence of Markov chain associated with the Feller kernel Π_μ. In order to ensure weak convergence of the sequence $\{\Pi^t(x;\cdot)\}_{t\in\mathbb{N}}$, however, we need an additional contraction condition which controls the dependence of the local specifications on the empirical fields.

Our uniform weighted Dobrushin-Vasserstein-Condition (Assumption 2.16) allows us to establish the following contraction property of the transition kernels $(\Pi_\tau)_{\tau\in\mathcal{M}_s(S)}$.

Proposition 2.19 *Let $\mu, \nu, \in \mathcal{M}(S)$ and $\tau \in \mathcal{M}_s(S)$. Under Assumption 2.16 we have that*

$$d(\mu\Pi_\tau, \nu\Pi_\tau) \leq \alpha d(\mu,\nu). \tag{2.62}$$

Proof: For any given $\tau \in \mathcal{M}_s(S)$, let the vector $r_a^\tau = (r_{a,i}^\tau)_{i\in\mathbb{A}}$ be a translation invariant estimate for the measures $\Pi_\tau(x;\cdot)$ and $\Pi_\tau(y;\cdot)$, where $x = y$ off a. Thus, for each $\tau \in \mathcal{M}_s(S)$, we have that

$$\Delta_a(\Pi_\tau f) \leq \sum_i r_{a-i,0}^\tau \Delta_i(f).$$

Using our weighted Dobrushin-Vasserstein-Condition (Assumption 2.16) we obtain

$$\begin{aligned}
&\sum_a 2^{\eta|a|}\Delta_a(\Pi_\tau f) \\
\leq\ & \sum_a \sum_i 2^{\eta|a|-\eta|i|} r_{a-i,0}^\tau 2^{\eta|i|}\Delta_i(f) \\
\leq\ & \sup_i \left\{\sum_a 2^{\eta|a-i|} r_{a-i,0}^\tau\right\} \sum_i 2^{\eta|i|}\Delta_i(f) \\
=\ & \sum_a 2^{\eta|a|} r_{a,0}^\tau \sum_i 2^{\eta|i|}\Delta_i(f) \\
\leq\ & \alpha \sum_i 2^{\eta|i|}\Delta_i(f).
\end{aligned}$$

In particular, we see that

$$\frac{\sum_a 2^{\eta|a|}\Delta_a(\Pi_\tau f)}{\sum_a 2^{\eta|a|}\Delta_a(f)} \leq \alpha \qquad (f \in \mathcal{C}(S)) \tag{2.63}$$

whenever $\sum_a 2^{\eta|a|}\Delta_a(f) < \infty$.

For $\mu, \nu \in \mathcal{M}(S)$, we have by definition of our metric $d(\cdot,\cdot)$ that

$$d(\mu\Pi_\tau, \nu\Pi_\tau) = \sup_{f\in\mathcal{C}(S)} \frac{|(\mu\Pi_\tau)(f) - (\nu\Pi_\tau)(f)|}{\sum_a 2^{\eta|a|}\Delta_a(f)}.$$

Of course, it suffices to take the above supremum over those continuous functions f on S which satisfy $\sum_a 2^{\eta|a|}\Delta_a(f) < \infty$.

Since, for any fixed $\tau \in \mathcal{M}_s(S)$, the transition probability Π_τ has the Feller property we have $\Pi_\tau f \in \mathcal{C}(S)$ for each τ and for all $f \in \mathcal{C}(S)$. This yields

$$\begin{aligned} d(\mu\Pi_\tau, \nu\Pi_\tau) &= \sup_{f\in\mathcal{C}(S)} \frac{|\mu(\Pi_\tau f) - \nu(\Pi_\tau f)|}{\sum_a 2^{\eta|a|}\Delta_a(\Pi_\tau f)} \frac{\sum_a 2^{\eta|a|}\Delta_a(\Pi_\tau f)}{\sum_a 2^{\eta|a|}\Delta_a(f)} \\ &\leq \alpha \sup_{f\in\mathcal{C}(S)} \frac{|\mu(\Pi_\tau f) - \nu(\Pi_\tau f)|}{\sum_a 2^{\eta|a|}\Delta_a(\Pi_\tau f)} \\ &\leq \alpha \sup_{g\in\mathcal{C}(S)} \frac{|\mu(g) - \nu(g)|}{\sum_a 2^{\eta|a|}\Delta_a(g)} = \alpha d(\mu,\nu), \end{aligned}$$

due to (2.63). This proves our assertion. □

Remark 2.20 *Observe that our Proposition 2.19 provides a new proof of Vasserstein's convergence theorem. For any fixed $\tau \in \mathcal{M}_s(S)$, the stochastic kernel Π_τ on $(S, \mathcal{S})$ has the Feller property, and so there exists a random field ν_τ on our configuration space $(S, \mathcal{S})$ such that $\nu_\tau = \nu_\tau\Pi_\tau$. Thus, we deduce from (2.62) that*

$$\mu\Pi_\tau^t \xrightarrow{w} \nu_\tau \qquad (t \to \infty) \tag{2.64}$$

for any initial distribution μ on S. In particular, the stochastic kernel Π_τ admits a unique equilibrium.

Our goal is now to show that Assumption 2.16 combined with the following contraction condition implies weak convergence of the sequence of empirical fields $\{R_t^x\}_{t\in\mathbb{N}}$ $(x \in S_0)$ to a unique probability measure μ^* on $(S, \mathcal{S})$.

Assumption 2.21 *There exists a constant $\beta < 1 - \alpha$ such that*

$$\sup_x d(\Pi_\mu(x;\cdot), \Pi_\nu(x;\cdot)) \leq \beta d(\mu,\nu) \tag{2.65}$$

for all $\mu, \nu \in \mathcal{M}_s(S)$.

Before we state and prove the main result of this subsection, let us introduce qualitative bounds for the dependence of the specifications on the parameter μ, which guarantee that Assumption 2.21 holds true.

Proposition 2.22 *(i) Suppose that the transition to a new state itself is made independently by different agents and that*

$$\sup_x \frac{1}{2} \|\pi_\mu(x;\cdot) - \pi_\nu(x;\cdot)\| \leq \beta d(\mu,\nu) \qquad (\mu,\nu \in \mathcal{M}_s(S)). \tag{2.66}$$

In this case, Assumption 2.21 is satisfied.

(ii) If the transition to a new configuration itself is interactive, then the following continuity condition implies Assumption 2.21:

$$b(\mu,\nu) := \sup_x \frac{1}{2} \int_S \|\gamma_0^{x,\mu}(\cdot;v) - \gamma_0^{x,\nu}(\cdot;v)\| \Pi_\mu(x;dv) \leq \beta\,(1-\hat{c})\, d(\mu,\nu),$$

where $\hat{c}$ is defined in (2.8). In particular, it is enough to require

$$\sup_{x,v} \frac{1}{2} \|\gamma_0^{x,\mu}(\cdot;v) - \gamma_0^{x,\nu}(\cdot;v)\| \leq \beta\,(1-\hat{c})\, d(\mu,\nu). \tag{2.67}$$

Proof: Let us first consider the case where the transition to a new configuration itself is made independently by different agents. It is easily seen that the vector $r^{\mu,\nu} = (r_a^{\mu,\nu})_{a \in \mathbb{A}}$ with components

$$r_a^{\mu,\nu} := \sup_x \frac{1}{2} \|\pi_\mu(x;\cdot) - \pi_\nu(x;\cdot)\| \qquad (a \in \mathbb{A}) \tag{2.68}$$

is an estimate for the measures $\Pi_\mu(x;\cdot)$ and $\Pi_\nu(x;\cdot)$ $(x \in S)$. We have that

$$\sup_x d(\Pi_\mu(x;\cdot), \Pi_\nu(x;\cdot)) = \sup_x \sup_{f \in \mathcal{C}(S)} \frac{|\int f(y)(\Pi_\mu(x;dy) - \Pi_\nu(x;dy))|}{\sum_a 2^{\eta|a|}\Delta_a(f)}.$$

This yields the following estimate:

$$\begin{aligned}\sup_x d(\Pi_\mu(x;\cdot), \Pi_\nu(x;\cdot)) &\leq \sup_{f \in \mathcal{C}(S)} \frac{\sum_a \Delta_a(f) r_a^{\mu,\nu}}{\sum_a 2^{\eta|a|}\Delta_a(f)} \\ &\leq \beta d(\mu,\nu) \sup_{f \in \mathcal{C}(S)} \frac{\sum_a \Delta_a(f)}{\sum_a 2^{\eta|a|}\Delta_a(f)} = \beta d(\mu,\nu).\end{aligned}$$

If the transition to a new state itself is interactive, then it follows from translation invariance of our local specifications and from Theorem 2.11 that the vector $(r_a^{\mu,\nu})_{a\in\mathbb{A}}$ with components

$$r_a^{\mu,\nu} := \sup_x \sum_{i\in\mathbb{A}} b(\mu,\nu) D_{i,0}(x,\mu) \qquad (a\in\mathbb{A}) \tag{2.69}$$

defines an estimate for the measures $\Pi_\mu(x;\cdot)$ and $\Pi_\nu(x;\cdot)$. The column sums of the matrix $D(x,\mu)$, however, are uniformly bounded above by $\frac{1}{1-\hat{c}}$, due to (2.47), and so

$$r_a^{\mu,\nu} \leq \beta d(\mu,\nu) \qquad (a\in\mathbb{A}). \tag{2.70}$$

This yields our assertion. □

Example 2.23 *Let us put $C=\{0,1\}$ and assume that the transition to a new state itself is made independently by different agents, i.e., for any $\mu\in\mathcal{M}_s(S)$ and for all configurations x, the random field $\Pi_\mu(x;\cdot)$ takes the product form*

$$\Pi_\mu(x;\cdot) = \prod_{a\in\mathbb{A}} \pi_\mu(\theta_a x;\cdot)$$

for some stochastic kernel π_μ from S to C. Given a configuration $x\in S_0$, we assume that the behaviour of agent $a\in\mathbb{A}$ depends on the local situation $(x^b)_{b\in N(a)}$ in the neighborhood of a and on the mean value

$$m(x) := \lim_{n\to\infty} \frac{1}{|\mathbb{A}_n|} \sum_{a\in\mathbb{A}_n} x^a. \tag{2.71}$$

Thus, there exists a measurable function $g: C^{2^{dl}+1}\times[0,1]\to[0,1]$ such that

$$\pi_\mu(\theta_a x,\{+1\}) = g\left((x^b)_{b\in N(a)}, m(\mu)\right).$$

Here, for $\mu\in\mathcal{M}_s(S)$, the quantity $m(\mu)$ is defined by

$$m(\mu) := \int x^0 d\mu.$$

We assume that the mapping g satisfies a uniform Lipschitz condition in its second argument, i.e.,

$$|g(\cdot,m) - g(\cdot,\hat{m})| \leq \beta|m-\hat{m}|.$$

Thus, with $f(x) := x^0$ we have, for all $\mu, \nu \in \mathcal{M}_s(S)$, that

$$\begin{aligned}\sup_x \frac{1}{2}\|\pi_\mu(x;\cdot) - \pi_\nu(x;\cdot)\| &\leq \beta|m(\mu) - m(\nu)| \\ &= \beta\frac{|\mu(f) - \nu(f)|}{\sum_a 2^{\eta|a|}\Delta_a(f)} \\ &\leq \beta d(\mu,\nu),\end{aligned}$$

and so it follows from Proposition 2.22 that our Assumption 2.21 is satisfied whenever $\beta < 1-\alpha$. Such a Lipschitz condition on the dependence on the mean value excludes critical phenomena as they appear in lattice models with sufficiently strong mean field interaction such as, e.g., the Curie-Weiss model.

We can now state and prove the main theorem of this subsection.

Theorem 2.24 *Suppose that our Assumptions 2.3, 2.4, 2.5, 2.16 and 2.21 are satisfied. In this case, there exists a unique shift-invariant random field ν on $(S, \mathcal{S})$ such that, for any initial distribution μ on S_0, we have*

$$\mu R_t(\cdot) := \int_S R_t^x(\cdot)\mu(dx) \xrightarrow{w} \nu(\cdot) \qquad (t \to \infty). \tag{2.72}$$

Proof: Let us fix $x \in S_0$. We are going to show that the sequence of empirical fields $\{R_t^x\}_{t\in\mathbb{N}}$ defined recursively by (2.38) satisfies a contraction condition with respect to the metric $d(\cdot,\cdot)$ introduced in (2.53).

1. Due to Proposition 2.19, we know already that Assumption 2.16 implies

$$d(\mu\Pi_\tau, \nu\Pi_\tau) \leq \alpha d(\mu,\nu) \tag{2.73}$$

for any $\mu, \nu, \tau \in \mathcal{M}_s(S)$.

2. For $\mu, \nu \in \mathcal{M}_s(S)$, we can now combine our Assumption 2.21 with (2.73) for $\tau = \mu$ in order to deduce that

$$d(\mu\Pi_\mu, \nu\Pi_\nu) \leq (\alpha+\beta)d(\mu,\nu). \tag{2.74}$$

Indeed, it follows from the definition of the metric $d(\cdot,\cdot)$ that

$$d(\nu\Pi_\mu, \nu\Pi_\nu) \leq \sup_x d(\Pi_\mu(x;\cdot), \Pi_\nu(x;\cdot))$$

and, due to (2.73), we have

$$\begin{aligned} d(\mu\Pi_\mu, \nu\Pi_\nu) &\leq d(\mu\Pi_\mu, \nu\Pi_\mu) + d(\nu\Pi_\mu, \nu\Pi_\nu) \\ &\leq \alpha d(\mu,\nu) + \sup_x d(\Pi_\mu(x;\cdot), \Pi_\nu(x;\cdot)) \\ &\leq (\alpha+\beta) d(\mu,\nu) \qquad (\alpha+\beta<1). \end{aligned}$$

3. Let us now concentrate on the process $\{\mu R_t\}_{t\in\mathbb{N}}$. First, we fix $x \in S_0$ and analyze the case $\mu = \delta_x$. Since $R(x) = R_0^x$ and because

$$R_{t+1}^x = R_t^x \Pi^t = R_0^x \Pi_{R_0^x} \cdots \Pi_{R_t^x} = R_t^x \Pi_{R_t^x} \qquad (t = 0, 1, 2, \ldots)$$

our estimate (2.74) yields the following contraction property for the sequence of ergodic empirical fields $\{R_t^x\}_{t\in\mathbb{N}}$:

$$\begin{aligned} d(R_{t+T}^x, R_t^x) &= d(R_{t+T-1}^x \Pi_{R_{t+T-1}^x}, R_{t-1}^x \Pi_{R_{t-1}^x}) \\ &\leq (\alpha+\beta) d(R_{t+T-1}^x, R_t^x) \\ &\leq (\alpha+\beta)^t d(R_T^x, R_0^x) \\ &\leq 2(\alpha+\beta)^t. \end{aligned}$$

Here, the last inequality follows from $d(\mu,\nu) \leq \|\mu - \nu\| \leq 2$; see Remark 2.14 (ii). In particular, we obtain that

$$\sup_T d(R_{t+T}^x, R_t^x) \leq 2(\alpha+\beta)^t \tag{2.75}$$

which shows that $\{R_t^x\}_{t\in\mathbb{N}}$ is a Cauchy sequence in the compact space $\mathcal{M}(S)$. Thus, the sequence $\{R_t^x\}_{t\in\mathbb{N}}$ converges weakly to some probability measure $\nu_x \in \mathcal{M}(S)$. Since $R_t^x \in \mathcal{M}_s(S)$ and because $\mathcal{M}_s(S)$ is a closed subset of $\mathcal{M}(S)$, the limit ν_x is a shift-invariant random field. As the set $\mathcal{M}_0(S)$ is dense in $\mathcal{M}_s(S)$ but not closed, there is no reason to expect $\nu_x \in \mathcal{M}_0(S)$. It is now easily seen that, for any initial distribution μ on S_0, there exists a shift-invariant random field ν_μ on S, such that $\mu R_t \stackrel{w}{\longrightarrow} \nu_\mu$ $(t \to \infty)$.

4. It remains to verify that $\nu_{\delta_x} = \nu_{\delta_y}$ for all $x, y \in S_0$. This, however, follows from

$$\begin{aligned} d(R_{t+1}^x, R_{t+1}^y) &= d(R_t^x \Pi_{R_t^x}, R_t^y \Pi_{R_t^y}) \\ &\leq (\alpha+\beta) d(R_t^x, R_t^y) \\ &\leq 2(\alpha+\beta)^{t+1} \stackrel{t\to\infty}{\longrightarrow} 0. \end{aligned} \tag{2.76}$$

This proves our assertion. □

Corollary 2.25 *Let $f \in C(S)$ and suppose that our Assumptions 2.3, 2.4, 2.5, 2.16 and 2.21 are satisfied. For any initial configuration $x \in S_0$, we have convergence of macroscopic quantities of the form $\int f(y)R(x_t)(dy)$ along $\mathbb{P}_x$-a.e. path of the microscopic process to $\int f d\nu$.*

We are now going to consider the case where the asymptotic behaviour of the macroscopic process depends on the initial configuration. To this end, we replace our Assumption 2.21 by the following weaker condition:

Assumption 2.26 *For any $\mu \in \mathcal{M}_0(S)$, there exists constants $t(\mu) \in \mathbb{N}$ and $\beta < 1 - \alpha$ such that*

$$\sup_x d(\Pi_{\mu_s}(x;\cdot), \Pi_{\mu_s \Pi_{\mu_s}}(x;\cdot)) \leq \beta d(\mu_s, \mu_s \Pi_{\mu_s}) \qquad (s \geq t(\mu)), \tag{2.77}$$

where $\mu_0 = \mu$ and $\mu_{s+1} = \mu_s \Pi_{\mu_s}$. That is, we require (2.65) to hold true for all random fields ν that take the form $\nu = \mu_s \Pi_{\mu_s}$, $s \geq t(\mu)$.

Let us study a simple example where Assumption 2.26 holds true, whereas our Assumption 2.21 is violated.

Example 2.27 *We put $C = \{0, 1\}$ and assume that the transition to a new state itself is made independently by different agents. Given a configuration $x \in S_0$, the behaviour of an individual agent $a \in \mathbb{A}$ depends on the average situation in his neighborhood $N(a)$ and on the average situation throughout the whole population described by the mean value $m(x)$ defined in (2.71). More precisely, we assume that the individual transition dynamics takes the form*

$$\pi^a(x; \{+1\}) = \pi_{R(x)}((x^b)_{b \in N(a)}; \{+1\}) = \frac{c}{|N(a)|} \sum_{b \in N(a)} x^b + f(m(x)) \tag{2.78}$$

for some constant $c \in \mathbb{R}$ and for a function $f : [0, 1] \to \mathbb{R}$. In particular, for any initial configuration $x \in S_0$ and for all $t \in \mathbb{N}$, we have that

$$\sup_y \frac{1}{2} \|\pi_{R(x_t)}(y;\cdot) - \pi_{R(x_t)\Pi_{R(x_t)}}(y;\cdot)\| = |f(m(x_t)) - f(m(x_{t+1}))| \qquad \mathbb{P}_x\text{-a.s.} \tag{2.79}$$

Due to the linear structure of the individual transition dynamics, the evolution of the sequence of empirical averages is almost surely described by the equation

$$m(x_{t+1}) = \hat{F}(m(x_t)) := cm(x_t) + f(m(x_t)) \qquad (t = 0, 1, 2, \ldots),$$

and our uniform Dobrushin condition (2.51) is satisfied with $\alpha_0 = \frac{c}{2^{ld}+1}$ $(c < 2^{ld}+1)$.

Let $m^* \in [0,1]$ *be a fixed-point of the mapping* $\hat{F} : [0,1] \to \mathbb{R}$ *defined above and let* $\varrho^* := (1-m^*, m^*)$ *be a probability measure on* C. *Obviously, the sequence of empirical distributions* $\{\varrho(x_t)\}_{t\in\mathbb{N}}$ *is* $\mathbb{P}_{\mu^*}$*-a.s. constant, where the random field* μ^* *on* $(S, \mathcal{S})$ *is given by the product measure*

$$\mu^* = \prod_{a\in\mathbb{A}} \varrho^*.$$

Consider now the function $f(m) := \frac{9}{2}m^2(1-m)$ *and put* $c = \frac{2^{ld}+1}{16}$. *The mapping* $\hat{F} : [0,1] \to \mathbb{R}$ *defined by* $\hat{F}(m) := \frac{1}{16}m + f(m)$ *has three fixed points:*

$$m_0 := 0, \quad m_1 := \frac{1}{2} - \sqrt{\frac{1}{24}}, \quad m_2 := \frac{1}{2} + \sqrt{\frac{1}{24}}.$$

Thus, our Assumption 2.21 is violated. However, Assumption 2.26 is still satisfied.

In order to see this, we fix an initial state $x \in S_0$. *An easy calculation shows that there exists a critical value* $m_c \in [0,1]$, $m_c \neq m_1$, *given by*

$$m_c = \hat{F}^{-1}(m_1)$$

such that the asymptotic behaviour of the sequence $\{m(x_t)\}_{t\in\mathbb{N}}$ *depends in the following manner on the initial configuration:*

$$\lim_{t\to\infty} m(x_t) = \begin{cases} 0 & \text{if } m(x) \in [0, m_1) \cup (m_c, 1] \\ m_1 & \text{if } m(x) \in \{m_1, m_c\} \\ m_2 & \text{otherwise} \end{cases} \qquad \mathbb{P}_x\text{-a.s.}$$

Since $f'(0) = 0$ *and* $|f'(m_2)| \approx 0.36$, *we see that*

$$|f(m(x_{t+1})) - f(m(x_t))| \le \beta |m(x_{t+1}) - m(x_t)| \qquad \mathbb{P}_x\text{-a.s.}$$

where $\beta < \frac{15}{16}$ *for all* t *sufficiently large. We can now proceed as in Example 2.23. Due to (2.79) and because of Proposition 2.22 (i), we get*

$$\sup_y d(\Pi_{R_t^x}(y;\cdot), \Pi_{R_t^x \Pi_{R_t^x}}(y;\cdot)) \le \beta d(R_t^x, R_t^x \Pi_{R_t^x}),$$

where $\alpha_0 + \beta < 1$ *for all* $t \in \mathbb{N}$ *large enough.*

Let us now establish a generalization of Theorem 2.24.

Theorem 2.28 *Suppose that Assumptions 2.3, 2.4, 2.5, 2.16 and 2.26 are satisfied. In this case, the following holds true:*

(i) For any $x \in S_0$, there exists a measure ν_x such that $R_t^x \xrightarrow{w} \nu_x$ as $t \to \infty$.

(ii) For any initial configuration μ concentrated on S_0, we have

$$\int R_t^x(\cdot)\mu(dx) \xrightarrow{w} \nu_\mu(\cdot) := \int \nu_x(\cdot)\mu(dx) \qquad (t \to \infty). \tag{2.80}$$

Proof: Let us fix $x \in S_0$. Without loss of generality we may assume that $t(R(x)) = 1$. Using the same arguments as in the proof of Theorem 2.24 we get

$$d(R_{t+1}^x, R_t^x) \leq 2(\alpha + \beta)^t.$$

In particular, for any $\epsilon > 0$, there exists $t_0 \in \mathbb{N}$ such that

$$\sup_T d(R_{t+T}^x, R_t^x) \leq 2 \sum_{s \geq t_0} (\alpha + \beta)^s < \epsilon$$

for all $t \geq t_0$. Thus, $\{R_t^x\}_{t \in \mathbb{N}}$ is again a Cauchy sequence with respect to the metric $d(\cdot, \cdot)$, and so there exists a shift invariant probability measure ν_x on $(S, \mathcal{S})$ such that

$$R_t^x \xrightarrow{w} \nu_x \qquad (t \to \infty).$$

Now, (ii) is obvious as the mapping $x \mapsto \nu_x$ from S_0 to $\mathcal{M}_s(S)$ is measurable. □

2.3.2 Microscopic Convergence

In this subsection, we are going to demonstrate that convergence on the macroscopic level of empirical fields implies local convergence on the microscopic level. Economically, this means that aggregate behaviour drives individual behaviour into equilibrium whenever the macroscopic process itself settles down in the long run. Under suitable contraction and continuity assumptions we show that the microscopic and macroscopic limit coincide. In such a situation, we have at the same time macroscopic and microscopic convergence to the same random field μ on $(S, \mathcal{S})$. The class of all possible limiting distributions can therefore be characterized by a fixed-point property.

Throughout this section, we assume that the macroscopic process $\{R(x_t)\}_{t \in \mathbb{N}}$ converges along $\mathbb{P}_x$-a.e. path of the microscopic process to some random field ν_x

on $(S, \mathcal{S})$ and that the weighted Dobrushin-Vasserstein-Condition (2.56) holds true. The dependence of the specification $\gamma^{x,\mu}$ on the parameter μ is assumed to be continuous. More precisely, for some constant $\beta^* > 0$, and for any two random fields μ, ν on $(S, \mathcal{S})$, we let the inequality

$$b(\mu, \nu) := \sup_x \frac{1}{2} \int_S \|\gamma_0^{x,\mu}(\cdot; v) - \gamma_0^{x,\nu}(\cdot; v)\| \Pi_\mu(x; dv) \leq \beta^* d(\mu, \nu) \tag{2.81}$$

be satisfied. Here, $d(\cdot, \cdot)$ denotes the metric given by (2.53) which induces the weak topology on $\mathcal{M}(S)$. For (2.81) to hold true, it is clearly enough to require

$$\sup_{x,v} \frac{1}{2} \|\gamma_0^{x,\mu}(\cdot; v) - \gamma_0^{x,\nu}(\cdot; v)\| \leq \beta^* d(\mu, \nu) \qquad (\mu, \nu \in \mathcal{M}_s(S)).$$

It follows from the proof of Proposition 2.22 that (2.81) implies

$$\sup_x d(\Pi_\mu(x; \cdot), \Pi_\nu(x; \cdot)) \leq \frac{\beta^*}{1 - \hat{c}} d(\mu, \nu). \tag{2.82}$$

Theorem 2.29 *Suppose that our Assumptions 2.3, 2.4 and 2.5 are satisfied, that the weighted Dobrushin-Vasserstein-Condition (2.56) is met, that the continuity assumption (2.81) holds true and that the initial distribution μ is concentrated on S_0. If, for μ-a.e. $x \in S_0$, the sequence of empirical fields $\{R_t^x\}_{t \in \mathbb{N}}$ converges in the weak topology to ν_x, then the following holds true:*

(i) The microscopic process $\{x_t\}_{t \in \mathbb{N}}$ converges in law to a probability measure $\bar{\nu}_\mu$. The random field $\bar{\nu}_\mu$ is the unique equilibrium of the Feller kernel Π_{ν_μ}, i.e.,

$$\bar{\nu}_\mu = \bar{\nu}_\mu \Pi_{\nu_\mu}. \tag{2.83}$$

Here, $\nu_\mu := \int \nu_x \mu(dx)$.

(ii) The macroscopic and the microscopic limit coincide, i.e., $\bar{\nu}_\mu = \nu_\mu$. Thus, we can characterize the class of all limiting distributions by the fixed-point property

$$\nu_\mu = \nu_\mu \Pi_{\nu_\mu}. \tag{2.84}$$

Proof: Our proof is related to an argument given in Föllmer (1979a). For any initial distribution μ, we denote by $\mathbb{E}_\mu$ the expectation with respect to the law $\mathbb{P}_\mu$. We shall first consider the case $\mu = \delta_x$ and demonstrate that our microscopic process converges in distribution to the unique equilibrium of the Feller kernel $\Pi_{\nu_{\delta_x}}$.

1. Let us fix $x \in S_0$, $A \in \mathcal{A}$ and $B \in S_A$. We are going to show that

$$\lim_{t\to\infty} \mathbb{E}_{\delta_x}[\Pi^t \mathbf{1}_B - \Pi^t_{\nu_x}\mathbf{1}_B] = 0. \tag{2.85}$$

Here, $\nu_x := \nu_{\delta_x}$. In Step 3 below, we use (2.85) and Vasserstein's convergence theorem in order to establish our assertion.

For $t, T \in \mathbb{N}$ we can write

$$\mathbb{E}_{\delta_x}\Pi^{t+T}(B) = \mathbb{E}_{\delta_x}[\Pi^t_{\nu_x}\mathbf{1}_B(x_T)] + R_{t,T}, \tag{2.86}$$

where we put

$$R_{t,T} := \mathbb{E}_{\delta_x}[(\Pi_{R^x_T}\cdots\Pi_{R^x_{T+t-1}} - \Pi^t_{\nu_x})\mathbf{1}_B(x_T)]. \tag{2.87}$$

In the next step we will show that $\lim_{T\to\infty}|R_{t,T}| = 0$ uniformly in $t \in \mathbb{N}$.

2. Note that

$$\begin{aligned}|R_{t,T}| &= \left|\sum_{k=1}^{t}\mathbb{E}_{\delta_x}\left[\Pi_{R^x_T}\cdots\Pi_{R^x_{T+k-2}}(\Pi_{R^x_{T+k-1}}\Pi^{t-k}_{\nu_x} - \Pi_{\nu_x}\Pi^{t-k}_{\nu_x})\mathbf{1}_B(x_T)\right]\right| \\ &\le \sum_{k=1}^{t}\mathbb{E}_{\delta_x}[\sup_y|(\Pi_{R^x_{T+k-1}} - \Pi_{\nu_x})(\Pi^{t-k}_{\nu_x}\mathbf{1}_B)(y)|].\end{aligned}$$

For any $k \in \mathbb{N}$, let us introduce a mapping $g_k : S \to \mathbb{R}$ by the relation

$$g_k(z) := \Pi^{t-k}_{\nu_x}\mathbf{1}_B(z)$$

so that

$$|R_{t,T}| \le \sum_{k=1}^{t}\sup_y\left|\int g_k(z)(\Pi_{R^x_{T+k-1}}(y;dz) - \Pi_{\nu_x}(y;dz))\right|.$$

Due to the Feller property of the transition kernel Π_{ν_x}, we have $g_k \in \mathcal{C}(S)$. For $k \in \mathbb{N}$, let the vector $r^{R^x_{T+k-1},\nu_x} = (r_i^{R^x_{T+k-1},\nu_x})_{i\in\mathbb{A}}$ be defined as in (2.69). Thus, $r^{R^x_{T+k-1},\nu_x}$ is an estimate for the measures $\Pi_{R^x_{T+k-1}}(y;\cdot)$ and $\Pi_{\nu_x}(y;\cdot)$ $(y \in S_0)$, and so we obtain the following inequality:

$$\sup_y\left|\int g_k(z)(\Pi_{R^x_{T+k-1}}(y;dz) - \Pi_{\nu_x}(y;dz))\right| \le \sum_i r_i^{R^x_{T+k-1},\nu_x}\Delta_i(g_k). \tag{2.88}$$

Due to our continuity assumption (2.81), we know that (2.82) holds true and this yields

$$r_i^{R^x_{T+k-1},\nu_x} \le \frac{\beta^*}{1-\hat{c}} d(R^x_{T+k-1},\nu_x) \qquad (i \in \mathbb{A});$$

see also (2.70). Thus, we have that

$$\begin{aligned} |R_{t,T}| &\le \frac{\beta^*}{1-\hat{c}} \sum_k \left[\sum_i \Delta_i(g_k) d(R^x_{T+k-1},\nu_x) \right] \\ &\le \sup_{t \ge T} d(R^x_t,\nu_x) \frac{\beta^*}{1-\hat{c}} \sum_{k,i} \Delta_i(g_k). \end{aligned}$$

Since the weighted uniform Dobrushin-Vasserstein-Condition (2.56) is satisfied it follows from (2.52) that

$$\sum_{k,i} \Delta_i(g_k) \le \sum_{k=1}^{t} \alpha_0^{t-k} |A| \le |A| \frac{1}{1-\alpha_0}.$$

Thus, uniformly in $t \in \mathbb{N}$, we have

$$\lim_{T\to\infty} |R_{t,T}| \le \lim_{T\to\infty} \sup_{t\ge T} d(R^x_t,\nu_x) \frac{|A|\beta^*}{(1-\hat{c})(1-\alpha)} = 0 \tag{2.89}$$

as the sequence of empirical fields $\{R^x_t\}_{t\in\mathbb{N}}$ converges to ν_x in the weak topology. This shows (2.85).

3. We shall now apply a basic result of Vasserstein (1969) in order to establish (i). Due to (2.89), we have that

$$\begin{aligned} &\lim_{t,T\to\infty} |\mathbb{E}_{\delta_x}[\Pi^{t+T}\mathbf{1}_B - \Pi^{t+T}_{\nu_x}\mathbf{1}_B]| \qquad (2.90) \\ = &\lim_{t,T\to\infty} \left| \mathbb{E}_{\delta_x} \Pi^t_{\nu_x} \mathbf{1}_B(x_T) + R_{t,T} - \mathbb{E}_{\delta_x} \Pi^t_{\nu_x} \mathbf{1}_B(x_T) \right| = 0. \end{aligned}$$

Due to (2.56), Vasserstein's theorem yields the existence of a unique random field $\bar{\nu}_x$ on $(S,\mathcal{S})$ such that $\Pi^t_{\nu_x}(y;\cdot) \xrightarrow{w} \bar{\nu}_x(\cdot)$ as $t\to\infty$ $(y \in S)$. Together with (2.90), this shows that

$$\lim_{t\to\infty} \Pi^t(x;B) = \lim_{t,T\to\infty} \Pi^{t+T}(x;B) = \lim_{t,T\to\infty} \Pi^{t+T}_{\nu_x}(x;B) = \bar{\nu}_x(B)$$

for any $B \in \mathcal{S}_A$ $(A \in \mathcal{A})$. This proves (i) for $\mu = \delta_x$.

4. Let μ be an initial distribution which is concentrated on the set S_0. From our preceding calculations it is easily seen that

$$\mu\Pi^t \xrightarrow{w} \bar{\nu}_\mu, \tag{2.91}$$

where $\bar{\nu}_\mu$ is the unique invariant measure of the kernel Π_{ν_μ}.

5. Let us now verify the fixed-point property (2.84) and show that the limiting distribution both on the macroscopic and on the microscopic level coincide. Due to our Assumption 2.16, the Feller kernel Π_{ν_μ} admits a unique equilibrium, and so it is enough to show that $\nu_\mu = \nu_\mu \Pi_{\nu_\mu}$.

   To this end, it suffices to consider the case $\mu = \delta_x$ ($x \in S_0$). It follows from Proposition 2.19, from the recursive definition of the sequence $\{R_t^x\}_{t\in\mathbb{N}}$ in (2.38) and from (2.82) that

$$\begin{aligned} d(\nu_x\Pi_{\nu_x}, \nu_x) &\le d(\nu_x\Pi_{\nu_x}, \nu_x\Pi_{R_t^x}) + d(\nu_x\Pi_{R_t^x}, R_t^x\Pi_{R_t^x}) + d(R_t^x\Pi_{R_t^x}, \nu_x) \\ &\le \sup_y d(\Pi_{\nu_x}(y;\cdot), \Pi_{R_t^x}(y;\cdot)) + d(\nu_x, R_t^x) + d(R_{t+1}^x, \nu_x) \\ &\le \frac{\beta^*}{1-\hat{c}} d(\nu_x, R_t^x) + d(\nu_x, R_t^x) + d(R_{t+1}^x, \nu_x) \to 0 \end{aligned}$$

   as $t \to 0$. Thus, $\nu_x = \nu_x\Pi_{\nu_x}$, and so it follows from (i) that $\nu_x = \bar{\nu}_x$, i.e., the limiting distribution on the microscopic and on the macroscopic level coincide.

This proves our assertion. □

Corollary 2.30 *We have the following variant of Theorem 2.29: Let $(X, \mathcal{X})$ be a measurable space and let $\Phi : \mathcal{M}_s(S) \to X$ be a measurable mapping. Suppose that, for a given configuration $x \in S_0$, an individual agent $a \in \mathbb{A}$ reacts to $\Phi(R(x))$, to the local situation $(x^b)_{b\in N(a)}$ in a neighborhood of a and to his microscopic environment. Assume moreover that the sequence $\{\Phi(R_t^x)\}_{t\in\mathbb{N}}$ converges $\mathbb{P}_x$-a.s. to $\Phi^x \in X$, that our uniform Dobrushin-Vasserstein-Condition holds true and suppose that the dependence of the local specifications on the parameter $\Phi(R(x))$ is continuous. It follows from the proof of Theorem 2.29 that, for any initial distribution μ on S_0, the microscopic process converges in distribution to the unique equilibrium $\bar{\nu}_\mu$ of the Feller kernel $\Pi_{\Phi^*(\mu)}$. Here, $\Phi^*(\mu) := \int \Phi^x \mu(dx)$.*

Remark 2.31 *Suppose that the microscopic process converges in law to a random field μ^* on $(S, \mathcal{S})$. Due to Theorem 2.29 (ii), this random field has the fixed point* *property* $\mu^* = \mu^*\Pi_{\mu^*}$. *If* μ^* *is ergodic, then* $\mu^* = \mu^*\Pi_{\mu^*} = \mu^*\Pi$. *In this case, the macroscopic process is almost surely constant under the law* $\mathbb{P}_{\mu^*}$ *and the underlying microscopic process is stationary. However, if* $\mu^* \in \mathcal{M}_s(S)\backslash\mathcal{M}_0(S)$ *then* μ^* *is not necessarily an invariant measure for our microscopic process as the kernel* Π *typically does not have the Feller property.*

2.3.3 Asymptotic Dynamics in Mean-Field-Models

In this section, we consider a mean-field type model and analyze the asymptotic behaviour both on the macroscopic level and on the microscopic level in greater detail. In particular, conditions for the existence of stationary distributions for the microscopic process are given.

The individual transition laws $(\pi^a(x;\cdot))_{a\in\mathbb{A}}$ are assumed to depend on the empirical field $R(x) \in \mathcal{M}_0(S)$ only through the empirical distribution $\varrho(x) \in \mathcal{M}(C)$. Thus, for any $x \in S_0$, the random field $\Pi(x;\cdot)$ takes the product form

$$\Pi(x;\cdot) = \prod_{a\in\mathbb{A}} \pi^a(x,;\cdot) = \prod_{a\in\mathbb{A}} \pi(x^a, \varrho(x);\cdot) \tag{2.92}$$

for some stochastic kernel π from $C \times \mathcal{M}(C)$ to C. We assume that the dependence of the transition kernel π on the empirical distribution ϱ is continuous and that the weighted uniform Dobrushin-Vasserstein-Condition is satisfied. In our present mean-field type setting, this assumption reduces to condition (2.57).

We are mow going to formulate sufficient conditions for the existence of stationary distributions for our microscopic process $\{x_t\}_{t\in\mathbb{N}}$. To this end, let ϱ_0 be a probability measure on the set of possible individual states C and let $\mu_0 := \prod_{a\in\mathbb{A}} \varrho_0 \in \mathcal{M}_0(S)$ be the initial distribution of our microscopic process. In this case, the dynamics on the microscopic level is described by a sequence of random fields $\{\mu_t\}_{t\in\mathbb{N}} = \{\mu_0\Pi^t\}_{t\in\mathbb{N}}$ on the configuration space $(S, \mathcal{S})$, where

$$\mu_1 = \mu_0\Pi = \int_S \prod_{a\in\mathbb{A}} \pi(x^a, \varrho_0;\cdot) \prod_{a\in\mathbb{A}} \varrho_0(dx^a) = \prod_{a\in\mathbb{A}} \int_C \pi(x^a, \varrho_0;\cdot)\varrho_0(dx^a)$$

and

$$\mu_t = \mu_{t-1}\Pi_{\mu_{t-1}} \qquad (t = 1, 2, \ldots).$$

Since μ_0 is a product measure, the dynamics on the macroscopic and on the microscopic level coincide, due to Proposition 2.8. The macroscopic process $\{R(x_t)\}_{t\in\mathbb{N}}$

is $\mathbb{P}_{\mu_0}$-almost surely described the sequence of empirical fields $\{\prod_{a\in\mathbb{A}} \varrho_t\}_{t\in\mathbb{N}}$, where the sequence of empirical distributions $\{\varrho_t\}_{t\in\mathbb{N}}$ is defined by the recursive relation

$$\varrho_{t+1}(\cdot) = G(\varrho_t) := \int_C \pi(c;\varrho_t;\cdot)\varrho_t(dc) \qquad (t = 0, 1, 2, \ldots). \tag{2.93}$$

Note that any fixed-point $\varrho^* \in \mathcal{M}(C)$ of the mapping $G : \mathcal{M}(C) \to \mathcal{M}(C)$ defined by (2.93) induces an equilibrium μ^* for our microscopic process. Indeed, the random field

$$\mu^* := \prod_{a\in\mathbb{A}} \varrho^* \in \mathcal{M}_0(S)$$

on $(S, \mathcal{S})$ is ergodic and has the fixed point property $\mu^* = \mu^*\Pi_{\mu^*}$. Thus, the microscopic process is stationary under the law $\mathbb{P}_{\mu^*}$.

Let us now fix an initial state $\varrho_0 \in \mathcal{M}(C)$ and assume that the sequence $\{\varrho_t\}_{t\in\mathbb{N}}$ governed by (2.93) converges to some limit $\varrho^*(\varrho_0)$. It follows from our preceding considerations that we have convergence in law of the microscopic process:

$$\mu_0\Pi^t = \left(\prod_{a\in\mathbb{A}} \varrho_0\right)\Pi^t \xrightarrow{w} \prod_{a\in\mathbb{A}} \varrho^*(\varrho_0) \qquad (t \to \infty).$$

Since $R(x_t) = \prod_{a\in\mathbb{A}} \varrho(x_t) = \mu_0\Pi^t$ for $\mu_0\Pi^t$-a.e. $x_t \in S$ $(t \in \mathbb{N})$, we see that convergence of the sequence of empirical fields $\{R(x_t)\}_{t\in\mathbb{N}}$ to some random field μ^* on $(S, \mathcal{S})$ reduces to convergence of the sequence of empirical distributions $\{\varrho(x_t)\}_{t\in\mathbb{N}}$ to a measure ϱ^* on C:

$$R(x_t) \xrightarrow{w} \prod_{a\in\mathbb{A}} \varrho^*(\varrho_0) =: \mu^*(\varrho_0) \in \mathcal{M}_0(S) \qquad \mathbb{P}_{\mu_0}\text{-a.s.} \qquad (t \to \infty).$$

Under the law $\mathbb{P}_{\mu^*}$, the microscopic process is stationary and the macroscopic process is almost surely constant. Thus, any limit of the sequence $\{\varrho_t\}_{t\in\mathbb{N}}$ governed by (2.93) induces a stationary distribution for our microscopic process.

Let us now show that the microscopic process in a simple mean-field model converges locally to a product measure on $(S, \mathcal{S})$ whenever the sequence of empirical distributions $\{\varrho(x_t)\}_{t\in\mathbb{N}}$ converges $\mathbb{P}_x$-almost surely to some measure $\varrho^*(x)$ on C. For any initial distribution μ on S_0, our microscopic process converges in distribution to the unique equilibrium $\bar{\nu}_\mu$ of the Feller kernel

$$\Pi_{\varrho^*(\mu)}(x;\cdot) = \prod_{a\in\mathbb{A}} \pi(x^a;\varrho^*(\mu);\cdot),$$

due to Corollary 2.30, where $\varrho^*(\mu) := \int \varrho^*(x)\mu(dx)$. Since $\Pi_{\varrho^*(\mu)}$ is a product measure, we deduce that the equilibrium $\bar{\nu}_\mu$ itself is also a product measure, and so there exists a measure ϱ^*_μ on C such that

$$\mu\Pi^t \xrightarrow{w} \bar{\nu}_\mu = \prod_{a\in\mathbb{A}} \varrho^*_\mu \qquad (t \to \infty).$$

In particular, for any initial distribution μ, the microscopic process converges in law to an *ergodic* random field μ^* on $(S, \mathcal{S})$ whenever the sequence of empirical distributions $\{\varrho(x_t)\}_{t\in\mathbb{N}}$ settles down in the long run. Thus, for any initial configuration $x \in S_0$, we have convergence on the macroscopic level to a product measure:

$$R(x_t) = R(x)\Pi^t \xrightarrow{w} \prod_{a\in\mathbb{A}} \varrho^*_{R(x)} \qquad \mathbb{P}_x\text{-a.s.} \qquad (t \to \infty)$$

2.4 Some Comments on the Induced Driving Sequence of the Asset Price Process

Let us now return to our asset price dynamics described by (1.20). We assume that, for some initial state $x \in S_0$, the sequence of empirical fields $\{R(x_t)\}_{t\in\mathbb{N}}$ converges almost surely to a random field μ^*_x on $(S, \mathcal{S})$ which has the fixed-point property $\mu^*_x = \mu^*_x\Pi_{\mu^*_x}$. If, as in a simple mean-field model, the random field μ^*_x is ergodic, then the macroscopic process is $\mathbb{P}_{\mu^*_x}$-almost surely constant, and the microscopic process is stationary under the law $\mathbb{P}_{\mu^*_x}$. In this case, randomness disappears on the macroscopic level of empirical fields. Economically, this means that the mood of the market is almost surely constant. In such a situation, our asset price process $\{p_t\}_{t\in\mathbb{N}}$ is driven by a sequence of independent and identically distributed random variables $\{\tilde{\varrho}_t\}_{t\in\mathbb{N}}$ whose law takes the form $\tilde{Q}(\Pr(\mu^*_x);\cdot)$. Here, the projection mapping $\Pr : \mathcal{M}_s(S) \to \mathcal{M}(C)$ is defined in (1.31). In Section 4.1.1, we are going to formulate conditions on the probability measure $\tilde{Q}(\Pr(\mu^*_x);\cdot)$ and on the mapping F introduced in (1.14) which guarantee that the sequence of temporary price equilibria $\{p_t\}_{t\in\mathbb{N}}$ defined recursively by (1.20) converges to a stationary regime as $t \to \infty$.

If $\mu^*_x \in \mathcal{M}_s(S)\backslash\mathcal{M}_0(S)$, then the random field μ^*_x is not necessarily an invariant measure for our microscopic process as the stochastic kernel Π typically does not have the Feller property. In this case, there is no reason to expect that the environment $\{\tilde{\varrho}_t\}_{t\in\mathbb{N}}$ for the evolution of the price process is stationary under the law $\mathbb{P}_{\mu^*_x}$. However, we are able to formulate an additional condition on the stochastic kernel $\tilde{Q}$ on $\mathcal{M}(C)$ which allows us to approximate the driving sequence $\{\tilde{\varrho}_t\}_{t\in\mathbb{N}}$ in law by a stationary environment. In such a situation, a stationarity assumption on the environment may serve as an approximation whenever the sequence of temporary equilibrium prices $\{p_t\}_{t\in\mathbb{N}}$ depends continuously on the driving process $\{\tilde{\varrho}_t\}_{t\in\mathbb{N}}$.

Definition 2.32 *Let (M_1, d_{M_1}) be a metric space and $(M_2, \mathcal{M}_2)$ be a measurable space. We say that a stochastic kernel $\hat{Q}$ from M_1 to $\mathcal{M}_2$ satisfies a* ***uniform Lipschitz condition****, if*

$$\sup_B \sup_{m,\hat{m}} \frac{|\hat{Q}(m;B) - \hat{Q}(\hat{m};B)|}{d_{M_1}(m,\hat{m})} \leq \tilde{L} < \infty. \tag{2.94}$$

It follows from Lemma A.4 that a stochastic kernel $\hat{Q}$ from M_1 to $\mathcal{M}_2$ satisfies a uniform Lipschitz condition if, for example, the measures $\hat{Q}(m;\cdot)$ $(m \in M_1)$ are absolutely continuous with respect to some law ν on $(M_2, \mathcal{M}_2)$ and if, moreover, the respective density functions are uniformly Lipschitz continuous.

Definition 2.33 *In the sequel, it will be convenient to denote by*

$$\mathrm{Law}(X, \mathbb{P}) \tag{2.95}$$

the law of a random variable X defined on some probability space $(\Omega, \mathcal{F}, \mathbb{P})$.

We are now going to show that any limit μ_x of the macroscopic process induces an ergodic random field ν_x on $(S, \mathcal{S})$ such that the environment $\{\tilde{\varrho}_t\}_{t\in\mathbb{N}}$ for the evolution of the stock price process is "approximately stationary" under the law $\mathbb{P}_{\nu_x}$. To this end, we shall first establish the following result.

Lemma 2.34 *Let (M_1, d_{M_1}) be a bounded metric space and let $u : M_1 \to M_1$ be a measurable mapping. For a starting point $m = m_0$, consider the deterministic sequence $\{m_t\}_{t\in\mathbb{N}}$ which is defined by the recursive relation*

$$m_{t+1} = u(m_t) \qquad (t \in \mathbb{N}).$$

We assume that

$$\lim_{t\to\infty} m_t = m^*(m) = u(m^*(m)) \in M_1$$

and that the contraction condition

$$d_{M_1}(m_t, m_{t+1}) \leq \alpha d_{M_1}(m_{t-1}, m_t) \qquad (\alpha < 1) \tag{2.96}$$

is satisfied. Moreover, we denote by $(M_2, \mathcal{M}_2)$ a measurable space and $\hat{Q}$ is stochastic kernel from M_1 to $\mathcal{M}_2$ which satisfies a uniform Lipschitz condition in the sense of (2.94).

For any initial value $m \in M_1$ of the process $\{m_t\}_{t\in\mathbb{N}}$, let $\{\tilde{m}_t\}_{t\in\mathbb{N}}$ be a sequence of random variables taking values in M_2. The sequence $\{\tilde{m}_t\}_{t\in\mathbb{N}}$ is defined on a probability space $(\Omega, \mathcal{F}, \mathbb{P}_m)$, and the law of the random variable $\tilde{m}_t$ takes the form

$$\mathrm{Law}(\tilde{m}_t, \mathbb{P}_m) = \hat{Q}(m_t; \cdot) \qquad (t \in \mathbb{N}).$$

Then there exists a constant $L < \infty$ such that

$$\|\mathrm{Law}(\{\tilde{m}_t\}_{t\in\mathbb{N}}, \mathbb{P}_m) - \mathrm{Law}(\{\tilde{m}_t\}_{t\in\mathbb{N}}, \mathbb{P}_{m^*(m)})\| \leq L d_{M_1}(m, m^*(m)).$$

In particular, we have that

$$\lim_{T\to\infty} \|\mathrm{Law}(\{\tilde{m}_t\}_{t\in\mathbb{N}}, \mathbb{P}_{m_T}) - \mathrm{Law}(\{\tilde{m}_t\}_{t\in\mathbb{N}}, \mathbb{P}_{m^*(m)})\| = 0,$$

i.e., the process $\{\tilde{m}_t\}_{t\in\mathbb{N}}$ behaves asymptotically like a sequence of i.i.d. random variables.

Proof: Let us fix $t \in \mathbb{N}$ and $B \in \otimes_{i=1}^{t} \mathcal{B}(M_1)$. First, we are going to verify that the mapping

$$m \mapsto \mathbb{P}_m[\{\tilde{m}_0, \tilde{m}_1, \ldots, \tilde{m}_t\} \in B]$$

from $\{m^*, m_0, m_1, \ldots\}$ to $[0, 1]$ is Lipschitz continuous with constant $L := \frac{\tilde{L}}{(1-\alpha)}$. It follows from (2.94) that

$$|\mathbb{P}_m[\tilde{m}_0 \in B] - \mathbb{P}_{\hat{m}}[\tilde{m}_0 \in B]| \leq \tilde{L} d_{M_1}(m, \hat{m}).$$

For any $t \in \mathbb{N}$, let us introduce the quantity

$$\alpha_t := \sup_B \sup_{m \neq \hat{m}} \frac{|\mathbb{P}_m[\{\tilde{m}_0, \tilde{m}_1, \ldots, \tilde{m}_t\} \in B] - \mathbb{P}_{\hat{m}}[\{\tilde{m}_0, \tilde{m}_1, \ldots, \tilde{m}_t\} \in B]|}{d_{M_1}(m, \hat{m})}.$$

Due to (2.96) and (2.94), we have that

$$\begin{aligned}
& \sup_B |\mathbb{P}_m[\{\tilde{m}_0, \tilde{m}_1, \ldots, \tilde{m}_{t+1}\} \in B] - \mathbb{P}_{\hat{m}}[\{\tilde{m}_0, \tilde{m}_1, \ldots, \tilde{m}_{t+1}\} \in B]| \\
\leq\ & \sup_B |\mathbb{P}_m[\tilde{m}_0 \in B] - \mathbb{P}_{\hat{m}}[\tilde{m}_0 \in B]| \\
& + \sup_B \left|\mathbb{P}_{u(m)}[\{\tilde{m}_0, \tilde{m}_1, \ldots, \tilde{m}_t\} \in B] - \mathbb{P}_{u(\hat{m})}[\{\tilde{m}_0, \tilde{m}_1, \ldots, \tilde{m}_t\} \in B]\right| \\
\leq\ & (\tilde{L} + \alpha\alpha_t) d_{M_1}(m, \hat{m}),
\end{aligned}$$

and so it follows by induction that $\alpha_{t+1} \leq \tilde{L}\sum_{l=0}^{t+1}\alpha^l$. Thus,

$$\alpha_t \leq \tilde{L}\sum_{i=0}^{\infty}\alpha^t = \frac{\tilde{L}}{(1-\alpha)}.$$

Now a simple monotone class argument yields our assertion. Indeed, let us fix $m \in M_1$ and denote by $\mathbb{G}$ the class of all $B \in \otimes_{i\geq 1}\mathcal{B}(M)$ satisfying

$$|\mathbb{P}_m[\{\tilde{m}_t\}_{t\in\mathbb{N}} \in B] - \mathbb{P}_{m^*(m)}[\{\tilde{m}_t\}_{t\in\mathbb{N}} \in B]| \leq Ld_M(m, m^*(m)).$$

It is easily seen that $\mathbb{G}$ is a monotone class including the σ-field $\otimes_{i=1}^{l}\mathcal{B}(M_1)$ $(l \in \mathbb{N})$. Thus, our assertion follows from the monotone class theorem. □

Corollary 2.35 *Assume that, for some initial state $x \in S_0$, the sequence of empirical fields $\{R_t^x\}_{t\in\mathbb{N}}$ given by (2.38) satisfies the contraction condition*

$$d(R_{t+1}^x, R_t^x) \leq \alpha d(R_t^x, R_{t-1}^x) \qquad (t = 0, 1, \ldots)$$

for some $\alpha < 1$ and that the macroscopic process converges almost surely to some random field μ_x^* on $(S, \mathcal{S})$ which satisfies the fixed point equation $\mu_x^* = \mu_x^*\Pi_{\mu_x^*}$.

Let $\{\tilde{m}_t\}_{t\in\mathbb{N}}$ be a sequence of i.i.d. random variables defined on some probability space $(\Omega, \mathcal{F}, \mathbb{P})$ with $Law(\tilde{m}_t, \mathbb{P}) = \tilde{Q}(\Pr(\mu_x^*); \cdot)$. In this case, we have

$$\lim_{T\to\infty} \|\mathrm{Law}(\{\tilde{\varrho}_t\}_{t\in\mathbb{N}}, \mathbb{P}_{R_T^x}) - \mathrm{Law}(\{\tilde{m}_t\}_{t\in\mathbb{N}}, \mathbb{P})\| = 0 \tag{2.97}$$

whenever the stochastic kernel $\tilde{Q}$ on $\mathcal{M}(C)$ satisfies a uniform Lipschitz condition. In particular, for any $\epsilon > 0$, there exists an ergodic random field μ on $(S, \mathcal{S})$, such that

$$\|\mathrm{Law}(\{\tilde{\varrho}_t\}_{t\in\mathbb{N}}, \mathbb{P}_\mu) - \mathrm{Law}(\{\tilde{m}_t\}_{t\in\mathbb{N}}, \mathbb{P})\| < \epsilon. \tag{2.98}$$

In this sense, any limit of the macroscopic process induces an ergodic random field μ on $(S, \mathcal{S})$ such that the environment $\{\tilde{\varrho}_t\}_{t\in\mathbb{N}}$ for the evolution of the price process is "approximately stationary" under the law $\mathbb{P}_\mu$.

Proof: The assertion follows immediately from Lemma 2.34. Indeed, let us put $(M_1, d_{M_1}) := (\mathcal{M}_s(S), d)$, $m_t := R_t^x$, $m^* := \mu_x^*$, $u(\mu) := \mu\Pi_\mu$ and $\hat{Q}(\mu; \cdot) := \tilde{Q}(\Pr(\mu); \cdot)$. In order to apply our Lemma 2.34 we just have to verify that the stochastic kernel $\hat{Q}$ from $\mathcal{M}_s(S)$ to $\mathcal{M}(C)$ satisfies a uniform Lipschitz condition in the sense of (2.94). This, however, follows from the Lipschitz condition imposed on the kernel $\tilde{Q}$ on $\mathcal{M}(C)$. Indeed, we have that

$$\|\hat{Q}(\mu;\cdot) - \hat{Q}(\hat{\mu};\cdot)\| \leq L \sum_{i=1}^{N} \left| \int_S \mathbf{1}_{c_i}(x^0)(\mu(dx) - \hat{\mu}(dx)) \right| \leq LNd(\mu, \hat{\mu}). \tag{2.99}$$

□

In Section 4.1.1, we will analyze the asymptotic behaviour of the sequence $\{p_t\}_{t\in\mathbb{N}}$ under the assumption that the mood of the market is already in equilibrium, i.e., we shall assume that our asset price process evolves in a stationary random environment. We shall provide conditions which guarantee that the sequence $\{p_t\}_{t\in\mathbb{N}}$ converges pathwise to a stationary process. For price dynamics of the log-linear form (1.15), we will show in Section 4.1.2 that the sequence $\{p_t\}_{t\in\mathbb{N}}$ converges to a stationary regime if the mood of the market settles down in the long run and if the destabilizing effects of the random environment are on average not too strong.

Chapter 3

Local and Global Interaction in a Random Environment

In this chapter, we analyze the asymptotic behaviour of both the *macroscopic* and the *microscopic* process in a financial market model with interacting agents in a random environment, i.e., in a situation where the dynamics on the macroscopic level of empirical fields does not necessarily proceed in a deterministic manner. Given a configuration $x \in S_0$, we assume that individual agents do not observe directly the average situation over the whole infinite system of all traders. Instead, they receive a common signal $e \in E$ whose law $Q(R(x); \cdot)$ depends on the empirical field $R(x)$.

In Section 3.1, we consider a model where an individual agent $a \in \mathbb{A}$ reacts to the local situation $(x^b)_{b \in N(a)}$ of the present configuration x in his neighborhood and to a random signal e about the empirical field $R(x)$. For any configuration $x \in S_0$ and for each fixed signal $e \in E$, the transition to a new configuration is described by a probability measure $\Pi_e(x; dy)$ on the configuration space S_0. Again, we do not define the transition kernels $(\Pi_e)_{e \in E}$ themselves. Instead we fix a family of local specifications $(\gamma^{x,e})_{x \in S, e \in E}$, and so each random field $\Pi_e(x; \cdot)$ is a Gibbs measure. As before, we formulate a Dobrushin condition on the local specifications $(\gamma^{x,e})_{x \in S, e \in E}$ which guarantees that $\gamma^{x,e}$ admits a unique global phase $\Pi_e(x; \cdot)$.

The dynamics of the microscopic process $\{x_t\}_{t \in \mathbb{N}}$ will be described by a Markov chain on the state space S_0 in a random environment. The environment is specified by a sequence $\{e_t\}_{t \in \mathbb{N}}$ of signals about the average behaviour throughout the entire population. If the interaction between different agents is not too strong, then the microscopic process $\{x_t\}_{t\in\mathbb{N}}$ induces almost surely the sequence of ergodic empirical fields $\{R(x_t)\}_{t\in\mathbb{N}}$, due to our spatial law of large numbers for ergodic empirical fields established in the previous chapter. In Theorem 3.1, we prove that the sequence $\{R(x_t)\}_{t\in\mathbb{N}}$ is a Markov chain on the state space $\mathcal{M}_0(S)$. Conditions on the local specifications $(\gamma^{x,e})_{x\in S,e\in E}$ and on the stochastic kernel Q which ensure that the macroscopic process converges in law to a unique equilibrium are stated in Theorem 3.10. The proof uses results from the theory of "random system with complete connections". In this case, we show in Theorem 3.16 that the underlying microscopic process has local asymptotic loss of memory. This means that in the long run the distribution of the state of an individual agent does not depend on the initial configuration. Here, we use again a variant of the Dobrushin-Vasserstein contraction technique. If the macroscopic process converges to some random absorbing point, then Theorem 3.26 shows that the microscopic process converges locally to a random field on $(S, \mathcal{S})$ which will typically depend on the starting point $x \in S_0$.

Finally, the dynamics of the microscopic process in a mean-field type model is analyzed in greater detail. In this case, a stronger result can be established. In Theorem 3.21, we prove convergence in law of the microscopic process under the assumption that the macroscopic process converges in distribution to a unique stationary measure. In this sense, the macroscopic process drives the microscopic process into equilibrium as soon as the sequence $\{R(x_t)\}_{t\in\mathbb{N}}$ settles down as $t \to \infty$. Moreover, we study the dynamics of *individual* opinions under the assumption that the mood of the market is already in equilibrium. In such a situation, the process $\{x_t^a\}_{t\in\mathbb{N}}$ $(a \in \mathbb{A})$ which describes the stochastic evolution of the individual state of agent a, may be viewed as a Markov chain in a stationary and ergodic random environment. It turns out that this sequence converges in the sense of a strong coupling to a stationary process $\{y_t^a\}_{t\in\mathbb{N}}$. The whole microscopic process $\{x_t\}_{t\in\mathbb{N}}$ will then converge locally in the sense of a strong coupling to the stationary process $\{y_t\}_{t\in\mathbb{N}} = \{(y_t^a)_{a\in\mathbb{A}}\}_{t\in\mathbb{N}}$.

In Section 3.2, we introduce an additional dependence of individual behaviour on random external conditions. The dynamics of the external conditions is described by a Markov chain on a compact state space. Again, we can apply results from the theory of random systems with complete connections in order to provide conditions which guarantee that the sequence of empirical fields $\{R(x_t)\}_{t\in\mathbb{N}}$ converges in law.

3.1 Constant External Conditions

Let us describe the dynamics of the microscopic process $\{x_t\}_{t\in\mathbb{N}}$ in a financial market model with interacting agents in a random environment. In this section, we consider the case where the conditional distribution of the state of an individual agent $a \in \mathbb{A}$ given the present configuration $x \in S_0$, does not only depend on the local situation $(x^b)_{b\in N(a)}$ of $x \in S_0$ in a neighborhood of a, but also on some random signal e whose law $Q(R(x);\cdot)$ depends on the empirical field $R(x)$. For example, e could be a signal about the present mood of the market, i.e., a signal about the empirical distribution $\varrho(x)$. The conditional law $Q(R(x);\cdot)$ of the signal $e \in E$ given the empirical field $R(x)$, is described by a stochastic kernel Q from $\mathcal{M}_s(S)$ to $\mathcal{E}$, where $(E,\mathcal{E})$ is an arbitrary measurable space; the "signal space". In Section 3.2, we introduce an additional dependence of individual behaviour on random external conditions.

In order to specify the transition dynamics of the process $\{x_t\}_{t\in\mathbb{N}}$ we fix, for any pair $(x,e) \in S \times E$, a local specification $\gamma^{x,e} = \{\gamma_A^{x,e}\}_{A\in\mathcal{A}}$ and assume that the mapping

$$(x,e) \mapsto \gamma_A^{x,e}(B;v) \qquad (A \in \mathcal{A}, B \in \mathcal{S}_A) \tag{3.1}$$

from $S \times E$ to $[0,1]$ is measurable for each boundary condition v on A^c. The local specifications $(\gamma^{x,e})_{x\in S, e\in E}$ are assumed to satisfy our Assumptions 2.3, 2.4 and 2.5 with μ replaced by e. Thus, each family of conditional probabilities $\gamma^{x,e}$ is spatially homogeneous and satisfies a Markov property of order l both in its dependence on the boundary condition and on the present configuration x. In particular, all agents react in the same manner to their environment and, for a given signal $e \in E$ about the average situation throughout the whole infinite system of all traders, the present state of any agent $a \in \mathbb{A}$ is influenced by just finitely many other agents.

The specification $\gamma^{x,e}$ determines a unique Markov random field

$$\Pi_e(x;\cdot) \tag{3.2}$$

on $(S,\mathcal{S})$, due to Dobrushin's uniqueness theorem. It follows from our measurability assumption (3.1) on the family $(\gamma^{x,e})_{x\in S}$ that (3.2) defines a stochastic kernel on $(S,\mathcal{S})$. For all $e \in E$ and for any $x \in S_0$, we have

$$\Pi_e(x;S_0) = 1, \tag{3.3}$$

due to Corollary 2.9 (1.). Thus, each transition kernel Π_e $(e \in E)$ may be viewed as a transition probability on the state space S_0. We can therefore introduce a stochastic kernel on S_0 by

$$\Pi(x;\cdot) := \int_E \Pi_e(x;\cdot)Q(R(x);de), \tag{3.4}$$

so that our microscopic process $\{x_t\}_{t\in\mathbb{N}}$ is described by a Markov chain on the state space S_0 with transition kernel Π. For a given configuration $x \in S_0$, we denote by $\mathbb{P}_x$ the distribution of the Markov chain on S_0 with transition kernel Π and with starting point x.

Given the present configuration x, the transition to a new state has a local and a global interactive structure. For any $a \in \mathbb{A}$, the interactive influence of the whole microscopic configuration $x \in S_0$ is felt through the local situation $(x^b)_{b\in N(a)}$ in the neighborhood of a and through the common signal e about the empirical field $R(x)$. Since the microscopic process lives on the set S_0, the sequence $\{x_t\}_{t\in\mathbb{N}}$ induces $\mathbb{P}_x$-almost surely the sequence of ergodic empirical fields $\{R(x_t)\}_{t\in\mathbb{N}}$ as soon as the starting point x belongs to S_0. Our aim is to analyze the asymptotic behaviour of the Markov chain $\{x_t\}_{t\in\mathbb{N}}$ on the state space S_0 defined by the transition kernel Π both on the microscopic level and on the macroscopic level of empirical fields.

In our present setting, the dynamics of the macroscopic process $\{R(x_t)\}_{t\in\mathbb{N}}$ typically does not proceed in a deterministic manner. In Chapter 3.1.1, we will show that the sequence $\{R(x_t)\}_{t\in\mathbb{N}}$ is a Markov chain on the state space $\mathcal{M}_0(S)$, i.e.,

$$\mathbb{E}_x[f(R(x_{t+1}))|R(x_t),\cdots,R(x_0)] = \mathbb{E}_x\left[f(R(x_{t+1}))|R(x_t)\right] \qquad \mathbb{P}_x\text{-a.s.}$$

We shall formulate conditions on the specifications and on the stochastic kernel Q from $\mathcal{M}_s(S)$ to $\mathcal{E}$ which guarantee that the macroscopic process converges in law to an equilibrium $\mu^* \in \mathcal{M}(\mathcal{M}_s(S))$ which does not depend on the initial configuration.

Let us now consider the dynamics on the microscopic level. The sequence $\{x_t\}_{t\in\mathbb{N}}$ may be viewed as a Markov chain in the random environment specified by the process $\{e_t\}_{t\in\mathbb{N}}$. This environment consists of a sequence of noisy signals about macroscopic properties of the configurations $\{x_t\}_{t\in\mathbb{N}}$ which are carried in the induced sequence of empirical fields $\{R(x_t)\}_{t\in\mathbb{N}}$.

By analogy with the situation analyzed in Chapter 2, our strong law of large numbers for ergodic empirical fields established in Proposition 2.8 yields a decoupling result which allows us to analyze the microscopic process $\{x_t\}_{t\in\mathbb{N}}$ and the macroscopic process $\{R(x_t)\}_{t\in\mathbb{N}}$ separately. More precisely, we are now going to show that the law of the environment $\{e_t\}_{t\in\mathbb{N}}$ is uniquely determined by the stochastic kernel Q from $\mathcal{M}_s(S)$ to $\mathcal{E}$ and by the initial empirical field $R(x)$.

To this end, we introduce a mapping $u : \mathcal{M}_s(S) \times E \to \mathcal{M}_s(S)$ by

$$u(R, e) := R\Pi_e(\cdot) = \int \Pi_e(x; \cdot)R(dx). \tag{3.5}$$

This mapping is well defined since the random field $\mu\Pi_e$ is shift-invariant whenever $\mu \in \mathcal{M}_s(S)$. Indeed, it follows from Lemma 2.7 (ii) that the stochastic kernel Π_e on $(S, \mathcal{S})$ is spatially homogeneous, and so

$$(\mu\Pi_e)(f \circ \theta_a) = \mu(\Pi_e(f \circ \theta_a)) = \mu(\Pi_e(f) \circ \theta_a) = \mu\Pi_e(f) \qquad (f \in \mathcal{C}(S)).$$

Due to Corollary 2.9 (i), the set $\mathcal{M}_0(S)$ is absorbing for the transformation u in the sense that

$$u(R, e) \in \mathcal{M}_0(S) \qquad (R \in \mathcal{M}_0(S),\ e \in E). \tag{3.6}$$

In the sequel it will be convenient to use the following notation. We put $E^{(t)} := \prod_{i=0}^{t} E$ with generic element

$$e_t^0 := (e_0, e_2, \dots, e_t),$$

and define a sequence of mappings $\{u_t\}_{t\in\mathbb{N}}$, $u_t : \mathcal{M}_s(S) \times E^{(t)} \to \mathcal{M}_s(S)$, by

$$u_0(R, e_0^0) := u(R, e_0) \quad \text{and} \quad u_t(R, e_t^0) := u(u_{t-1}(R, e_{t-1}^0), e_t) \qquad (t = 1, 2, \dots).$$

Abusing our notation we suppress a t-index and put

$$u(R, e_t^0) := u_t(R, e_t^0) \qquad (t \in \mathbb{N}). \tag{3.7}$$

Let us now fix an initial configuration $x \in S_0$. For a given signal sequence $\{e_t\}_{t\in\mathbb{N}}$, we can define a sequence of empirical fields $\{\xi_t^x\}_{t\in\mathbb{N}}$ by the relation

$$\xi_0^x := R(x) \quad \text{and} \quad \xi_t^x := u(\xi_{t-1}^x, e_{t-1}) = u(R(x), e_{t-1}^0) \qquad (t \geq 1). \tag{3.8}$$

Given the signals $\{e_t\}_{t\in\mathbb{N}}$, the macroscopic process $\{R(x_t)\}_{t\in\mathbb{N}}$ is $\mathbb{P}_x$-a.s. uniquely determined by the initial empirical field $R(x)$, due to Corollary 2.9. More precisely, we have that

$$R(x_{t+1}) = u(R(x_t), e_t) = u(R(x), e_t^0) = \xi_{t+1}^x \qquad \mathbb{P}_x\text{-a.s.} \qquad (t \in \mathbb{N}). \tag{3.9}$$

In particular, the distribution of the random variable e_t given $R(x_t)$, is $\mathbb{P}_x$-almost surely of the form

$$\mathbb{P}_x[e_t \in \cdot | R(x_t)] = \mathbb{P}_x[e_t \in \cdot | \xi_t^x] = Q(u(R(x), e_{t-1}^0); \cdot).$$

Thus, given an initial configuration $x \in S_0$, the law the sequence $\{e_t\}_{t\in\mathbb{N}}$ is uniquely determined by the initial empirical field $R(x)$. Hence, for any starting point $x \in S_0$, the distribution of the microscopic process under the law $\mathbb{P}_x$ at time $t+1$ takes the from

$$\begin{aligned}
\Pi^{t+1}(x;\cdot) &= \int_E \cdots \int_E [\Pi_{e_0}\cdots\Pi_{e_t}](x;\cdot)Q(R(x)\Pi_{e_0}\cdots\Pi_{e_{t-1}};de_t)\cdots \\
&\quad \cdots Q(R(x)\Pi_{e_0};de_1)Q(R(x);de_0) \\
&= \int_E \cdots \int_E [\Pi_{e_0}\cdots\Pi_{e_t}](x;\cdot)Q(u(\xi^x,e_{t-1}^0);de_t)\cdots \\
&\quad \cdots Q(u(\xi^x,e_0);de_1)Q(\xi^x;de_0). \qquad (3.10)
\end{aligned}$$

Under the assumption that the macroscopic process converges in law to a unique measure μ^* on $\mathcal{M}_s(S)$ we will show in Section 3.1.2 that the sequence $\{e_t\}_{t\in\mathbb{N}}$ obeys a strong ergodicity property. In the long run, i.e., as $T \to \infty$, the law of the environment $\{e_{t+T}\}_{t\in\mathbb{N}}$ does not depend on the initial configuration. From this, we will then deduce that the microscopic process has "local asymptotic loss of memory". That is, asymptotically, the distribution of the random variables $(x_t^a)_{a\in A}$ $(A \in \mathcal{A})$ does not depend on the initial configuration.

3.1.1 Dynamics of the Macroscopic Process

This section is devoted to the analysis of the dynamics of the sequence of ergodic empirical fields $\{R(x_t)\}_{t\in\mathbb{N}}$. Due to (3.9), the law of the random variable $R(x_{t+1})$ depends on the microscopic configuration x_t in period t just through the empirical field $R(x_t)$. The following theorem shows that the process $\{R(x_t)\}_{t\in\mathbb{N}}$ is a Markov chain on the state space $\mathcal{M}_0(S)$. Later, we state conditions on the local specifications $(\gamma^{x,e})_{x\in S, e\in E}$ and on the stochastic kernel Q from $\mathcal{M}_s(S)$ to $\mathcal{E}$ which guarantee that the macroscopic process converges in distribution to a unique equilibrium μ^* on $\mathcal{M}_s(S)$ as $t \to \infty$.

Theorem 3.1 *Under the measure $\mathbb{P}_x$ $(x \in S_0)$ the sequence of ergodic empirical fields $\{R(x_t)\}_{t\in\mathbb{N}}$ is a Markov chain on the state space $\mathcal{M}_0(S)$ with initial value $R(x)$. The transition operator U acts on the set of bounded measurable functions f on $\mathcal{M}_0(S)$ according to the formula*

$$Uf(R) = \int f(u(R,e))Q(R;de). \qquad (3.11)$$

Proof: Let f be any bounded measurable function on $\mathcal{M}_0(S)$. Using the recurrence relation (3.9) and the law of conditional iterated expectation we get

$$\begin{aligned}
& \mathbb{E}_x\left[f(R(x_{t+1}))|R(x_t),\cdots,R(x_1)\right] \\
= \; & \mathbb{E}_x\left[\mathbb{E}_x[f(R(x_{t+1}))|R(x_t),\cdots,R(x_1),e_t]|R(x_t),\cdots,R(x_1)\right] \\
= \; & \mathbb{E}_x\left[f(u(R(x_t),e_t))|R(x_t),\cdots,R(x_1)\right] \\
= \; & \int f(u(R(x_t),e_t))Q(R(x_t);de_t) \qquad \mathbb{P}_x\text{-a.s.}
\end{aligned}$$

This proves our assertion. □

Since, conditioned on the environment $\{e_t\}_{t\in\mathbb{N}}$, our macroscopic process follows almost surely a deterministic dynamics, we propose a "random system with complete connections" as a suitable mathematical framework for analyzing the Markov chain $\{R(x_t)\}_{t\in\mathbb{N}}$.

Definition 3.2 *Let (M_1, d_{M_1}) be a metric space and $(M_2, \mathcal{M}_2)$ be a measurable space. Let Z denote a stochastic kernel from M_1 to $\mathcal{M}_2$ and let $v : M_1 \times M_2 \to M_1$ be a measurable mapping.*

(i) Following Iosefescu and Theodorescu (1968), we call the quadruple

$$\Sigma := ((M_1, d_{M_1}), (M_2, \mathcal{M}_2), Z, v) \tag{3.12}$$

***a homogeneous random system with complete connections** (RSCC).*

(ii) Given an initial value $\xi \in M_1$, a RSCC induces two stochastic processes $\{\xi_t\}_{t=0,1,2,..}$ and $\{\zeta_t\}_{t=0,1,2,...}$ on the canonical probability space $(\Omega, \mathcal{F}, \mathbb{P}_\xi)$ taking values in M_1 and in M_2, respectively, by

$$\xi_{t+1} = v(\xi_t, \zeta_t) \qquad (\xi_0 = \xi \quad \mathbb{P}_\xi\text{-a.s.}) \tag{3.13}$$

and by

$$\mathbb{P}_\xi(\zeta_t \in \cdot|\xi_t, \zeta_{t-1}, \xi_{t-1}, \zeta_{t-2}, \ldots) = Z(\xi_t; \cdot). \tag{3.14}$$

*These processes are called the **associated Markov process** and the **signal sequence**, respectively.*

*(iii) We call a random system with complete connections a **distance-diminishing model**, if the transformation $v : M_1 \times M_2 \to M_1$ satisfies the following **contraction property**: There exists a constant $\theta < 1$ such that*

$$d_{M_1}(v(\xi,\zeta), v(\hat{\xi},\zeta)) \leq \theta d_{M_1}(\xi, \hat{\xi}) \tag{3.15}$$

uniformly in $\zeta \in M_2$ $(\xi, \hat{\xi} \in M_1)$.

(iv) *We call the signal sequence* $\{\zeta_t\}_{t\in\mathbb{N}}$ ***uniformly ergodic in the strong sense*** *if, for any* $t \in \mathbb{N}$, *there exists a measure* Z_t^* *on* $(M_2^{(t)}, \otimes_{i=0}^t \mathcal{M}_2)$ *such that*

$$\lim_{T\to\infty} \sup_{t,\xi} \|Z_t^T(\xi;\cdot) - Z_t^*(\cdot)\| = 0. \tag{3.16}$$

Here, $Z_t^T(\xi;\cdot) := \text{Law}(\{\zeta_T, \ldots, \zeta_{T+t}\}, \mathbb{P}_\xi)$.

The main results about distance-diminishing random systems with complete connections whose associated Markov process takes values in a compact metric space (M_1, d_{M_1}) are summarized in the appendix.

Remark 3.3 (i) *Observe that the transition operator* U *of the Markov process* $\{\xi_t\}$ *on* M_1 *associated with a random system with complete connections* Σ *acts on the class of all bounded measurable functions* f *on* M_1 *according to the formula*

$$Uf(\xi) = \int_{M_2} f(v(\xi,\zeta))Z(\xi; d\zeta). \tag{3.17}$$

If the transition kernel Z *from* M_1 *to* $\mathcal{M}_2$ *satisfies a suitable continuity condition, then the process* $\{\xi_t\}_{t\in\mathbb{N}}$ *has the Feller property.*

(ii) *For a given signal sequence* $\{\zeta_t\}_{t\in\mathbb{N}}$, *the Markov process* $\{\xi_t\}_{t\in\mathbb{N}}$ *on* M_1 *associated with the random system* Σ *given by (3.12) satisfies* $\mathbb{P}_\xi$*-almost surely the deterministic recursive relation*

$$\xi_{t+1} = v_t(\xi, \zeta_t^0). \tag{3.18}$$

Here, $\zeta_t^0 := (\zeta_0, \zeta_1, \ldots, \zeta_t) \in M_2^{(t)} := \prod_{i=0}^t M_2$ $(t \in \mathbb{N})$, *and the sequence of mappings* $\{v_t\}_{t\in\mathbb{N}}$, $v_t : M_1 \times M_2^{(t)} \to M_1$, *is defined recursively by the relation*

$$v_0(\xi,\zeta_0^0) \;=\; v(\xi,\zeta_0) \quad \text{and} \quad v_t(\xi,\zeta_t^0) = v(v_{t-1}(\xi,\zeta_{t-1}^0),\zeta_t) \qquad (t \geq 1).$$

We are now going to introduce a random system with complete connections Σ^* whose associated Markov chain $\{\xi_t\}_{t\in\mathbb{N}}$ coincides in law with our macroscopic process $\{R(x_t)\}_{t\in\mathbb{N}}$. It is then enough to analyze the asymptotic behaviour of the process $\{\xi_t\}_{t\in\mathbb{N}}$ in order to study the long run behaviour of the sequence of empirical fields $\{R(x_t)\}_{t\in\mathbb{N}}$. Most of the results about distance-diminishing random systems with complete connections provided in, e.g., Iosefescu and Theodorescu (1968) or Norman

(1972), are formulated for random systems whose associated Markov process takes values in a compact metric space. Therefore, we are going to regard our macroscopic process $\{R(x_t)\}_{t\in\mathbb{N}}$ as a Markov chain taking values in the metric space $(\mathcal{M}_s(S), d)$. The metric $d(\cdot,\cdot)$ is defined in (2.53) and $(\mathcal{M}_s(S), d)$ is a compact metric space, due to Proposition 2.15.

Let us now introduce the random system with complete connections

$$\Sigma^* := ((\mathcal{M}_s(S), d), (E, \mathcal{E}), Q, u), \tag{3.19}$$

where u is the mapping defined in (3.5). We denote by $(\Omega, \mathcal{F}, \{\xi_t\}_{t\in\mathbb{N}}, (\mathbb{P}_\xi)_{\xi\in\mathcal{M}_s(S)})$ the canonical model for the Markov chain associated with Σ^*, i.e., $\mathbb{P}_\xi$ is the probability measure on the path space $\Omega = \mathcal{M}_s(S)^{\mathbb{N}}$ which corresponds to start in ξ. By $\{\zeta_t\}_{t\in\mathbb{N}}$ we denote the associated signal sequence. In our present setting where the dynamics on the macroscopic level of empirical fields does not necessarily proceed in a deterministic manner, the Markov chain $\{\xi_t\}_{t\in\mathbb{N}}$ on $\mathcal{M}_s(S)$ with starting point $R(x)$ is the analogue of the process $\{R_t^x\}_{t\in\mathbb{N}}$ analyzed in the previous chapter.

For a given initial configuration $x \in S_0$, the sequence $\{\xi_t^x\}_{t\in\mathbb{N}}$ specified in (3.8) may be viewed as the Markov chain with initial value $R(x)$ associated with the random system with complete connections Σ^*. More precisely, we can easily establish the following results.

Proposition 3.4 *For any initial distribution $\mu \in \mathcal{M}(S_0)$ of the microscopic process $\{x_t\}_{t\in\mathbb{N}}$, let us define a probability measure $\hat{\mu}$ on $\mathcal{M}_0(S)$ by*

$$\hat{\mu}(B) := \int_S \mathbf{1}_B(R(x))\mu(dx) \qquad (B \in \mathcal{B}(\mathcal{M}_0(S))). \tag{3.20}$$

Then the following holds true:

(i) The Markov chain $\{\xi_t\}_{t\in\mathbb{N}}$ on $\mathcal{M}_s(S)$ with initial distribution $\hat{\mu}$ associated with the random system Σ^* defined in (3.19) has the same distribution as the macroscopic process $\{R(x_t)\}_{t\in\mathbb{N}}$, i.e.,

$$\mathrm{Law}(\{\xi_t\}_{t\in\mathbb{N}}, \mathbb{P}_{\hat{\mu}}) = \mathrm{Law}(\{R(x_t)\}_{t\in\mathbb{N}}, \mathbb{P}_\mu). \tag{3.21}$$

Here, the law $\mathbb{P}_{\hat{\mu}}$ on $\mathcal{M}_s(S)^{\mathbb{N}}$ is defined by $\mathbb{P}_{\hat{\mu}}(\cdot) = \int_{\mathcal{M}_s(S)} \mathbb{P}_\xi(\cdot)\hat{\mu}(d\xi)$. In particular, given an initial configuration $x \in S_0$, the macroscopic process $\{R(x_t)\}_{t\in\mathbb{N}}$ may be viewed as the Markov chain with starting point $R(x)$ associated with the random system with complete connections Σ^*.

(ii) The signal sequences $\{\zeta_t\}_{t\in\mathbb{N}}$ and $\{e_t\}_{t\in\mathbb{N}}$ on E coincide in distribution in the sense that

$$\mathrm{Law}(\{\zeta_t\}_{t\in\mathbb{N}}, \mathbb{P}_{\hat{\mu}}) = \mathrm{Law}(\{e_t\}_{t\in\mathbb{N}}, \mathbb{P}_{\mu}). \tag{3.22}$$

Proof:

(i) Let us fix an initial distribution $\mu \in \mathcal{M}(S_0)$ of the microscopic process $\{x_t\}_{t\in\mathbb{N}}$. We have

$$\mathbb{P}_{\mu}[R(x_0) \in B] = \int_S \mathbf{1}_B((R(x))\mu(dx) = \hat{\mu}(B) \qquad (B \in \mathcal{B}(\mathcal{M}_0(S)).$$

Thus, under the law $\mathbb{P}_{\mu}$ the macroscopic process $\{R(x_t)\}_{t\in\mathbb{N}}$ is a Markov chain on the state space $\mathcal{M}_0(S)$ with initial distribution $\hat{\mu}$; cf. Theorem 3.1.

Observe that $\hat{\mu}(\mathcal{M}_0(S)) = 1$. Thus, under the measure $\mathbb{P}_{\hat{\mu}}$, the sequence $\{\xi_t\}_{t\in\mathbb{N}}$ is Markov chain with state space $\mathcal{M}_0(S)$ and with initial distribution $\hat{\mu}$, due to (3.6). Now (i) is obvious as the transition operator of both the macroscopic process $\{R(x_t)\}_{t\in\mathbb{N}}$ and the Markov chain $\{\xi_t\}_{t\in\mathbb{N}}$ act on the set of bounded measurable functions f on $\mathcal{M}_0(S)$ according to (3.11).

(ii) The assertion follows from (i) as the law of the signal sequences $\{e_t\}_{t\in\mathbb{N}}$ and $\{\zeta_t\}_{t\in\mathbb{N}}$, respectively, is uniquely determined by the stochastic kernel Q from $\mathcal{M}_s(S)$ to $\mathcal{E}$ and by the distribution of the respective processes $\{R(x_t)\}_{t\in\mathbb{N}}$ and $\{\xi_t\}_{t\in\mathbb{N}}$.

□

The following proposition shows that a Markov chain $\{\xi_t\}_{t\in\mathbb{N}}$ associated with the random system Σ^* whose initial distribution is concentrated on the set $\mathcal{M}_0(S)$ induces a macroscopic process which coincides in law with the sequence $\{\xi_t\}_{t\in\mathbb{N}}$.

Proposition 3.5 *Let $\hat{\mu} \in \mathcal{M}(\mathcal{M}_s(S))$ be an initial distribution of the Markov chain $\{\xi_t\}_{t\in\mathbb{N}}$ associated with the random system with complete connections Σ^*. Suppose that $\hat{\mu}$ is concentrated on the set $\mathcal{M}_0(S)$ and define a probability measure $\tilde{\mu}$ on the configuration space $(S, \mathcal{S})$ by*

$$\tilde{\mu}(B) := \int_{\mathcal{M}_0(S)} \mu(B)\hat{\mu}(d\mu) \qquad (B \in \mathcal{S}). \tag{3.23}$$

Then we have

$$\mathrm{Law}(\{\xi_t\}_{t\in\mathbb{N}}, \mathbb{P}_{\hat{\mu}}) = \mathrm{Law}(\{R(x_t)\}_{t\in\mathbb{N}}, \mathbb{P}_{\tilde{\mu}}) \tag{3.24}$$

and

$$\mathrm{Law}(\{\zeta_t\}_{t\in\mathbb{N}}, \mathbb{P}_{\tilde{\mu}}) = \mathrm{Law}(\{e_t\}_{t\in\mathbb{N}}, \mathbb{P}_{\tilde{\mu}}). \tag{3.25}$$

Proof: For any ergodic random field μ on S, we have $R(x) = \mu$ for μ-a.e. $x \in S$. Thus, $\tilde{\mu}(S_0) = 1$, and so we can take $\tilde{\mu}$ as the initial distribution for our microscopic process. Since

$$\mathbb{P}_{\tilde{\mu}}[R(x_0) \in B] = \int_{\mathcal{M}_0(S)} \int_S \mathbf{1}_B((R(x_0))\mu(dx_0)\hat{\mu}(d\mu) = \int_{\mathcal{M}_0(S)} \mathbf{1}_B(\mu)\hat{\mu}(d\mu) = \hat{\mu}(B),$$

the assertion follows as in the proof of the preceding proposition. □

Existence and Uniqueness of Invariant Measures

We are now ready to state conditions on the stochastic kernel Q and on the local specifications $(\gamma^{x,e})_{x\in S, e\in E}$ which guarantee that the macroscopic process $\{R(x_t)\}_{t\in\mathbb{N}}$ converges in law to a unique equilibrium μ^* on $\mathcal{M}_s(S)$ as $t \to \infty$. Using general convergence results for distance-diminishing random systems with complete connections provided in, e.g., Norman (1972), we shall see that the sequence of empirical fields $\{R(x_t)\}_{t\in\mathbb{N}}$ converges in distribution as $t \to \infty$ if the interaction between different agents is not too strong and if the stochastic kernel Q from $\mathcal{M}_s(S)$ to $\mathcal{E}$ satisfies a Doeblin-type and a uniform Lipschitz condition.

Definition 3.6 *Let $(M_i, \mathcal{M}_i)$, $i = 1, 2$, be measurable spaces and let Z be a stochastic kernel from M_1 to $\mathcal{M}_2$. We say that Z has a* **lower bound**, *if there exists a constant $\lambda > 0$ and a probability measure ν on $(M_2, \mathcal{M}_2)$ such that*

$$\inf_{m\in M_1} Z(m;\cdot) \geq \lambda\nu(\cdot). \tag{3.26}$$

Theorem 3.7 *Suppose that the local specifications $(\gamma^{x,e})_{x\in S, e\in E}$ satisfy our Assumptions 2.3, 2.4 and 2.5 with μ replaced by e and assume that the uniform weighted Dobrushin-Vasserstein-Condition (2.56) is met. Then the following holds true:*

(i) The random system with complete connections Σ^* given by (3.19) is distance-diminishing in the sense of Definition 3.2 (iii).

(ii) If the transition kernel Q satisfies a uniform Lipschitz condition in the sense of Definition 2.32, then the Markov process $\{\xi_t\}_{t\in\mathbb{N}}$ associated with the random system with complete connections Σ^* admits an invariant measure.

(iii) If, moreover, the kernel Q has a lower bound in the sense of (3.26), then the process $\{\xi_t\}_{t\in\mathbb{N}}$ converges in law to a stationary distribution which does not depend on the starting point.

(iv) Any invariant measure μ^* for the Markov chain associated with Σ^* satisfies

$$\mu^*(\mathcal{M}_0(S)) \in \{0,1\}, \tag{3.27}$$

i.e., μ^* is trivial on the set of all ergodic random fields on $(S,\mathcal{S})$.

Proof:

(i) It follows from our weighted Dobrushin-Vasserstein condition (2.56) and from Proposition 2.19 with $\tau = e$ that

$$d(u(R,e),u(\hat{R},e)) \leq \alpha d(R,\hat{R}) \qquad (\alpha < 1) \tag{3.28}$$

uniformly in $e \in E$ $(R,\hat{R} \in \mathcal{M}_s(S))$.

(ii) This assertion follows from (i) and from Proposition A.5.

(iii) This follows from (i) and from Proposition A.8.

(iv) Let $\{\mu_1^*,\dots,\mu_k^*\}$ be set of all extreme invariant measures for the Markov chain associated with Σ^*. This set is finite, due to Theorem 3.4.2 in Norman (1972). Suppose that $\mu_1^*(\mathcal{M}_0(S)) > 0$. We claim that the probability measure $\hat{\mu}$ on $\mathcal{M}_s(S)$ defined by

$$\hat{\mu}(B) := \frac{\mu_1^*(B \cap \mathcal{M}_0(S))}{\mu_1^*(\mathcal{M}_0(S))}$$

is invariant for the Markov chain $\{\xi_t\}_{t\in\mathbb{N}}$.

In order to verify our assertion, we denote by $\widehat{\Pi}$ the transition kernel of the process $\{\xi_t\}_{t\in\mathbb{N}}$. Due to (3.6), the set of all ergodic probability measures on $(S,\mathcal{S})$ is an absorbing set for the mapping $u : \mathcal{M}_s(S) \times E \to \mathcal{M}_s(S)$ defined by (3.5). Thus, we have that

$$\begin{aligned}
\mu_1^*(\mathcal{M}_0(S)) &= \int_{\mathcal{M}_0(S)} \widehat{\Pi}(\xi;\mathcal{M}_0(S))\mu_1^*(d\xi) + \int_{\mathcal{M}_0(S)^c} \widehat{\Pi}(\xi;\mathcal{M}_0(S))\mu_1^*(d\xi) \\
&= \mu_1^*(\mathcal{M}_0(S)) + \int_{\mathcal{M}_0(S)^c} \widehat{\Pi}(\xi;\mathcal{M}_0(S))\mu_1^*(d\xi),
\end{aligned}$$

and so we have either $\mu_1^*(\mathcal{M}_0(S)^c) = 0$, i.e., $\mu_1^*(\mathcal{M}_0(S)) = 1$, or $\widehat{\Pi}(\xi; \mathcal{M}_0(S)) = 0$ for μ_1^*-a.e. $\xi \in \mathcal{M}_0(S)^c$. In the first case we are done. In the latter case we obtain for any $B \in \mathcal{B}(\mathcal{M}_s(S))$ that

$$\begin{aligned}
\hat{\mu}(B) &= \frac{1}{\mu_1^*(\mathcal{M}_0(S))} \int_{\mathcal{M}_s(S)} \widehat{\Pi}(\xi; B \cap \mathcal{M}_0(S)) \mu_1^*(d\xi) \\
&= \frac{1}{\mu_1^*(\mathcal{M}_0(S))} \int_{\mathcal{M}_0(S)} \widehat{\Pi}(\xi; B \cap \mathcal{M}_0(S)) \mu_1^*(d\xi) \\
&= \frac{1}{\mu_1^*(\mathcal{M}_0(S))} \int_{\mathcal{M}_0(S)} \widehat{\Pi}(\xi; B) \mu_1^*(d\xi) \\
&= \int_{\mathcal{M}_0(S)} \widehat{\Pi}(\xi; B) \hat{\mu}(d\xi),
\end{aligned}$$

and so $\hat{\mu}$ is an equilibrium for the kernel $\widehat{\Pi}$. Since $\hat{\mu} \in \text{Conv}\{\mu_1^*, \ldots, \mu_k^*\}$ and because the probability measures $\{\mu_i^*\}_{i=1}^k$ are mutually singular, we deduce that $\hat{\mu} = \mu_1^*$. Thus, $\mu_1^*(\mathcal{M}_0(S)) = 1$.

This proves the theorem. □

Remark 3.8 *Under the heading "iterated function systems", the case of a finite signal space E is also studied in Barnsley, Demko, Elton, and Geronimo (1988) and in Barnsley and Elton (1988). In this case, conditions for the existence and attractiveness of invariant distributions for the Markov chain $\{\xi_t\}_{t\in\mathbb{N}}$ on $\mathcal{M}_s(S)$ can be established under weaker continuity assumptions on the stochastic kernel Q from $\mathcal{M}_s(S)$ to $\mathcal{E}$.*

Let us now apply our results about the existence and attractiveness of stationary distributions for the Markov chain $\{\xi_t\}_{t\in\mathbb{N}}$ on $\mathcal{M}_s(S)$ associated with Σ^*, in order to formulate conditions which guarantee that the macroscopic process admits an invariant measure.

Theorem 3.9 *Let μ^* be a stationary distribution for the Markov chain $\{\xi_t\}_{t\in\mathbb{N}}$ on $\mathcal{M}_s(S)$ associated with the random system Σ^*. Suppose that μ^* is concentrated on the set $\mathcal{M}_0(S)$. Then the macroscopic process is stationary under the law $\mathbb{P}_{\tilde{\mu}}(\cdot) = \int_S \mathbb{P}_x(\cdot)\tilde{\mu}(dx)$, where the random field $\tilde{\mu}$ on $(S, \mathcal{S})$ is defined by*

$$\tilde{\mu}(\cdot) := \int_{\mathcal{M}_0(S)} \mu(\cdot)\mu^*(d\mu). \tag{3.29}$$

Proof: Let μ^* be an invariant distribution for the Markov chain $\{\xi_t\}_{t\in\mathbb{N}}$ on $\mathcal{M}_s(S)$ associated with the random system Σ^* which is concentrated on the set $\mathcal{M}_0(S)$. We have $\tilde{\mu}(S_0) = 1$, and so it follows from Proposition 3.5 that

$$\text{Law}(\{R(x_t)\}_{t\in\mathbb{N}}, \mathbb{P}_{\tilde{\mu}}) = \text{Law}(\{\xi_t\}_{t\in\mathbb{N}}, \mathbb{P}_{\mu^*}). \tag{3.30}$$

Since the process $\{\xi_t\}_{t\in\mathbb{N}}$ is stationary under the law $\mathbb{P}_{\mu^*}$, the sequence of empirical fields $\{R(x_t)\}_{t\in\mathbb{N}}$ is stationary under the law $\mathbb{P}_{\tilde{\mu}}$. □

We can now combine Proposition 3.5 with Theorem 3.7 in order to establish the main result of this section. For our financial market model, the following theorem provides a bound for the strength of interaction between different types of traders which guarantees that the dynamics on the level of aggregate behaviour settles down to a unique equilibrium as $t \to \infty$.

Theorem 3.10 *Suppose that the local specifications $(\gamma^{x,e})_{x\in S, e\in E}$ satisfy our Assumptions 2.3, 2.4, 2.5 and 2.16 with μ replaced by e. Let the transition kernel Q from $\mathcal{M}_s(S)$ to $\mathcal{E}$ satisfy a uniform Lipschitz condition and assume that Q has a lower bound in the sense of (3.26). Then our macroscopic process $\{R(x_t)\}_{t\in\mathbb{N}}$ converges in law to a unique probability measure μ^* on $\mathcal{M}_s(S)$ as $t \to \infty$.*

Proof: Let us fix $x \in S_0$. It follows from Proposition 3.5 and Theorem 3.7 that

$$\text{Law}(R(x_t), \mathbb{P}_x) = \text{Law}(\xi_t, \mathbb{P}_{R(x)}) \xrightarrow{w} \mu^* \qquad (t \to \infty).$$

This proves our assertion. □

The model analyzed in this section may be viewed as a randomized version of the model studied in the previous chapter. In Chapter 2, we established almost sure convergence of the macroscopic process under the assumption that the local interaction in the kernels Π_μ is not too strong and given that the dependence of the specifications on the parameter μ is weak enough. In our present setting, the transition to a new state depends on the current empirical field $R(x_t)$ through some random variable e_t whose law depends on $R(x_t)$. This provides and an additional smoothing effect, and so we can establish a convergence result, namely convergence in law of the macroscopic process, without any condition which controls the dependence of the local specifications on the signal e. We just have to control the local interaction in the kernels $(\Pi_e)_{e\in E}$ by means of a uniform Dobrushin-Vasserstein-type condition. Observe, however, that our condition (3.26) excludes the case $Q(R(x);\cdot) = \delta_{R(x)}(\cdot)$, i.e., the situation analyzed in the previous chapter.

The Macroscopic Process in a Mean-Field-Model

We are now going to analyze the dynamics on the macroscopic level in a mean-field type setting in greater detail. In particular, we provide conditions which guarantee that the macroscopic process admits an invariant distribution. In our present mean-field setting, we assume that the average situation over the whole infinite system of all traders is described by the empirical distribution of the agents' states. For any signal $e \in E$ about the mood of the market, we fix a stochastic kernel π_e on the set of possible individual states C and assume that the random field $\Pi_e(x; \cdot)$ takes the product form

$$\Pi_e(x; \cdot) = \prod_{a \in \mathbb{A}} \pi_e(x^a; \cdot). \tag{3.31}$$

The conditional law $\bar{Q}(\varrho(x_t); \cdot)$ of the random variable e_t given the empirical distribution $\varrho(x_t) \in \mathcal{M}(C)$, is described by a stochastic kernel $\bar{Q}$ on $\mathcal{M}(C)$.

Let us fix $\varrho_0 \in \mathcal{M}(C)$ and suppose that the initial distribution μ_0 of our microscopic process is given by the product measure

$$\mu_0 = \prod_{a \in \mathbb{A}} \varrho_0.$$

For any given environment $\{e_t\}_{t \in \mathbb{N}}$, the evolution of the sequence of empirical distributions $\{\varrho(x_t)\}_{t \in \mathbb{N}}$ proceeds almost surely in a deterministic manner, due to Proposition 1.5. More precisely, we have that

$$\varrho(x_{t+1}) = v(\varrho(x_t), e_t) := \varrho(x_t)\pi_{e_t} \qquad \mathbb{P}_{\mu_0}\text{-a.s.}$$

Thus, the sequence $\{\varrho(x_t)\}_{t \in \mathbb{N}}$ may be viewed as the Markov chain $\{\varrho_t\}_{t \in \mathbb{N}}$ on $\mathcal{M}(C)$ with starting point ϱ_0 associated with the random system with complete connections

$$\Sigma' := ((\mathcal{M}(C), |\cdot|), (E, \mathcal{E}), \bar{Q}, v). \tag{3.32}$$

We assume that the dependence of the probability measure $\pi_e(x^a; \cdot)$ on the present state x^a of agent a is not too strong, i.e., we require (2.57) to hold true with ϱ replaced by e. In this case, the random system Σ' given by (3.32) is distance-diminishing in the sense of Definition 3.2 (iii), and so the Markov chain $\{\varrho_t\}_{t \in \mathbb{N}}$ admits an invariant measure ϱ^* whenever the stochastic kernel $\bar{Q}$ on $\mathcal{M}(C)$ satisfies a uniform Lipschitz condition; cf. Proposition A.5.

In order to show that each such $\varrho^* \in \mathcal{M}(\mathcal{M}(C))$ induces a stationary distribution for our macroscopic process, we introduce a random field μ^* on $(S, \mathcal{S})$ by the relation

$$\mu^*(dx) := \int_{\mathcal{M}(C)} \prod_{a \in \mathbb{A}} \varrho(dx^a)\varrho^*(d\varrho) \tag{3.33}$$

and claim that the macroscopic process $\{R(x_t)\}_{t\in\mathbb{N}}$ is stationary under the law $\mathbb{P}_{\mu^*}$. In order to verify our assertion, it is enough to show that $\text{Law}(R(x_0), \mathbb{P}_{\mu^*}) = \text{Law}(R(x_1), \mathbb{P}_{\mu^*})$ as the sequence $\{R(x_t)\}_{t\in\mathbb{N}}$ is a Markov chain. Since the random field μ^* on $(S, \mathcal{S})$ is a mixture of product measures, we have

$$R(x_0) = \prod_{a\in\mathbb{A}} \varrho(x_0) \qquad \mathbb{P}_{\mu^*}\text{-a.s.}$$

and so

$$\mathbb{P}_{\mu^*}[R(x_0) \in B] = \int_S \mathbf{1}_B \circ \left(\prod_{a\in\mathbb{A}} \varrho(x_0)\right) \mu^*(dx_0) = \left(\prod_{a\in\mathbb{A}} \varrho^*\right)(B).$$

For any $\varrho \in \mathcal{M}(C)$, let us now put

$$\mu_\varrho := \prod_{a\in\mathbb{A}} \varrho \in \mathcal{M}_0(S)$$

and introduce the stochastic kernels

$$\Pi_\varrho(x;\cdot) := \int_E \Pi_e(x;\cdot)\bar{Q}(\varrho;de) \qquad \text{and} \qquad \pi_\varrho(c;\cdot) := \int_E \pi_e(c;\cdot)\bar{Q}(\varrho;de)$$

on S and C, respectively. It follows from our Lemma 2.7 (ii) that the transition kernel Π_ϱ is spatially homogeneous so that $\mu\Pi_\varrho \in \mathcal{M}_s(S)$ whenever $\mu \in \mathcal{M}_s(S)$. Thus, due to Corollary 2.9 (1.) we have $\mu_\varrho\Pi_\varrho \in \mathcal{M}_0(S)$ as $\mu_\varrho \in \mathcal{M}_0(S)$. This yields

$$\begin{aligned}
\mathbb{P}_{\mu^*}[R(x_1) \in B] &= \int \cdots \int \mathbf{1}_B(R(x_1))\Pi_{e_0}(x_0; dx_1)\bar{Q}(\varrho(x_0); de_0)\mu_\varrho(dx_0)\varrho^*(d\varrho) \\
&= \int_{\mathcal{M}(C)} \int_S \mathbf{1}_B(R(x_1))\mu_\varrho\Pi_\varrho(dx_1)\varrho^*(d\varrho) \\
&= \int_{\mathcal{M}(C)} \mu_\varrho\Pi_\varrho(B)\varrho^*(d\varrho) \\
&= \int_{\mathcal{M}(C)} \prod_{a\in\mathbb{A}} (\varrho\pi_\varrho)(B)\varrho^*(d\varrho) \\
&= \left(\prod_{a\in\mathbb{A}} \varrho^*\right)(B).
\end{aligned}$$

Here, the last equality holds true because ϱ^* is an invariant measure for the Markov chain $\{\varrho_t\}_{t\in\mathbb{N}}$ on $\mathcal{M}(C)$ associated with the random system with complete connections Σ'. Thus, we have shown:

Proposition 3.11 *Each invariant distribution ϱ^* for the Markov chain associated with the random system Σ' defined in (3.32) induces a random field μ^* on S such that the macroscopic process $\{R(x_t)\}_{t\in\mathbb{N}}$ is stationary under the law $\mathbb{P}_{\mu^*}$.*

Let us now assume that the macroscopic process $\{R(x_t)\}_{t\in\mathbb{N}}$ converges in law to a unique measure μ^* on $\mathcal{M}_s(S)$ as $t \to \infty$. If the initial distribution μ_0 on $(S, \mathcal{S})$ takes a product form, then we have almost surely that $R(x_t) = \prod_{a\in\mathbb{A}} \varrho(x_t)$. In particular, this yields convergence in law of the sequence of empirical distributions $\{\varrho(x_t)\}_{t\in\mathbb{N}}$ to a unique probability measure ϱ^* on $\mathcal{M}(C)$ and the macroscopic process converges in law to the product measure

$$\mu^* = \prod_{a\in\mathbb{A}} \varrho^* \in \mathcal{M}\left(\prod_{a\in\mathbb{A}} \mathcal{M}(C)\right) \subset \mathcal{M}(\mathcal{M}_0(S)).$$

Hence, in our present mean-field setting Theorem 3.9 yields the following result:

Proposition 3.12 *(i) The Markov chain associated with the random system Σ^* defined in (3.19) admits a unique invariant distribution μ^* on $\mathcal{M}_s(S)$ if and only if the Markov chain associated with the random system Σ' given by (3.32) admits a unique stationary measure ϱ^* on $\mathcal{M}(C)$ and $\mu^* = \prod_{a\in\mathbb{A}} \varrho^*$. The probability measure μ^* is concentrated on the set of product measures on S, and so we have $\mu^*(\mathcal{M}_0(S)) = 1$.*

(ii) If the macroscopic process $\{R(x_t)\}_{t\in\mathbb{N}}$ converges in law to a unique equilibrium, then there exists random field $\tilde{\mu}$ on $(S, \mathcal{S})$ such that the sequence $\{R(x_t)\}_{t\in\mathbb{N}}$ is stationary under the law $\mathbb{P}_{\tilde{\mu}}$.

3.1.2 Dynamics of the Microscopic Process

This section is devoted to an analysis of the asymptotic behaviour of the microscopic process $\{x_t\}_{t\in\mathbb{N}}$. We study the interplay between the long behaviour on the macroscopic level of empirical fields and the asymptotic behaviour on the microscopic level. We are going to demonstrate that convergence in law of the *macroscopic* process implies local asymptotic loss of memory of the *microscopic* process. That is, whenever the macroscopic process settles down to a unique limit, the distribution of the states of any finite set of agents does asymptotically not depend on the starting point of the microscopic process. If, under some law $\mathbb{P}_{\tilde{\mu}}$, the macroscopic process is stationary, then the stochastic kernel Π on S_0 admits a unique invariant distribution ν. In this case, the microscopic process $\{x_t\}_{t\in\mathbb{N}}$ converges in distribution to

ν. Furthermore, we shall see that the microscopic process $\{x_t\}_{t\in\mathbb{N}}$ converges in law whenever the macroscopic process converges to some random absorbing point.

Existence of Stationary Distributions

In this subsection, we will apply our results about the existence of stationary distributions for the macroscopic process in order to provide conditions which guarantee that the underlying microscopic process admits an equilibrium.

Theorem 3.13 *Let μ^* be a stationary distribution for the Markov chain $\{\xi_t\}_{t\in\mathbb{N}}$ on $\mathcal{M}_s(S)$ associated with the random system Σ^* given by (3.19). If μ^* is concentrated on the set $\mathcal{M}_0(S)$, then both the microscopic and the macroscopic process are stationary under the law $\mathbb{P}_{\tilde{\mu}}(\cdot) = \int_S \mathbb{P}_x(\cdot)\tilde{\mu}(dx)$, where the random field $\tilde{\mu}$ on $(S,\mathcal{S})$ is defined by*

$$\tilde{\mu}(\cdot) := \int_{\mathcal{M}_0(S)} \mu(\cdot)\mu^*(d\mu).$$

Proof: It follows from Theorem 3.9 that the macroscopic process $\{R(x_t)\}_{t\in\mathbb{N}}$ is stationary under the measure $\mathbb{P}_{\tilde{\mu}}$. Thus, it remains to show that the underlying microscopic process $\{x_t\}_{t\in\mathbb{N}}$ is also stationary under the law $\mathbb{P}_{\tilde{\mu}}$.

To this end, we fix $B \in \mathcal{S}$. In a first step, we are going to verify that

$$\tilde{\mu}(B) = \mathbb{E}_{\tilde{\mu}}[R(x_0)(B)].$$

Indeed, since $R(x) = \mu$ for μ-a.e. $x \in S$ whenever $\mu \in \mathcal{M}_0(S)$, we have

$$\begin{aligned}\mathbb{E}_{\tilde{\mu}}[R(x_0)(B)] &= \int_{\mathcal{M}_0(S)}\int_{S_0} R(x_0)(B)\mu(dx_0)\mu^*(d\mu) = \int_{\mathcal{M}_0(S)} \mu(B)\mu^*(d\mu)\\ &= \tilde{\mu}(B).\end{aligned}$$

Our goal is now to show that

$$\mathbb{P}_{\tilde{\mu}}[x_1 \in B] = \mathbb{E}_{\tilde{\mu}}[R(x_1)(B)].$$

Let μ be an ergodic random field on $(S,\mathcal{S})$ and $e \in E$. Due to Corollary 2.9 (i), we have $\mu\Pi_e \in \mathcal{M}_0(S)$. In particular, $\mu\Pi_e = R(x)$ for $\mu\Pi_e$-a.e. $x \in S$. This yields

$$\begin{aligned}\mathbb{E}_{\tilde{\mu}}[R(x_1)(B)] &= \int_{S_0}\int_E\int_{S_0} R(x_1)(B)\Pi_{e_0}(x_0;dx_1)Q(R(x_0);de_0)\tilde{\mu}(dx_0)\\ &= \int_{\mathcal{M}_0(S)}\int_E\int_S R(x_1)(B)\mu\Pi_{e_0}(dx_1)Q(\mu;de_0)\mu^*(d\mu)\\ &= \int_{\mathcal{M}_0(S)}\int_E \mu\Pi_{e_0}(B)Q(\mu;de_0)\mu^*(d\mu)\\ &= \mathbb{P}_{\tilde{\mu}}[x_1 \in B].\end{aligned}$$

Since the macroscopic process is stationary under the law $\mathbb{P}_{\tilde{\mu}}$, we deduce that

$$\tilde{\mu}(B) = \mathbb{E}_{\tilde{\mu}}[R(x_0)(B)] = \mathbb{E}_{\tilde{\mu}}[R(x_1)(B)] = \mathbb{P}_{\tilde{\mu}}[x_1 \in B] = \tilde{\mu}\Pi(B) \qquad (B \in \mathcal{S}). \quad (3.34)$$

Thus, $\tilde{\mu}$ is an invariant measure for the stochastic kernel Π, and so both the microscopic and the macroscopic process are stationary under the law $\mathbb{P}_{\tilde{\mu}}$. □

The next theorem shows that the microscopic process admits a stationary distribution whenever there exists a random field $\tilde{\mu}$ on S such that the macroscopic process is stationary under the law $\mathbb{P}_{\tilde{\mu}}$.

Theorem 3.14 *If, under some law $\mathbb{P}_{\mu}$, the sequence of empirical fields $\{R(x_t)\}_{t\in\mathbb{N}}$ is stationary, then the underlying microscopic process $\{x_t\}_{t\in\mathbb{N}}$ is stationary under the law $\mathbb{P}_{\tilde{\mu}}$, where the random field $\tilde{\mu}$ on $(S, \mathcal{S})$ is defined by*

$$\tilde{\mu}(\cdot) = \int_S R(x)(\cdot)\mu(dx). \quad (3.35)$$

Moreover, we have

$$\mathrm{Law}(\{R(x_t)\}_{t\in\mathbb{N}}, \mathbb{P}_{\mu}) = \mathrm{Law}(\{R(x_t)\}_{t\in\mathbb{N}}, \mathbb{P}_{\tilde{\mu}}).$$

Proof: Let μ be a random field on S_0 such that the sequence of ergodic empirical fields $\{R(x_t)\}_{t\in\mathbb{N}}$ is stationary under the law $\mathbb{P}_{\mu}$.

We denote by $\{\xi_t\}_{t\in\mathbb{N}}$ the Markov chain on $\mathcal{M}_s(S)$ associated with our random system with complete connections Σ^* and let $\hat{\mu}$ be the random field defined in (3.20). Due to Proposition 3.4, we have

$$\mathrm{Law}(\{R(x_t)\}_{t\in\mathbb{N}}, \mathbb{P}_{\mu}) = \mathrm{Law}(\{\xi_t\}_{t\in\mathbb{N}}, \mathbb{P}_{\hat{\mu}}). \quad (3.36)$$

In particular, the process $\{\xi_t\}_{t\in\mathbb{N}}$ is stationary under the measure $\mathbb{P}_{\hat{\mu}}$.

The random field $\tilde{\mu}$ on $(S, \mathcal{S})$ introduced in (3.35) is concentrated on the set S_0 and satisfies the relation

$$\tilde{\mu}(\cdot) = \int_{\mathcal{M}_0(S)} \mu(\cdot)\hat{\mu}(d\mu).$$

Thus, it follows from Proposition 3.5 and from (3.36) that

$$\mathrm{Law}(\{R(x_t)\}_{t\in\mathbb{N}}, \mathbb{P}_{\tilde{\mu}}) = \mathrm{Law}(\{\xi_t\}_{t\in\mathbb{N}}, \mathbb{P}_{\hat{\mu}}) = \mathrm{Law}(\{R(x_t)\}_{t\in\mathbb{N}}, \mathbb{P}_{\mu}).$$

According to Theorem 3.13, the microscopic process $\{x_t\}_{t\in\mathbb{N}}$ is stationary under the law $\mathbb{P}_{\tilde{\mu}}$ as the sequence $\{\xi_t\}_{t\in\mathbb{N}}$ is stationary under the measure $\mathbb{P}_{\hat{\mu}}$. □

Example 3.15 *Consider the mean-field model in a random environment introduced in (3.31). Due to Proposition 3.11, any invariant distribution* $\varrho^* \in \mathcal{M}(\mathcal{M}(C))$ *for the Markov chain associated with the random system* Σ' *defined in (3.32) induces a random field* μ^* *on* $(S, \mathcal{S})$ *such that the macroscopic process is stationary under the law* $\mathbb{P}_{\tilde{\mu}}$*. Thus, it follows from Theorem 3.14 that any such* ϱ^* *induces an equilibrium for our microscopic process.*

Asymptotic Loss of Memory and Uniqueness of Stationary Distributions

Armed with our results about the long run behaviour of the macroscopic process $\{R(x_t)\}_{t\in\mathbb{N}}$ established in the previous section, we are now able to analyze the asymptotics of the underlying microscopic process $\{x_t\}_{t\in\mathbb{N}}$. Throughout this section, we assume that the macroscopic process converges in law to a unique equilibrium μ^* on $\mathcal{M}_s(S)$. Our goal is to show that the underlying microscopic process has local asymptotic loss of memory. To this end, we combine a uniform convergence property of the signal sequence associated with the distance-diminishing random system with complete connections Σ^* defined in (3.19) with a variant of the Dobrushin-Vasserstein contraction technique: If the macroscopic process converges in law, then the signal sequence $\{e_t\}_{t\in\mathbb{N}}$ is uniformly ergodic in the strong sense. This means that asymptotically the microscopic process evolves in a random environment whose distribution does not depend on the initial configuration. Moreover, for any *fixed* environment $\{e_t\}_{t\in\mathbb{N}}$, the sequence $\{x_t\}_{t\in\mathbb{N}}$ is weakly ergodic in the sense that

$$\lim_{t\to\infty} \Delta(\Pi_{e_0}\cdots\Pi_{e_t}\mathbf{1}_B) = 0 \qquad (B \in \mathcal{S}_A, A \in \mathcal{A}) \tag{3.37}$$

whenever our uniform Dobrushin-Vasserstein-Condition is satisfied; cf. Remark 2.13. Thus, in the long run as $t \to \infty$, the distribution of the random variables $(x_t^a)_{a\in A}$ $(A \in \mathcal{A})$ should not depend on the initial configuration. More precisely, we have

Theorem 3.16 *Suppose that the local specifications* $(\gamma^{x,e})_{x\in S, e\in E}$ *satisfy our Assumptions 2.3, 2.4, 2.5 and the weighted Dobrushin-Vasserstein-Condition 2.16 with* μ *replaced by* e*. If the stochastic kernel* Q *from* $\mathcal{M}_s(S)$ *to* $\mathcal{E}$ *satisfies a uniform Lipschitz condition and has a lower bound in the sense of (3.26), then the microscopic process has local asymptotic loss of memory. More precisely, for each* $A \in \mathcal{A}$*, for any* $B \in \mathcal{S}_A$ *and for all* $\mu, \nu \in \mathcal{M}(S_0)$*, we have that*

$$\lim_{t\to\infty} \left| \int_{S_0} \Pi^t(x; B)\mu(dx) - \int_{S_0} \Pi^t(x; B)\nu(dx) \right| = 0. \tag{3.38}$$

We shall prove this theorem below.

Let us now provide a condition which guarantees that our microscopic process converges in distribution to a unique equilibrium as $t \to \infty$.

Theorem 3.17 *Suppose that the local specifications $(\gamma^{e,x})_{x\in S, e\in E}$ satisfy our Assumptions 2.3, 2.4, 2.5 and the weighted Dobrushin-Vasserstein-Condition 2.16 with μ replaced by e. Assume moreover that the stochastic kernel Q from $\mathcal{M}_s(S)$ to $\mathcal{E}$ satisfies a uniform Lipschitz condition and has a lower bound in the sense of (3.26). If the unique stationary distribution μ^* of the Markov chain associated with the random system Σ^* is concentrated on the set $\mathcal{M}_0(S)$, then the stochastic kernel Π on S_0 admits a unique invariant measure $\tilde{\mu}$. For any starting point $x \in S_0$, the microscopic process converges in law to $\tilde{\mu}$, and so we have at the same time convergence on the macroscopic level to μ^* and convergence on the microscopic level to $\tilde{\mu}$.*

Proof: It follows from Theorem 3.16 that the stochastic kernel Π on S_0 admits at most one invariant distribution. Due to Theorem 3.13, there exists a random field $\tilde{\mu}$ on the configuration space $(S, \mathcal{S})$ such that the sequence $\{x_t\}_{t\in\mathbb{N}}$ is stationary under the law $\mathbb{P}_{\tilde{\mu}}$, and so $\tilde{\mu} = \tilde{\mu}\Pi$. Thus, weak convergence of the microscopic process follows from Theorem 3.16. Convergence of the macroscopic process follows from Theorem 3.10. □

Corollary 3.18 *Consider the mean-field model in a random environment introduced in (3.31) and suppose that the Markov chain $\{\varrho_t\}_{t\in\mathbb{N}}$ on $\mathcal{M}(C)$ associated with the random system Σ' given by (3.32) admits a unique stationary distribution. It follows from Proposition 3.12 that the macroscopic process $\{R(x_t)\}_{t\in\mathbb{N}}$ converges in law. Due to Theorem 3.17, the stochastic kernel Π admits a unique equilibrium, and so we have at the same time convergence in distribution of the underlying microscopic process $\{x_t\}_{t\in\mathbb{N}}$.*

Let us now prepare the proof of Theorem 3.16. To this end, we introduce some additional notation. For $t, T \in \mathbb{N}$ we put $e_t^T := (e_T, \ldots, e_{T+t})$ and for $x \in S_0$ we define a probability measure $Q_t^T(R(x); \cdot)$ on $(E^{(t)}, \mathcal{E}^{(t)}) := (\otimes_{i=0}^t E, \otimes_{i=0}^t \mathcal{E})$ by

$$Q_t^T(R(x); \cdot) := \text{Law}(\{e_T, \ldots, e_{T+t}\}, \mathbb{P}_x). \tag{3.39}$$

For a given signal vector $e_t^T \in E^{(t)}$, we consider the transition kernels $\Pi(\cdot; e_t^T; \cdot)$ on $(S, \mathcal{S})$ defined by

$$\Pi(x; e_t^T; B) := \left[\Pi_{e_T} \cdots \Pi_{e_{T+t}}\right](x; B) \qquad (B \in \mathcal{S}). \tag{3.40}$$

For any configuration $v = (v^a)_{a\in\mathbb{A}} \in S$, for each $x \in S, e \in E$ and for all local sets $A \in \mathcal{A}$, we write $\gamma_A^{x,e}(\cdot; v)$ for the probability measure $\gamma_A^{x,e}(\cdot; (v^a)_{a\in A^c})$ on C^A with boundary condition $(v^a)_{a\in A^c}$ on A^c. Moreover, we put

$$\Pi_v^{A_0,\dots,A_t}(x; e_t^0; \cdot) := \int_S \cdots \int_S \gamma_{A_0}^{x,e_0}(dx_1; v) \cdots \gamma_{A_{t-1}}^{x_{t-1},e_{t-1}}(dx_t; v)\gamma_{A_t}^{x_t,e_t}(\cdot; v),$$

where $A_0, A_2, \dots, A_t$ $(t \in \mathbb{N})$ are local sets.

In order to avoid a problem of measurability, it will be convenient to use the following approximation result.

Lemma 3.19 *For any local set $A \in \mathcal{A}$, for each $t \in \mathbb{N}$ and for all $\epsilon > 0$, there exits local sets $A_0 \supset A_2 \supset \cdots \supset A_t$ such that*

$$\sup_{B\in\mathcal{S}_A} |\Pi_v^{A_0,\dots,A_t}(x; e_t^0; B) - \Pi(x; e_t^0; B)| < \epsilon \tag{3.41}$$

uniformly in $x \in S$, in $e_t^0 \in E^{(t)}$ and in the boundary condition $v \in S$.

Proof: Let us fix $\epsilon > 0$ and $A \in \mathcal{A}$. For $t = 0$ we have to establish the existence of a local set $A_0 \in \mathcal{A}$ such that

$$\sup_{x,e_0,v}\sup_{B\in\mathcal{S}_A} |\Pi_{e_0}(x; B) - \gamma_{A_0}^{x,e_0}(B; v)| < \epsilon.$$

This, however, follows from our uniform Dobrushin-Condition (Assumption 2.5) together with Theorem 8.23 (ii) and with Remark 8.26 in Georgii (1989): There exists constants $\lambda > 0$ and $c(\lambda) < 1$ such that, for any $A_0 \in \mathcal{A}$, the following estimate holds true:

$$\sup_{x,e_0,v}\left|\Pi_{e_0}(x; B) - \gamma_{A_0}^{x,e_0}(B; v)\right| \le \frac{|A|}{1-c(\lambda)}\exp(-\lambda s(A, A_0^c)) \qquad (B \in \mathcal{S}_A); \tag{3.42}$$

see also (2.12) and (2.15) above.

Now we can proceed as follows. We fix a sequence of signals $\{e_t\}_{t\in\mathbb{N}}$ and let $A_0 \supset \cdots \supset A_{t+1}$ be local sets to be specified below. Observe that

$$\left|\Pi(x; e_{t+1}^0; B) - \int_S \cdots \int_S \gamma_{A_0}^{x,e_0}(dx_1; v) \cdots \gamma_{A_t}^{x_t,e_t}(dx_{t+1}; v)\gamma_{A_{t+1}}^{x_{t+1},e_{t+1}}(B; v)\right|$$

$$\le \left|\int_S \gamma_{A_{t+1}}^{y,e_{t+1}}(B; v)\left\{\Pi(x; e_t^0; dy) - \int_S \cdots \int_S \gamma_{A_0}^{x,e_0}(dx_1; v) \cdots \gamma_{A_t}^{x_t,e_t}(dy; v)\right\}\right| \tag{3.43}$$

$$+\left|\int_S \left\{\Pi(y; e_{t+1}; B) - \gamma_{A_{t+1}}^{y,e_{t+1}}(B; v)\right\}\Pi(x; e_t^0; dy)\right|. \tag{3.44}$$

Due to (3.42), there exists a local set $A_{t+1} \in \mathcal{A}$ such that (3.44) is uniformly bounded above by $\frac{\epsilon}{t+1}$. In order to control (3.43), we can proceed by induction.

Our Markov property of order l implies that the mapping $y \mapsto \gamma^{y,e}_{A_{t+1}}(B;v)$ is a local function. More precisely, for any given local set $A_{t+1} \in \mathcal{A}$, there exists a local set $\hat{A} \in \mathcal{A}$, $A_{t+1} \subset \hat{A}$ which does depend neither on $e \in E$ nor on the boundary condition v on A^c_{t+1} such that $y \mapsto \gamma^{y,e}_{A_{t+1}}(B;v)$ is $\mathcal{S}_{\hat{A}}$- measurable. Thus, (3.43) can be estimated by

$$\begin{aligned}
&\sup_{\hat{B}\in\mathcal{S}_{\hat{A}}} \left| \Pi(x;e^0_t;\hat{B}) - \int_S \cdots \int_S \gamma^{x,e_0}_{A_0}(dx_1;v)\cdots\gamma^{x_{t-1},e_{t-1}}_{A_{t-1}}(dx_t;v)\gamma^{x_t,e_t}_{A_t}(\hat{B};v)\right| \\
\leq\ &\sup_{\hat{B}\in\mathcal{S}_{\hat{A}}} \left| \int_S \gamma^{y,e_t}_{A_t}(\hat{B};v)\left\{\Pi(x;e^0_{t-1};dy) - \gamma^{x,e_0}_{A_0}(dx_1;v)\cdots\gamma^{x_{t-1},e_{t-1}}_{A_{t-1}}(dy;v)\right\}\right| \\
&+ \sup_{\hat{B}\in\mathcal{S}_{\hat{A}}} \left| \int_S \left\{\Pi(y;e_t;\hat{B}) - \gamma^{y,e_t}_{A_t}(\hat{B};v)\right\}\Pi(x;e^0_{t-1};dy)\right|.
\end{aligned}$$

Now we can choose $A_t \supset \hat{A} \supset A_{t+1}$ such that the second term in the last inequality is bounded by $\frac{\epsilon}{t+1}$ and proceed as above. By induction we see that

$$\sup_{B\in\mathcal{S}_A}\ \sup_{e^0_t,v} |\Pi^{A_0,\ldots,A_t}_v(x;e^0_t;B) - \Pi(x;e^0_t;B)| < \epsilon. \tag{3.45}$$

This proves our assertion. □

Observe that, for any given configuration $v \in S$, for all $t \in \mathbb{N}, A \in \mathcal{A}, B \in \mathcal{S}_A$ and for any fixed local sets $A_0, A_2, \ldots, A_t$, the mapping

$$e^0_t \mapsto \sup_x \Pi^{A_0,\ldots,A_t}_v(x;e^0_t;B) \tag{3.46}$$

is measurable as we just have to calculate the supremum of finitely many measurable functions. We are now ready to establish the main result of this section.

Proof of Theorem 3.16:

Let us fix $A \in \mathcal{A}$ and $B \in \mathcal{S}_A$. It is obviously enough to show that

$$\lim_{t\to\infty} \sup_{x,y} |\Pi^t(x;B) - \Pi^t(y;B)| = 0. \tag{3.47}$$

For any initial configuration $x \in S_0$ and for all $t \in \mathbb{N}$, it follows from our strong law of large numbers for ergodic empirical fields established in Proposition 2.8 that

$$\Pi^{t+1}(x;B) = \int_E \cdots \int_E [\Pi_{e_0}\cdots\Pi_{e_t}](x;B)Q(u(R(x),e^0_{t-1});de_t)\cdots Q(R(x);de_0);$$

see also (3.10). Using the notation introduced in (3.39) and (3.40), this amounts to

$$\begin{aligned}
&\Pi^{T+t+1}(x;B)\\
&= \int\cdots\int \Pi(y;e_t^T;B)Q_t^0(u(R(x),e_{T-1}^0);de_t^T)\Pi(x;e_{T-1}^0;dy)Q_{T-1}^0(R(x);de_{T-1}^0).
\end{aligned}$$

Let us now fix $t\in\mathbb{N}$ and $\epsilon>0$. Due to Lemma 3.19, we can choose local sets $A_0\supset\cdots\supset A_t$ such that

$$\sup_{v,x,B,e_t^T} |\Pi(x;e_t^T;B)-\Pi_v^{A_0,\dots,A_t}(x;e_t^T;B)|<\epsilon. \tag{3.48}$$

Thus, uniformly in $B\in\mathcal{S}_A$, the quantity $\Pi^{t+T+1}(x;B)$ is bounded above by

$$\int\int\{\sup_z \Pi_v^{A_0,\dots,A_t}(z;e_t^T;B)\}Q_t^0(u(R(x),e_{T-1}^0);de_t^T)Q_{T-1}^0(R(x);de_{T-1}^0)+\epsilon$$

and bounded below by

$$\int\int\{\inf_z \Pi_v^{A_0,\dots,A_t}(z;e_t^T;B)\}Q_t^0(u(R(x),e_{T-1}^0);de_t^T)Q_{T-1}^0(R(x);de_{T-1}^0)-\epsilon.$$

This yields the following estimate:

$$\begin{aligned}
&\sup_{x,y}|\Pi^{T+t+1}(x;B)-\Pi^{T+t+1}(y;B)|\\
&\le\sup_{x,y}\Bigg|\int\int\{\sup_z \Pi_v^{A_0,\dots,A_t}(z;e_t^T;B)\}Q_t^0(u(R(x),e_{T-1}^0);de_t^T)Q_{T-1}^0(R(x);de_{T-1}^0)\\
&\quad-\int\int\{\inf_z \Pi_v^{A_0,\dots,A_t}(z;e_t^T;B)\}Q_t^0(u(R(y),e_{T-1}^0);de_t^T)Q_{T-1}^0(R(y);de_{T-1}^0)\Bigg|+2\epsilon\\
&\le\sup_{x,y}\left|\int\{\sup_z \Pi_v^{A_0,\dots,A_t}(z;e_t^T;B)\}\left[Q_t^T(R(x);de_t^T)-Q_t^T(R(y);de_t^T)\right]\right| \qquad (3.49)\\
&\quad+\sup_y\int\{\sup_z \Pi_v^{A_0,\dots,A_t}(z;e_t^T;B)-\inf_z \Pi_v^{A_0,\dots,A_t}(z;e_t^T;B)\}Q_t^T(R(y);de_t^T) \qquad (3.50)\\
&\quad+2\epsilon.
\end{aligned}$$

Here, the second inequality follows from the definition of the transition kernel Q_t^T from S_0 to $\mathcal{E}^{(t)}$ defined in (3.39). We are going to analyze the quantities (3.49) and (3.50) separately.

1. Since $Q_t^T(R(x);\cdot)-Q_t^T(R(y);\cdot)$ is a signed measure on $(E^{(t)},\mathcal{E}^{(t)})$ with total mass zero, we can estimate (3.49) by

$$\sup_{x,y}\|Q_t^T(R(x);\cdot)-Q_t^T(R(y);\cdot)\|.$$

Due to Theorem 3.7, the Markov chain associated with the random system Σ^* converges in law to a unique invariant distribution. Thus, it follows from Proposition A.10 that the signal sequence $\{e_t\}_{t\in\mathbb{N}}$ is uniformly ergodic in the strong sense, i.e., for any $t \in \mathbb{N}$, there exists a measure Q_t^* on $(E^{(t)}, \mathcal{E}^{(t)})$ such that

$$\lim_{T\to\infty} \sup_{x,t} \|Q_t^T(R(x);\cdot) - Q_t^*(\cdot)\| = 0. \tag{3.51}$$

In particular, for any fixed sequence of local sets $\{A_t\}_{t\in\mathbb{N}}$, we have that

$$\lim_{T\to\infty} \sup_{t,x,y} \left| \int \sup_z \Pi_v^{A_0,\ldots,A_t}(z; e_t^T; B) \left[Q_t^T(R(x); de_t^T) - Q_t^T(R(y); de_t^T)\right] \right| = 0.$$

2. Let us now analyze the integral in (3.50). For any given local sets $A_0 \supset \cdots \supset A_t$, it follows from (3.51) that

$$\begin{aligned} &\lim_{T\to\infty} \sup_y \left| \int \{\sup_z \Pi_v^{A_0,\ldots,A_t}(z; e_t^T; B) - \inf_z \Pi_v^{A_0,\ldots,A_t}(z; e_t^T; B)\} Q_t^T(R(y); de_t^T) \right| \\ &= \left| \int \{\sup_z \Pi_v^{A_0,\ldots,A_t}(z; e_t^0; B) - \inf_z \Pi_v^{A_0,\ldots,A_t}(z; e_t^0; B)\} Q_t^*(de_t^0) \right| \end{aligned} \tag{3.52}$$

Using the triangle inequality and Lemma 3.19, it is easily seen that the local sets $A_0 \supset \cdots \supset A_t$ can be chosen such that

$$\begin{aligned} \Delta(\Pi_v^{A_0,\ldots,A_t}(\cdot; e_t^0; B)) &:= \sup_z \Pi_v^{A_0,\ldots,A_t}(z; e_t^0; B) - \inf_z \Pi_v^{A_0,\ldots,A_t}(z; e_t^0; B) \\ &\leq \Delta(\Pi(\cdot; e_t^0; B)) + 2\epsilon \end{aligned}$$

uniformly in $e_t^0 \in E^{(t)}$, in $B \in \mathcal{S}_A$, and in the boundary condition $v \in S$. Hence

$$\begin{aligned} &\int \Delta(\Pi_v^{A_0,\ldots,A_t}(\cdot; e_t^0; B)) Q_t^*(de_t^0) \\ &\leq \int \{\sup_z \Pi(z; e_t^0; B) - \inf_z \Pi(z; e_t^0; B)\} Q_t^*(de_t^0) + 2\epsilon. \end{aligned}$$

For any fixed environment $\{e_t\}_{t\in\mathbb{N}}$, our uniform Dobrushin-Vasserstein-Condition (Assumption 2.16) implies that

$$\sup_{x,y} |\Pi(x; e_t^0; B) - \Pi(y; e_t^0; B)| \leq c\alpha^{t+1} \tag{3.53}$$

for some constants $c = c(|A|) < \infty$ and $\alpha < 1$ which do neither depend on $B \in \mathcal{S}_A$ nor on the environment $\{e_t\}_{t\in\mathbb{N}}$; see, e.g., Remark 2.13. Thus, for any given $\epsilon > 0$, there exists large enough $t_0, T_0 \in \mathbb{N}$ such that

$$\sup_{x,y,e_t^0} \left|\Pi(x, e_t^0; B) - \Pi(y, e_t^0; B)\right| < \epsilon \qquad (t \geq t_0)$$

and such that

$$\sup_{x,y,t} \|Q_t^T(R(x); \cdot) - Q_t^*(\cdot)\| < \epsilon \qquad (T \geq T_0).$$

Hence, for all $t \geq t_0$ and for any $T \geq T_0$, we can fix local sets $A_0, A_1, \ldots, A_t$ and a configuration $v \in S$ such that the following estimate holds true:

$$\begin{aligned} (3.50) \quad &\leq \sup_{x,y} \|Q_t^T(R(x); \cdot) - Q_t^*(\cdot)\| + \sup_{e_t^0} \Delta(\Pi_v^{A_0,\ldots,A_t}(\cdot; e_t^0; B)) \\ &\leq 3\epsilon + \Delta(\Pi(\cdot; e_t^0; B)) \leq 4\epsilon. \end{aligned}$$

Thus, for any $t \geq t_0$ and for all $T \geq T_0$, we have that

$$\sup_{x,y\in S_0} |\Pi^{t+T+1}(x; B) - \Pi^{t+T+1}(y; B)| < 7\epsilon.$$

Since $\epsilon > 0$ is arbitrary, the assertion follows. □

The Microscopic Process in a Mean-Field Model in a Stationary Random Environment

We are now going to analyze the asymptotics of individual behaviour in the mean-field type model given by (3.31) under the assumption that the macroscopic process is already in equilibrium. More precisely, we assume that there exists a probability measure $\tilde{\mu}$ on $(S, \mathcal{S})$ such that the sequence of ergodic empirical fields $\{R(x_t)\}_{t\in\mathbb{N}}$ is stationary under the law $\mathbb{P}_{\tilde{\mu}}$. Due to Proposition 3.11, such a random field exists whenever the Markov process associated with the random system with complete connections Σ' introduced in (3.32) admits a stationary distribution. Given that the assumptions of Theorem 3.16 are satisfied, the sequence $\{x_t\}_{t\in\mathbb{N}}$ converges in law to a unique equilibrium as $t \to \infty$; cf. Corollary 3.18. In our present mean-field setting, however, we can establish a stronger result. Applying a general convergence result for Markov chains in a stationary random environment provided in Borovkov (1998), we are able to show that our microscopic process converges locally in the sense of a strong coupling to a stationary process.

Remark 3.20 *It follows from our Proposition 3.5 and from Theorem A.10 that the signal sequence* $\{e_t\}_{t\in\mathbb{N}}$ *is stationary and ergodic under the law* $\mathbb{P}_{\tilde{\mu}}$. *Thus, the microscopic process may be viewed as a Markov chain evolving in a stationary and ergodic random environment. The stationary sequence* $\{e_t\}_{t\in\mathbb{N}}$ *can always be extended to a sequence defined for all integers* $-\infty < t < \infty$, *due to Kolmogorov's extension theorem.*

Without loss of generality, we assume that the sequence $\{(x_t, e_t)\}_{t\in\mathbb{N}}$ is defined on the canonical probability space $(\Omega, \mathcal{F}, \mathbb{P}_{\tilde{\mu}})$ and that $(x_t, e_t)(\omega) = \omega_t$ for all $t \in \mathbb{N}$. Here, $\omega = (\omega_t)_{t\in\mathbb{N}} \in \Omega$. We introduce the shift transformation θ which acts on the path space Ω according to the formula

$$\theta((\omega_t, \omega_{t+1}, \ldots)) = (\omega_{t+1}, \omega_{t+2}, \ldots).$$

Theorem 3.21 *Suppose that the macroscopic process is already in equilibrium and that the individual transition probabilities* $(\pi_e)_{e\in E}$ *are uniformly bounded away from zero in the sense that* $\inf_{c,\hat{c},e} \pi_e(c;\hat{c}) > 0$. *Then there exists a stationary sequence of random variables* $Y = \{Y_t\}_{t\in\mathbb{N}}$, $Y_t = (y_t^a)_{a\in\mathbb{A}}$, *defined on a common probability space* $(\Omega, \mathcal{F}, \mathbb{P}_{\tilde{\mu}})$ *with the process* $\{(x_t, e_t)\}_{t\in\mathbb{N}}$ *such that the microscopic process converges locally to* Y *in the sense of a strong coupling. More precisely, for any local set* $A \in \mathcal{A}$ *the following holds true:*

$$\lim_{t\to\infty} \mathbb{P}_{\tilde{\mu}}[y_k^a = x_k^a \quad \textit{for all } k \geq t \textit{ and for all } a \in A] = 1. \tag{3.54}$$

Proof: Let us fix a local set $A \in \mathcal{A}$ and put $x_t^A := (x_t^a)_{a\in A}$. Thus, $\{x_t^A\}_{t\in\mathbb{N}}$ is a Markov chain in the random environment specified by the sequence $\{e_t\}_{t\in\mathbb{N}}$. Due to the conditional independence of the random variables $(x_{t+1}^a)_{a\in A}$ given the common signal e_t and because of Theorem 13.3 in Borovkov (1998), there exists a measurable transformation $f : C \times E \times [0,1] \to C$ such that the process $\{x_t^A\}_{t\in\mathbb{N}}$ admits the following representation:

$$x_{t+1}^a = f(x_t^a, e_t, \alpha_t^a) \qquad (a \in A). \tag{3.55}$$

Here, $\{\alpha_t^a\}_{t\in\mathbb{Z}}$ $(a \in \mathbb{A})$ is an i.i.d. sequence of random variables taking values in $[0,1]$, and the sequences $\{e_t\}_{t\in\mathbb{Z}}$, $\{\alpha_t^a\}_{t\in\mathbb{Z}}$ $(a \in A)$ are independent.

Let us now fix a possible individual state $c \in C$. For any $t \in \mathbb{N}$, we put

$$B_t := \{x_t^a = c \text{ for all } a \in A\}.$$

Thus, $\{B_t\}_{t\in\mathbb{N}}$ is a sequence of renovating events in the sense of Definition 11.2 in Borovkov (1998). Since the individual transition dynamics are uniformly bounded away from zero, we have $\mathbb{P}_{\tilde{\mu}}(B_t) > 0$ for all $t \in \mathbb{N}$ and

$$\lim_{n\to\infty} \mathbb{P}\left(\cup_{t=1}^{n} B_t \cap \theta^{-s} B_{t+s}\right) = 1$$

uniformly in $s \in \mathbb{N}$. This allows us to apply Theorem 11.3 in Borovkov (1998): On a common probability space $(\Omega, \mathcal{F}, \mathbb{P}_{\tilde{\mu}})$ with the sequence $\{(x_t, e_t)\}_{t\in\mathbb{N}}$ we can define a stationary sequence of random variables $Y^A = \{Y_t^A\}_{t\in\mathbb{N}}$, $Y_t^A = (y_t^a)_{a\in A}$ such that

$$y_{t+1}^a = f(y_t^a, e_t, \alpha_t^a),$$

and such that

$$\lim_{n\to\infty} \mathbb{P}(Y_t^A = x_t^A \quad \text{for all } t \geq n) = 1. \tag{3.56}$$

Now we can define the desired process $Y = \{Y_t\}_{t\in\mathbb{N}}$ by the relation $Y_t = (y_t^a)_{a\in\mathbb{A}}$. Obviously, this process is stationary and the sequences $\{y_t^a\}_{t\in\mathbb{N}}$ $(a \in \mathbb{A})$ are conditionally independent given the common signals $\{e_t\}_{t\in\mathbb{N}}$. □

Absorbing Macroscopic Processes and Local Convergence

In the last but one subsection, we established local asymptotic loss of memory on the microscopic level under the assumption that the macroscopic level settles down to a unique limit in the long run. In this subsection, we shall assume that our macroscopic process converges along almost all paths of the microscopic process to some random absorbing point. We show that the underlying microscopic process converges in law to a random field which typically depends on the initial configuration.

Definition 3.22 *Let $(\{\eta_t\}_{t\in\mathbb{N}}, (\mathbb{P}_\eta)_{\eta\in X})$ be a Markov chain on $(\Omega, \mathcal{F})$ with compact metric state space (X, d_X). The Markov chain $\{\eta_t\}_{t\in\mathbb{N}}$ is called* ***absorbing****, if there exist finitely many points $\nu^1, \ldots, \nu^k \in X$ and functions $g_1, \ldots, g_k$ on X such that*

$$\sum_{j=1}^{k} g_j(\eta) = 1 \qquad \textit{and} \qquad \mathbb{P}_\eta[\lim_{t\to\infty} \eta_t = \nu^j] = g_j(\eta) \qquad (j = 1, \ldots, k). \tag{3.57}$$

In the sequel, we denote by $\{\xi_t\}_{t\in\mathbb{N}}$ the Markov chain on $\mathcal{M}_s(S)$ associated with our random system with complete connections Σ^* defined in (3.19) and assume that the stochastic kernel Q from $\mathcal{M}_s(S)$ to $\mathcal{E}$ satisfies a uniform Lipschitz condition in the sense of Definition 2.32.

Remark 3.23 *It follows from Theorem 3.4.2 in Norman (1972) that the Markov chain* $\{\xi_t\}_{t\in\mathbb{N}}$ *associated with* Σ^* *is absorbing in the sense of Definition 3.22 whenever there exists a dense subset* $\hat{M}_1 \subset \mathcal{M}_s(S)$ *such that (3.57) holds true for all* $\xi \in \tilde{M}_1$.

The next result follows from Theorem 3.4.2 in Norman (1972).

Lemma 3.24 *If the Markov chain* $\{\xi_t\}_{t\in\mathbb{N}}$ *is absorbing in the sense of Definition 3.22, then the set*

$$\{\delta_{\nu^1}(\cdot), \ldots, \delta_{\nu^k}(\cdot)\}$$

is a basis for the set of all invariant measures for the process $\{\xi_t\}_{t\in\mathbb{N}}$.

Below, we shall verify that the signal sequence $\{\zeta_t\}_{t\in\mathbb{N}}$ associated with the random system Σ^* behaves asymptotically like an i.i.d. sequence of random variables if the associated Markov process is absorbing. From this we will then deduce that, for any starting point $x \in S_0$, our microscopic process converges in law, i.e.,

$$\Pi^t(x; \cdot) \xrightarrow{w} \mu_x(\cdot) \qquad (t \to \infty) \tag{3.58}$$

for some random field μ_x on $(S, \mathcal{S})$. The limiting distribution μ_x turns out to be a weighted average of the unique stationary distributions μ_j of the (Feller) kernels

$$\Pi_j(x; \cdot) := \int_E \Pi_e(x; \cdot) Q(\nu^j; de) \qquad (j = 1, \ldots, k). \tag{3.59}$$

Here, $\nu^1, \ldots, \nu^k$ are the absorbing points of the macroscopic process.The weights $\{w^1, \ldots, w^k\}$ take the form $w^j = g_j(R(x))$ $(j = 1, \ldots, k)$.

In the sequel, it will be convenient to use the following notation; cf. (3.39):

$$Q_t^T(\xi; \cdot) := \mathrm{Law}(\{\zeta_T, \ldots, \zeta_{T+t}\}, \mathbb{P}_\xi) \qquad (\xi \in \mathcal{M}_s(S),\ t, T \in \mathbb{N}).$$

Proposition 3.25 *Suppose that the Markov chain* $\{\xi_t\}_{t\in\mathbb{N}}$ *associated with our random system with complete connections* Σ^* *converges almost surely to some random absorbing point* $\nu \in \{\nu^1, \ldots, \nu^k\}$. *In this case, the following holds true:*

$$\lim_{T\to\infty} \sup_{t,\xi} \left\| Q_t^T(\xi; \cdot) - \sum_{j=1}^k g_j(\xi) \otimes_{i=0}^t Q(\nu^j; \cdot) \right\| = 0, \tag{3.60}$$

i.e., the signal process $\{\zeta_{T+t}\}_{t\in\mathbb{N}}$ *behaves like an i.i.d. sequence of random variables as* $T \to \infty$.

Proof: For $\xi \in \mathcal{M}_s(S)$ and for $t \in \mathbb{N}$, let us define a probability measure $Q_t^*(\xi;\cdot)$ on $(E^{(t)}, \mathcal{E}^{(t)})$ by

$$Q_t^*(\xi;\cdot) := \sum_{j=1}^{k} g_j(\xi) Q_t^0(\nu^j;\cdot).$$

These probability measures satisfy

$$\lim_{T\to\infty} \sup_{t,\xi} \|Q_t^T(\xi;\cdot) - Q_t^*(\xi;\cdot)\| = 0;$$

see, e.g., Iosefescu and Theodorescu (1968), Lemma 2.1.60 and Theorem 2.1.66. It is therefore enough to verify that the law $Q_t^0(\nu^j;\cdot)$ takes the product form

$$Q_t^0(\nu^j;\cdot) = \otimes_{i=0}^t Q(\nu^j;\cdot) \qquad (t \in \mathbb{N}).$$

Since the set $\{\delta_{\nu^1}(\cdot), \ldots, \delta_{\nu^k}(\cdot)\}$ is a basis for the set of all invariant measures of the process $\{\xi_t\}_{t\in\mathbb{N}}$, we have, for any absorbing point $\nu^j \in \mathcal{M}_s(S)$, that

$$Q(\nu^j; \{\zeta : u(\xi,\zeta) \in B\}) = \delta_{\nu^j}(B) \qquad (B \in \mathcal{E}).$$

This shows that the measure $Q(\nu^j;\cdot)$ $(j = 1, 2, \ldots, k)$ is concentrated on the set $M(\nu^j) := \{\zeta : u(\nu^j,\zeta) = \nu^j\}$. Thus, for arbitrary sets $B_1, B_2 \in \mathcal{E}$, we have that

$$\begin{aligned} Q_1^0(\nu^j; B_0 \times B_1) &= \int_{B_0} Q(\nu^j; d\zeta) Q(u(\nu^j,\zeta); B_1) \\ &= \int_{B_0 \cap M(\nu^j)} Q(\nu^j; d\zeta) Q(u(\nu^j,\zeta); B_1) \\ &= Q(\nu^j; B_0 \cap M(\nu^j)) Q(\nu^j; B_1) \\ &= Q(\nu^j; B_0) Q(\nu^j; B_1). \end{aligned}$$

For $t \geq 2$, the assertion follows by induction. □

We are now ready to analyze the asymptotic dynamics of our microscopic process. If the macroscopic process converges to some random absorbing point in the sense of Definition 3.22, then the signal process $\{e_t\}_{t\in\mathbb{N}}$ behaves asymptotically like an i.i.d. sequence of random variables. Thus, asymptotically, the microscopic process evolves with probability $g_j(R(x))$ in a random environment which is generated by a sequence of independent and $Q(\nu^j;\cdot)$-distributed random variables. In this case, the asymptotic transition dynamics of the sequence $\{x_t\}_{t\in\mathbb{N}}$ is described by the stochastic kernel Π_j defined in (3.59), and so local convergence follows from a perturbation of Vasserstein's convergence theorem.

For notational convenience, we will assume that the mapping

$$e_t^0 \mapsto \sup_x \Pi(x; e_t^0; B) \qquad (B \in \mathcal{S}_A, A \in \mathcal{A})$$

is measurable. Otherwise, an ϵ-approximation argument as in the proof of Theorem 3.16 yields the desired result.

Theorem 3.26 *Suppose that our local specifications $(\gamma^{x,e})_{x\in S\, e\in E}$ satisfy the standard Assumptions 2.3, 2.4, 2.5 and 2.16 with μ replaced by e, and assume that the stochastic kernel Q from $\mathcal{M}_s(S)$ to $\mathcal{E}$ satisfies a uniform Lipschitz condition. Let the macroscopic process $\{R(x_t)\}_{t\in\mathbb{N}}$ be absorbing in the sense that there exists finitely many functions $g_1, g_2, \ldots, g_k : \mathcal{M}_s(S) \to [0,1]$ and random fields $\nu^1, \ldots, \nu^k$ on $(S, \mathcal{S})$ such that*

$$\mathbb{P}_x[\lim_{t\to\infty} R(x_t) = \nu^j] = g_j(R(x)) \qquad \left(\sum_j g_j(R(x)) = 1\right). \tag{3.61}$$

In this case, the microscopic process $\{x_t\}_{t\in\mathbb{N}}$ converges in distribution to a random field on $(S, \mathcal{S})$. More precisely, for any $x \in S_0$, we have that

$$\lim_{t\to\infty} \left| \Pi^t(x; B) - \sum_{j=1}^k g_j(R(x))\mu_j(B) \right| = 0 \qquad (B \in \mathcal{S}_A, A \in \mathcal{A}). \tag{3.62}$$

Here, μ_j denotes the unique invariant measure of the kernel Π_j defined in (3.59).

Proof: Let $A \in \mathcal{A}$ and $B \in \mathcal{S}_A$ be given. For each $x \in S_0$ and for any $t \in \mathbb{N}$, we introduce a measure $\mu_t(x; \cdot)$ on $(E^{(t)}, \mathcal{E}^{(t)})$ by the relation

$$\mu_t(x; de_t^0) := \sum_{j=1}^k g_j(R(x)) \otimes_{l=0}^t Q(\nu^j; de_l). \tag{3.63}$$

Let us fix $A \in \mathcal{A}$ and $B \in \mathcal{S}_A$. In a first step, we are going to show that

$$\lim_{t,T\to\infty} \left| \Pi^{t+T+1}(x; B) - \int \Pi(x; e_t^0; B)\mu_t(x; de_t^0) \right| = 0. \tag{3.64}$$

Using the notation introduced in (3.39) and (3.40), we have

$$\begin{aligned} &\Pi^{T+t+1}(x; B) \\ = &\int \cdots \int \Pi(y; e_t^T; B)\Pi(x; e_{T-1}^0; dy)Q_t^0(u(R(x), e_{T-1}^0); de_t^T)Q_{T-1}^0(R(x); de_{T-1}^0), \end{aligned}$$

due to (3.10), and so it is easily seen that

$$\int \sup_z \Pi(z; e_t^0; B) Q_t^T(R(x); de_t^0) - \int \inf_z \Pi^t(z; e_t^0; B) \mu_t(x; de_t^0) \tag{3.65}$$

$$\geq \Pi^{t+T}(x; B) - \int \Pi(x; e_t^0; B) \mu_t(x; de_t^0)$$

$$\geq \int \inf_z \Pi(z; e_t^0; B) Q_t^T(R(x); de_t^0) - \int \sup_z \Pi^t(z; e_t^0; B) \mu_t(x; de_t^0). \tag{3.66}$$

Observe that

$$(3.65) = \int \sup_z \Pi(z; e_t^0; B)[Q_t^T(R(x); de_t^0) - \mu_t(x; de_t^0)] \tag{3.67}$$

$$- \int \{\sup_z \Pi(z; e_t^0; B) - \inf_z \Pi(z; e_t^0; B)\} \mu_t(x; de_t^0). \tag{3.68}$$

Since the Markov process associated with the random system Σ^* is assumed to be absorbing, it follows from Proposition 3.25 that (3.67) converges to zero as $T \to \infty$ uniformly $t \in \mathbb{N}$ and in $x \in S_0$. Moreover, our uniform Dobrushin-Vasserstein-Condition (Assumption 2.16) implies convergence of (3.68) to zero as $t \to \infty$; cf. Remark 2.13. For the same reason, (3.66) converges to 0 as $t, T \to \infty$. This yields (3.64).

We can now apply Vasserstein's convergence theorem in order to establish our result. We have

$$\sup_x \left| \int \Pi(x; e_t^0; B) \mu_t(x; de_t^0) - \sum g_{j=1}^k (R(x)) \mu_j(B) \right|$$

$$= \sup_x \left| \sum_{j=1}^k g_j(R(x)) \left(\int_E \Pi_e(x; dx_1) Q(\nu^j; de) \cdots \int_E \Pi_e(x_t; dx_{t+1}) Q(\nu^j; de) \right) \mathbf{1}_B(x_{t+1}) \right.$$

$$\left. - \sum_{j=1}^k g_j(R(x)) \mu_j(B) \right|$$

$$= \sup_x \left| \sum_{j=1}^k g_j(R(x)) (\Pi_j^{t+1}(x; B) - \mu_j(B)) \right|.$$

Since μ_j is the unique invariant measure of the stochastic kernel Π_j, the sequence of random fields $\{\Pi_j^t(x; \cdot)\}_{t \in \mathbb{N}}$ converges weakly to the equilibrium μ_j as $t \to \infty$, due to Vasserstein's convergence theorem. This completes the proof. □

Let us now analyze a simple example, where the long run dynamics of the macroscopic process depends on the initial distribution of our microscopic process.

Example 3.27 *Let us assume that the agents are located on the one-dimensional integer lattice $\mathbb{Z}$, that $l = 1$ and that the transition to a neu state itself is made independently by different agents. We put $C = E = \{0, +1\}$, and for any fixed signal $e \in E$, we specify the individual transition dynamics as*

$$\pi_e(\theta_a x; \{+1\}) = \frac{1}{12} \sum_{|b-a| \leq 1} x^b + \frac{2}{3} e.$$

As before, we denote by $m(x)$ the empirical average induced by the configuration $x \in S_0$, i.e.,

$$m(x) = \lim_{n \to \infty} \frac{1}{|\mathbb{A}_n|} \sum_{a \in \mathbb{A}_n} x^a.$$

Thus, for any starting point $x \in S_0$, the sequence $\{m(x_t)\}_{t \in \mathbb{N}}$ satisfies $\mathbb{P}_x$-almost surely the relation

$$m(x_{t+1}) = \frac{1}{4} m(x_t) + \frac{2}{3} e_t \qquad (t \in \mathbb{N}).$$

We assume that, for any configuration $x \in S_0$, the signal $e \in E$ depends on the empirical field $R(x)$ only through the induced empirical average $m(x)$. The conditional law $Q(m(x_t); \cdot)$ of the signal e_t given the average situation $m(x_t)$, is described by the following stochastic kernel Q from $[0, +1]$ to $\{0, +1\}$:

$$Q(m; \{+1\}) = \begin{cases} 0 & \text{if } m \leq \frac{1}{3} \\ 3m - 1 & \text{if } \frac{1}{3} < m < \frac{2}{3} \\ 1 & \text{if } m \geq \frac{2}{3}. \end{cases}$$

It is easily seen that the transition kernel Q satisfies a uniform Lipschitz condition.

Whenever $m_T \leq \frac{1}{3}$ for some $T \in \mathbb{N}$, we have almost surely that $e_{t+T} = 0$ for all $t \in \mathbb{N}$. Conversely, $e_{t+T} = 1$ $(t \in \mathbb{N})$ as soon as $m_T \geq \frac{2}{3}$. In particular, for any starting point $x \in S_0$, we obtain

$$Q(m(x_1); +1) \in \{0, 1\} \qquad \mathbb{P}_x\text{-a.s.} \tag{3.69}$$

Thus, there exists a constant $c = c(x) >\in [0, 1]$ such that

$$\lim_{t \to \infty} m(x_t) = \frac{8}{9} \quad \text{with probability } c$$

and

$$\lim_{t \to \infty} m(x_t) = 0 \quad \text{with probability } 1 - c.$$

Let us now introduce the Feller kernels

$$\Pi_+(x;\cdot) := \prod_{a\in\mathbb{A}} \pi_+(\theta_a x;\cdot) \qquad \text{and} \qquad \Pi_-(x;\cdot) := \prod_{a\in\mathbb{A}} \pi_-(\theta_a x;\cdot)$$

on the configuration space S_0. Here, $\pi_\pm$ are stochastic kernels from S to C which take the form

$$\pi_+(x;\{+1\}) = \frac{1}{12}\sum_{|a|\le 1} x^a + \frac{2}{3} \qquad \text{and} \qquad \pi_-(x;\{+1\}) = \frac{1}{12}\sum_{|a|\le 1} x^a.$$

We denote by $\mu_\pm$ the unique stationary distribution of the kernel $\Pi_\pm$. For any $x \in S_0$, we deduce from (3.69) that

$$R(x_t) = R(x)\Pi_+^t \xrightarrow{w} \mu_+ \qquad \text{with probability } c(x) \qquad (t\to\infty)$$

and

$$R(x_t) = R(x)\Pi_-^t \xrightarrow{w} \mu_- \qquad \text{with probability } 1-c(x) \qquad (t\to\infty).$$

Thus, the Markov process associated with the random system Σ^* is absorbing in the sense of Definition 3.22, and so we can apply Theorem 3.26 in order to analyze the asymptotic behaviour of the underlying microscopic process. For any starting point $x \in S_0$, our microscopic process converges in law to the probability measure

$$\nu^*(\cdot) = Q(m(x);\{+1\})\mu_+(\cdot) + (1 - Q(m(x);\{+1\}))\mu_-(\cdot). \tag{3.70}$$

In particular, the asymptotic behaviour of the microscopic process depends on the initial empirical average $m(x)$.

3.1.3 Some Comments on the Induced Driving Sequence of the Asset Price Process

Let us now return to our asset price dynamics described by (1.20). We assume that the Markov chain associated with the random system with complete connections Σ^* admits an invariant measure μ^*. If $\mu^*(\mathcal{M}_0(S)) > 0$, then $\mu^*(\mathcal{M}_0(S)) = 1$, due to Theorem 3.7. In this case, there exists a random field $\tilde{\mu}$ on $(S, \mathcal{S})$ such that both the microscopic and the macroscopic process are stationary under the law $\mathbb{P}_{\tilde{\mu}}$; cf. Theorem 3.13. In such a situation, the random environment $\{\tilde{\varrho}_t\}_{t\in\mathbb{N}}$ for the evolution of the price process is stationary. In Section 4.1.1, we will formulate conditions on the law of the driving sequence $\{\tilde{\varrho}_t\}_{t\in\mathbb{N}}$ and on the mapping F introduced in (1.14) which guarantee that the sequence of temporary price equilibria $\{p_t\}_{t\in\mathbb{N}}$ converges pathwise to a stationary process as $t \to \infty$.

If $\mu^*(\mathcal{M}_0(S)) = 0$, then there does not necessarily exist an initial distribution for our microscopic process which induces a stationary macroscopic process. In special cases, however, there exists random fields $\tilde{\mu}$ on S_0 such that the sequence of empirical distributions $\{\varrho(x_t)\}_{t\in\mathbb{N}}$ is stationary under the law $\mathbb{P}_{\tilde{\mu}}$. In this case, the random environment $\{\tilde{\varrho}_t\}_{t\in\mathbb{N}}$ defined on $(\Omega, \mathcal{F}, \mathbb{P}_{\tilde{\mu}})$ is also stationary.

Example 3.28 *Let us put $C = \{0, 1\}$ and consider a model with linear individual transition dynamics where the transition to a new state itself is made independently by different agents. We fix a constant $c \in \mathbb{R}$ and a measurable mapping $f : E \to \mathbb{R}$. Given a configuration $x \in S_0$ and a signal $e \in E$, the individual transition dynamics is described by a stochastic kernel π_e from $C^{2^{ld}+1}$ to C which takes the form*

$$\pi_e^a(x; \{+1\}) = \pi_e((x^b)_{b\in N(a)}; \{+1\}) = \frac{c}{|N(a)|} \sum_{b\in N(a)} x^b + f(e). \qquad (3.71)$$

Thus, an individual agent reacts to the average situation in his neighborhood and to a random signal about the average situation throughout the entire population.

For a given initial configuration $x \in S_0$ and for each fixed signal sequence $\{e_t\}_{t\in\mathbb{N}}$, the evolution of the sequence of empirical averages $\{m(x_t)\}_{t\in\mathbb{N}}$ proceeds almost surely in a deterministic manner:

$$m(x_{t+1}) = cm(x_t) + f(e_t) =: v(m(x_t), e_t) \qquad \mathbb{P}_x\text{-}a.s.$$

We assume that the signal e_t about the average situation in the whole infinite system of all agents depends on the empirical field $R(x_t)$ only through the mean value $m(x_t)$. Thus, the conditional law $\bar{Q}(m(x_t); \cdot)$ of the signal e_t given the empirical average $m(x_t)$, can be described by a stochastic kernel $\bar{Q}$ from $[0, 1]$ to $\mathcal{E}$. The process $\{m(x_t)\}_{t\in\mathbb{N}}$ may therefore be viewed as the Markov chain $\{m_t\}_{t\in\mathbb{N}}$ on $[0, 1]$ which is associated with the random system with complete connections

$$\Sigma' = (([0, 1], |\cdot|), (E, \mathcal{E}), \bar{Q}, v).$$

Any stationary distribution ϱ^* on $[0, 1]$ for the process $\{m_t\}_{t\in\mathbb{N}}$ induces a random field μ^* on S_0 such that the sequence $\{m(x_t)\}_{t\in\mathbb{N}}$ is stationary under the law $\mathbb{P}_{\mu^*} = \int_S \mathbb{P}_x \mu^*(dx)$. Indeed, for any $m \in [0, 1]$, let $\varrho(m) = (1 - m, m)$ be a probability distribution on C and put

$$\mu^*(dx) = \int_0^1 \prod_{a\in\mathbb{A}} \varrho(m)(dx^a)\varrho^*(dm).$$

In this case, we have $\text{Law}(\{m(x_t)\}_{t\in\mathbb{N}}, \mathbb{P}_{\mu^*}) = \text{Law}(\{m_t\}_{t\in\mathbb{N}}, \mathbb{P}_{\varrho^*})$, *and so the sequence of empirical averages* $\{m(x_t)\}_{t\in\mathbb{N}}$ *is stationary under the law* $\mathbb{P}_{\mu^*}$. *Thus, under the measure* $\mathbb{P}_{\mu^*}$ *the price process is driven by a stationary sequence* $\{\tilde{\varrho}_t\}_{t\in\mathbb{N}}$.

In a more general financial market model with locally and globally interacting agents in a random environment there does not necessarily exist an initial distribution for the microscopic process such that the sequence $\{x_t\}_{t\in\mathbb{N}}$ induces a stationary environment for the evolution of the price process. However, the following variant of Lemma 2.34 shows that we can approximate the driving sequence $\{\tilde{\varrho}_t\}_{t\in\mathbb{N}}$ in law by a stationary environment if the stochastic kernel $\tilde{Q}$ on $\mathcal{M}(C)$ satisfies a uniform Lipschitz condition in the sense of Definition 2.32. In such a situation, a stationarity assumption on the sequence $\{\tilde{\varrho}_t\}_{t\in\mathbb{N}}$ may serve as an approximation whenever the price process depends continuously on the environment.

Lemma 3.29 *Let* $(\{\xi_t\}_{t\in\mathbb{N}}, (\mathbb{P}_\xi)_{\xi\in M_1})$ *be the Markov chain on* $(\Omega, \mathcal{F})$ *associated with the distance-diminishing random system* $\Sigma := ((M_1, d_{M_1}), (M_2, \mathcal{M}_2), Z, v)$. *Let* $(M_3, \mathcal{M}_3)$ *be a measurable space and* $\hat{Q}$ *be a stochastic kernel from* M_1 *to* $\mathcal{M}_3$. *For* $\xi \in M_1$, *let* $\{\tilde{\xi}_t\}_{t\in\mathbb{N}}$ *be a sequence of random variables defined on* $(\Omega, \mathcal{F}, \mathbb{P}_\xi)$ *such that*

$$\mathbb{P}_\xi[\tilde{\xi}_t \in \cdot | \xi_t, \ldots, \xi_0, \tilde{\xi}_{t-1}, \ldots, \tilde{\xi}_0] = \hat{Q}(\xi_t; \cdot). \tag{3.72}$$

If the stochastic kernels Z *and* $\hat{Q}$ *satisfy a uniform Lipschitz condition in the sense of Definition 2.32, then the mapping* $\xi \mapsto \text{Law}(\{\tilde{\xi}_t\}_{t\in\mathbb{N}}, \mathbb{P}_\xi)$ *from* M_1 *to* $[0,1]$ *is Lipschitz continuous. More precisely, there exist a constant* $L < \infty$ *such that*

$$\|\text{Law}(\{\tilde{\xi}_t\}_{t\in\mathbb{N}}, \mathbb{P}_\xi) - \text{Law}(\{\tilde{\xi}_t\}_{t\in\mathbb{N}}, \mathbb{P}_{\hat{\xi}})\| \le L d_{M_1}(\xi, \hat{\xi}) \qquad (\xi, \hat{\xi} \in M_1). \tag{3.73}$$

Proof: Due to the monotone class argument given in the proof of Lemma 2.34, it is enough to the establish the existence of a constant $L < \infty$ such that, uniformly in $t \in \mathbb{N}$ and in $B \in \otimes_{i=1}^t \mathcal{B}(M_1)$, we have that

$$\left|\mathbb{P}_\xi[\{\tilde{\xi}_0, \ldots, \tilde{\xi}_t\} \in B] - \mathbb{P}_{\hat{\xi}}[\{\tilde{\xi}_0, \ldots, \tilde{\xi}_t\} \in B]\right| \le L d_{M_1}(\xi, \hat{\xi}) \qquad (\xi, \hat{\xi} \in M_1). \tag{3.74}$$

To this end, we denote by $L_{\hat{Q}}$ and by L_Z the Lipschitz constants for the stochastic kernels $\hat{Q}$ and Z, respectively. By analogy with the proof of Lemma 2.34 we introduce the quantity

$$\alpha_t := \sup_B \sup_{\xi \neq \hat{\xi}} \frac{\left|\mathbb{P}_\xi[\{\tilde{\xi}_0, \tilde{\xi}_2, \ldots, \tilde{\xi}_t\} \in B] - \mathbb{P}_{\hat{\xi}}[\{\tilde{\xi}_0, \tilde{\xi}_2, \ldots, \tilde{\xi}_t\} \in B]\right|}{d_{M_1}(\xi, \hat{\xi})}.$$

Due to the contraction property of the transformation v and because of the uniform Lipschitz conditions imposed on the stochastic kernel Z and $\hat{Q}$, we have that

$$\begin{aligned}
&\left|\mathbb{P}_{\xi}[\{\tilde{\xi}_0,\ldots,\tilde{\xi}_{t+1}\}\in B]-\mathbb{P}_{\hat{\xi}}[\{\tilde{\xi}_0,\ldots,\tilde{\xi}_{t+1}\}\in B]\right| \\
\leq\ & \sup_{B_1}\left|\mathbb{P}_{\xi}[\tilde{\xi}_0\in B_1]-\mathbb{P}_{\hat{\xi}}[\tilde{\xi}_0\in B_1]\right|+\sup_{\xi,B_2}\left|\hat{Q}(\xi;B_2)-\hat{Q}(\hat{\xi};B_2)\right| \\
& \sup_{B_3,\zeta}\left|\mathbb{P}_{v(\xi,\zeta)}[\{\tilde{\xi}_0,\ldots,\tilde{\xi}_t\}\in B_3]-\mathbb{P}_{v(\hat{\xi},\zeta)}[\{\tilde{\xi}_0,\ldots,\tilde{\xi}_t\}\in B_3]\right| \\
\leq\ & (L_{\hat{Q}}+L_Z+\alpha\alpha_t)d_{M_1}(\xi,\hat{\xi}),
\end{aligned}$$

and so

$$\alpha_t\leq(L_{\hat{Q}}+L_Z)\sum_{i\in\mathbb{N}}\alpha^i\leq\frac{L_{\hat{Q}}+L_Z}{1-\alpha}.$$

This proves our assertion. □

Corollary 3.30 *Suppose that the Markov chain $\{\xi_t\}_{t\in\mathbb{N}}$ on M_1 associated with the distance-diminishing random system $\Sigma=((M_1,d_{M_1}),(M_2,\mathcal{M}_2),Z,v)$ converges in law to a unique invariant measure μ^*. Then the sequence of random variables $\{\tilde{\xi}_t\}_{t\in\mathbb{N}}$ defined by (3.72) is stationary under the law $\mathbb{P}_{\mu^*}$ and*

$$\lim_{t\to\infty}\sup_{\xi}\|\mathbb{P}_{\xi}-\mathbb{P}_{\mu^*}\|_{\hat{\mathcal{F}}_t}=0, \tag{3.75}$$

where $\hat{\mathcal{F}}_t:=\sigma(\{\tilde{\xi}_s\}_{s\geq t})$. In this respect, the sequence $\{\tilde{\xi}_t\}_{t\in\mathbb{N}}$ becomes stationary in the long run.

Proof: Let us fix $B\in\otimes_{t\geq 1}\mathcal{M}_3$ and denote by U^t the t-fold iteration of the transition operator U associated with the Markov chain $\{\xi_t\}_{t\in\mathbb{N}}$. Due to Lemma 3.29, there exists a constant $L<\infty$ which does not depend on B such that the mapping

$$\xi\mapsto\mathbb{P}_{\xi}[\{\tilde{\xi}_t\}_{t\in\mathbb{N}}\in B]$$

from M_1 to $[0,1]$ is Lipschitz continuous with Lipschitz constant L. Thus, we can apply Proposition A.9. There are constants $\bar{L}<\infty$ and $\alpha<1$ such that

$$\begin{aligned}
\sup_{\xi}\|\mathbb{P}_{\xi}-\mathbb{P}_{\mu^*}\|_{\hat{\mathcal{F}}_t} &= \sup_{\xi,B}\left|(U^t\mathbb{P}_{\bullet}[\{\tilde{\xi}_t\}_{t\in\mathbb{N}}\in B])(\xi)-\int_{M_1}\mathbb{P}_{\hat{\xi}}[\{\tilde{\xi}_t\}_{t\in\mathbb{N}}\in B]\mu^*(d\hat{\xi})\right| \\
&\leq \bar{L}\alpha^t.
\end{aligned}$$

This yields our assertion. □

Remark 3.31 *Observe that the sequence $\{\tilde{\xi}_t\}_{t\in\mathbb{N}}$ specified by (3.72) may be viewed as an additional signal sequence associated with the random system with complete connections $\Sigma = ((M_1, d_{M_1}), (M_2, \mathcal{M}_2), Z, v)$. In this sense, our Lemma 3.29 is closely related to Proposition 2.2.10 in Iosefescu and Theodorescu (1968).*

We are now going to show how one can approximate the driving sequence for the price process in law by an stationary environment. To this end, let μ^* be an invariant measure for the Markov process $\{\xi_t\}_{t\in\mathbb{N}}$ on $\mathcal{M}_s(S)$ associated with our random system with complete connections Σ^* and assume that the stochastic kernel $\tilde{Q}$ on $\mathcal{M}(C)$ introduced in (1.19) satisfies a uniform Lipschitz condition.

Let $\{\tilde{\xi}_t\}_{t\in\mathbb{N}}$ be a sequence of random variables defined on a common probability space with the Markov chain $\{\xi_t\}_{t\in\mathbb{N}}$ whose conditional dynamics takes the form

$$\mathbb{P}_\xi[\tilde{\xi}_t \in \cdot | \xi_t, \ldots, \xi_0, \tilde{\xi}_{t-1}, \ldots, \tilde{\xi}_0] = \tilde{Q}(\mathrm{Pr}(\xi_t); \cdot) =: \hat{Q}(\xi_t; \cdot).$$

Here, $\mathrm{Pr} : \mathcal{M}_s(S) \to \mathcal{M}(C)$ denotes the projection mapping which assigns to every stationary random field on S its' marginal distribution at site 0.

We denote by d_V the Vasserstein distance on the class of all probability measures on $\mathcal{M}_s(S)$. In view of (2.99) it follows from Lemma 3.29 that there exists a constant $L < \infty$ such that

$$\|\mathrm{Law}(\{\tilde{\xi}_t\}_{t\in\mathbb{N}}, \mathbb{P}_{\hat{\mu}}) - \mathrm{Law}(\{\tilde{\xi}_t\}_{t\in\mathbb{N}}, \mathbb{P}_{\mu^*})\| \leq L d_V(\hat{\mu}, \mu^*)$$

for all $\hat{\mu} \in \mathcal{M}(\mathcal{M}_s(S))$. Since the set $\mathcal{M}_0(S)$ is dense in the class of all shift-invariant random fields on $(S, \mathcal{S})$, there exists, for any $\epsilon > 0$, a measure $\hat{\mu}$ on $\mathcal{M}_0(S)$ such that $d_V(\hat{\mu}, \mu^*) < \epsilon/L$, and so

$$\|\mathrm{Law}(\{\tilde{\xi}_t\}_{t\in\mathbb{N}}, \mathbb{P}_{\hat{\mu}}) - \mathrm{Law}(\{\tilde{\xi}_t\}_{t\in\mathbb{N}}, \mathbb{P}_{\mu^*})\| < \epsilon.$$

By analogy with (3.29) we can now introduce a random field $\tilde{\mu}$ on S_0 such that

$$\mathrm{Law}(\{\tilde{\varrho}_t\}_{t\in\mathbb{N}}, \mathbb{P}_{\tilde{\mu}}) = \mathrm{Law}(\{\tilde{\xi}_t\}_{t\in\mathbb{N}}, \mathbb{P}_{\hat{\mu}}),$$

and so

$$\|\mathrm{Law}(\{\tilde{\varrho}_t\}_{t\in\mathbb{N}}, \mathbb{P}_{\tilde{\mu}}) - \mathrm{Law}(\{\tilde{\xi}_t\}_{t\in\mathbb{N}}, \mathbb{P}_{\mu^*})\| < \epsilon. \tag{3.76}$$

In this sense, each invariant distribution for the Markov chain associated with our random system with complete connections Σ^* given by (3.19) induces a random field $\tilde{\mu}$ on S_0 such that, under the measure $\mathbb{P}_{\tilde{\mu}}$, the law of the driving sequence for the price process is close to the law of a stationary sequence of random variables. In such a situation, a stationarity assumption on the environment may serve as an approximation whenever the sequence of temporary equilibrium prices depends continuously on the environment.

3.2 Random External Conditions

Let us now introduce an additional dependence of individual behaviour on random economic fundamentals. The dynamics of the external conditions is described by a Markov chain $\{h_t\}_{t\in\mathbb{N}}$ with transition kernel K on the compact metric space (H, d_H). Given a configuration $x \in S_0$ and a fundamental value $h \in H$. an individual agent $a \in \mathbb{A}$ reacts to the local situation $(x_b)_{b\in N(a)}$ in his neighborhood $N(a)$, to a random signal $e \in E$ about the average situation in the whole infinite system of all traders described by the empirical field $R(x)$ and to the external condition $h \in H$.

By analogy with the situation analyzed in Chapter 3.1 we fix, for any triple $(x, e, h) \in S \times E \times H$, a local specification $\gamma^{x,e,h}$ and assume that the mapping

$$(x, e, h) \mapsto \gamma_A^{x,e,h}(B; v) \qquad (A \in \mathcal{A}, B \in \mathcal{S}_A) \tag{3.77}$$

from $S \times E \times H$ to $[0, 1]$ is measurable for each boundary condition v on A^c. The local specifications $(\gamma^{x,e,h})_{x\in S, e\in E, h\in H}$ are assumed to satisfy our Assumptions 2.3, 2.4 and 2.5 with μ replaced by (e, h). Thus, each family of conditional probabilities $\gamma^{x,e,h}$ is spatially homogeneous and satisfies a Markov property of order l both in its dependence on the boundary condition and on the present configuration x. In particular, all agents react in the same manner to their environment.

The specification $\gamma^{x,e,h}$ determines a unique Markov random field

$$\Pi_{e,h}(x; \cdot) \tag{3.78}$$

on $(S, \mathcal{S})$, due to Dobrushin's uniqueness theorem. It follows from our measurability assumption (3.77) on the family $(\gamma^{x,e,h})_{x\in S}$ that (3.78) defines a stochastic kernel $\Pi_{e,h}$ on $(S, \mathcal{S})$. For all $(e, h) \in E \times H$ and for any $x \in S_0$, we have

$$\Pi_{e,h}(x; S_0) = 1, \tag{3.79}$$

due to Corollary 2.9 (i). Thus, the transition kernel $\Pi_{e,h}$ may be viewed as a transition probability on the state space S_0. Our microscopic process may therefore be viewed as a Markov chain on the state space S_0 in a random environment. The environment is specified by the sequence $\{(e_t, h_t)\}_{t\in\mathbb{N}}$ which describes the evolution of both the economic fundamentals and the signals about aggregate behaviour. The full dynamics can be described by a Markov chain $\{(x_t, h_t)\}_{t\in\mathbb{N}}$ on $S_0 \times H$ with transition kernel

$$P((x,h);\cdot) = \left(\int_E \Pi_{e,h}(x;\cdot)Q(R(x);de)\right) \otimes K(h;\cdot). \tag{3.80}$$

In order to analyze the asymptotic dynamics of the macroscopic process, we can proceed as in Chapter 3.1. To start with, we define a mapping $u : \mathcal{M}_s(S) \times E \times H \to \mathcal{M}_s(S)$ by

$$u(R,e,h) := R\Pi_{e,h}. \tag{3.81}$$

By analogy with (3.6), the class of all ergodic random fields on $(S, \mathcal{S})$ is an absorbing set for the transformation u in the sense that

$$u(R,e,h) \in \mathcal{M}_0(S) \qquad (R \in \mathcal{M}_0(S),\ e \in E,\ h \in H).$$

Next, we specify a metric $d_{\mathcal{M}_s \times H}$ on the product space $\mathcal{M}_s(S) \times H$ by

$$d_{\mathcal{M}_s \times H}((R,h),(\hat{R},\hat{h})) := d(R,\hat{R}) + d_H(h,\hat{h})$$

and introduce the following random system with complete connections $\widetilde{\Sigma}$:

$$\widetilde{\Sigma} := ((\mathcal{M}_s \times H, d_{\mathcal{M}_s \times H}), (E \times H, \mathcal{E} \otimes H), Z, v). \tag{3.82}$$

Here, the stochastic kernel Z from $\mathcal{M}_s(S) \times H$ to $\mathcal{E} \otimes \mathcal{H}$ takes the product form

$$Z((R,h);\cdot) := Q(R;\cdot) \otimes K(h;\cdot)$$

and the mapping $v : \mathcal{M}_s(S) \times H \times E \times H \to \mathcal{M}_s(S) \times H$ is given by

$$v((R,h),(e,\hat{h})) := (u(R,e,h),\hat{h}). \tag{3.83}$$

We denote by $\{\xi_t\}_{t\in\mathbb{N}}$ and $\{\zeta_t\}_{t\in\mathbb{N}}$ the Markov chain on $\mathcal{M}_s(S) \times H$ and the signal sequence on $E \times H$, respectively, associated with the random system $\widetilde{\Sigma}$ defined by (3.82). Observe that the these processes take the form $\{\xi_t\}_{t\in\mathbb{N}} = \{(R_t, h_t)\}_{t\in\mathbb{N}}$ and $\{\zeta_t\}_{t\in\mathbb{N}} = \{(e_t, h_{t+1})\}_{t\in\mathbb{N}}$, respectively.

Let us now state a condition on the dependence of the microscopic characteristics of an agent on the economic fundamentals which guarantees that the random system $\widetilde{\Sigma}$ is distance-diminishing.

Proposition 3.32 *Suppose that the local specifications* $(\gamma^{x,e,h})_{x\in S, e\in E, h\in H}$ *satisfy our Assumptions 2.3, 2.4, 2.5 and 2.16 with* μ *replaced by* (e,h) *and let* $\hat{c}$ *be the uniform Dobrushin constant defined in (2.8). If the dependence of individual behaviour on the external economic fundamentals satisfies the continuity condition*

$$\sup_{x,e} \frac{1}{2} \int_S \|\gamma^{x,e,h}(\cdot; v) - \gamma^{x,e,\hat{h}}(\cdot; v)\| \Pi_{e,h}(x; dv) \le \alpha(1-\hat{c}) d_H(h,\hat{h}), \tag{3.84}$$

then the random system $\widetilde{\Sigma}$ *is distance-diminishing. In particular, it is enough to require*

$$\sup_{x,e,v} \|\gamma^{x,e,h}(\cdot; v) - \gamma^{x,e,\hat{h}}(\cdot; v)\| \le \alpha(1-\hat{c}) d_H(h.\hat{h}).$$

Proof: It follows from Proposition 2.19 with $\tau = (e,h)$ that

$$d(u(R,e,h), u(\hat{R},e,h)) \le \alpha d(R,\hat{R}).$$

Moreover, we can use the same arguments as in the proof of Proposition 2.22 (ii) in order to verify that

$$d(R\Pi_{e,h}, R\Pi_{e,\hat{h}}) \le \alpha d_H(h,\hat{h}) \qquad (R \in \mathcal{M}_s(S),\ \epsilon \in E).$$

Thus, the triangle inequality yields

$$d_{\mathcal{M}_s \times H}(u(R,e,h), u(\hat{R},e,\hat{h})) \le \alpha(d(R,\hat{R}) + d_H(h,\hat{h})).$$

This proves our assertion. □

By analogy with Theorem 3.7, we have the following result:

Theorem 3.33 *Suppose that the stochastic kernels* Q *and* K *satisfy a uniform Lipschitz condition in the sense of Definition 2.32, that they have a lower bound and that our standard Assumptions 2.3, 2.4, 2.5 and 2.16 hold true with* μ *replaced by* (e,h). *If the contraction condition (3.84) is satisfied, then the sequence of empirical fields* $\{R(x_t)\}_{t\in\mathbb{N}}$ *converges in law to a probability measure on* $\mathcal{M}_s(S)$ *which does not depend on the starting point* (x,h) *of the process* $\{(x_t,h_t)\}_{t\in\mathbb{N}}$.

Proof: Let us denote L_Q and by L_K the Lipschitz constants corresponding to the stochastic kernels Q and K, respectively. Moreover, let $\mathbb{G}$ be the set of all $B \in \mathcal{E} \otimes \mathcal{H}$ such that

$$\sup_{(\xi,h)\neq(\hat{\xi},\hat{h})} \frac{|Z((R,h);B) - Z((\hat{R},\hat{h});B)|}{d(R,\hat{R}) + d_H(h,\hat{h})} \le L_K + L_Q. \tag{3.85}$$

Observe that $\mathbb{G}$ is a monotone class which contains a generator of the σ-field $\mathcal{E} \otimes \mathcal{H}$. Thus, (3.85) holds true for all $B \in \mathcal{E} \otimes \mathcal{E}$, due to the monotone class theorem. For the same reason the stochastic kernel Z from $\mathcal{M}_s(S) \times H$ to $\mathcal{E} \otimes \mathcal{H}$ has a lower bound, and so our assertion follows from Proposition A.8. □

Let μ^* be an invariant measure for the Markov chain associated with the random system $\widetilde{\Sigma}$ which is concentrated on the set $\mathcal{M}_0(S) \times H$. By analogy with Proposition 3.9, we could establish the existence of a random field $\tilde{\mu}$ on $S_0 \times H$, such that the macroscopic process $\{R(x_t)\}_{t \in \mathbb{N}}$ is stationary under the law $\mathbb{P}_{\tilde{\mu}}$. Thus, under the measure $\mathbb{P}_{\tilde{\mu}}$ our asset price process evolves in a stationary random environment. If the stochastic kernel $\tilde{Q}$ on $\mathcal{M}(C)$ satisfies a suitable Lipschitz condition, then any stationary measure for the Markov chain $\{\xi_t\}_{t \in \mathbb{N}}$ on $\mathcal{M}_s(S) \times H$ associated with the random system $\widetilde{\Sigma}$ induces a random field $\tilde{\mu}$ on $S_0 \times H$ such that the driving sequence for the price process is approximately stationary under the law $\mathbb{P}_{\tilde{\mu}}$; cf. Lemma 3.29 and Corollary 3.30. More precisely, for any $\epsilon > 0$, there exists a stationary sequence of random variables $\{\tilde{\xi}_t\}_{t \in \mathbb{N}}$ defined on a probability space $(\Omega, \mathcal{F}, \mathbb{P})$ such that

$$\|\mathrm{Law}(\{\tilde{\varrho}_t\}_{t \in \mathbb{N}}, \mathbb{P}_{\tilde{\mu}}) - \mathrm{Law}(\{\tilde{\xi}_t\}_{t \in \mathbb{N}}, \mathbb{P})\| < \epsilon.$$

Let us now consider the dynamics of the microscopic process. By analogy with Theorems 3.16 and 3.17 we have the following result:

Theorem 3.34 *Suppose that the process $\{(R(x_t), h_t)\}_{t \in \mathbb{N}}$ converges in law to a random field μ^* on $S \times H$ which does not depend on the starting point (x, h) of the sequence $\{(x_t, h_t)\}_{t \in \mathbb{N}}$. Then the following holds true:*

(i) The microscopic process has local asymptotic loss of memory.

(ii) If μ^* is concentrated on the set $\mathcal{M}_0(S) \times H$, then the stochastic kernel P on $S_0 \times H$ admits a unique stationary measure ν. For any starting point $(x, h) \in S_0 \times H$, the process $\{(x_t, h_t)\}_{t \in \mathbb{N}}$ converges in distribution to ν.

(iii) In the case of a mean-field type interaction, the sequence $\{x_t\}_{t \in \mathbb{N}}$ converges locally in the sense of a strong coupling to a stationary process.

Proof: Since the Markov chain associated with the random system $\widetilde{\Sigma}$ converges in law to a unique equilibrium, it follows from Proposition A.10 that the sequence $\{(e_t, h_{t+1})\}_{t \in \mathbb{N}}$ – and hence the sequence $\{(e_t, h_t)\}_{t \in \mathbb{N}}$ – is uniformly ergodic in the strong sense. Thus, we can apply the same arguments as in the proof of Theorems 3.16, 3.17 and 3.21 in order to establish our assertion. □

Chapter 4

Dynamics of Equilibrium Prices

In this chapter, we analyze the asymptotic behaviour of the price process $\{p_t\}_{t\in\mathbb{N}}$. The sequence of temporary price equilibria is defined recursively by the relation

$$p_{t+1} = F(\tilde{\varrho}_{t+1}, p_t) \qquad (t = 0, 1, 2, \ldots), \tag{4.1}$$

where $F : \mathcal{M}(C) \times \mathbb{R} \longrightarrow \mathbb{R}$ denotes the measurable transformation introduced in (1.14). Thus, the price process may be viewed as a recursive sequence in a random environment. The random environment is specified by the process $\{\tilde{\varrho}_{t+1}\}_{t\in\mathbb{N}}$ defined on a common probability space $(\Omega, \mathcal{F}, \mathbb{P})$ with our microscopic process $\{x_t\}_{t\in\mathbb{N}}$. The driving sequence $\{\tilde{\varrho}_{t+1}\}_{t\in\mathbb{N}}$ is generated by the sequence of empirical distributions $\{\varrho(x_{t+1})\}_{t\in\mathbb{N}}$ which describes the evolution of the mood of the market; cf. (1.20).

In Section 4.1.1, we consider a stationary reference model. We shall assume that the microscopic process induces a stationary sequence of empirical distributions $\{\varrho(x_t)\}_{t\in\mathbb{N}}$, i.e., we study a situation where the mood of the market is already in equilibrium. In this case, the environment $\{\tilde{\varrho}_{t+1}\}_{t\in\mathbb{N}}$ is stationary under the law $\mathbb{P}$, and so we can apply results provided in Borovkov (1998) in order to analyze the asymptotic behaviour of the price process. If the random environment is on average not too destabilizing, then the sequence $\{p_t\}_{t\in\mathbb{N}}$ converges pathwise to a stationary process $\{P_t^*\}_{t\in\mathbb{N}}$ in the sense that

$$\mathbb{P}[\lim_{t\to\infty} |p_t - P_t^*| = 0] = 1. \tag{4.2}$$

Nonetheless, the price process might be highly volatile. Consider, for example, the situation where the sequence $\{p_t\}_{t\in\mathbb{N}}$ is defined recursively by the log-linear equation

$$\log p_{t+1} - \log p_t = f(\tilde{\varrho}_{t+1}) \log p_t + g(\tilde{\varrho}_{t+1}) \qquad (t = 0, 1, 2, \ldots) \tag{4.3}$$

in the random environment described by the sequence $\{(f(\tilde{\varrho}_{t+1}), g(\tilde{\varrho}_{t+1}))\}_{t\in\mathbb{N}}$. In periods where the random variable $f(\tilde{\varrho}_{t+1})$ takes positive values, the process $\{p_t\}_{t\in\mathbb{N}}$ may become highly unstable. Economically, this feature can be interpreted as the temporary occurrence of bubbles or crashes in a financial market model whose overall behaviour is ergodic.

For our purposes, such a stationarity assumption on the mood of the market is rather restrictive. Instead, it seems natural to investigate the asymptotic behaviour of the price process under the assumption that the random environment is out of equilibrium, i.e., under the assumption that the environment for the evolution of the sequence $\{p_t\}_{t\in\mathbb{N}}$ is specified by a non-stationary stochastic process. However, given that the mood of the market settles down in the long run, it is desirable to have sufficient conditions which ensure that the price process is driven into a stationary regime. In Section 4.1.3, we concentrate on a log-linear price dynamics of the form

$$\log p_{t+1} = f(\tilde{\varrho}_{t+1}) \log p_t + g(\tilde{\varrho}_{t+1}) \qquad (t \in \mathbb{N}).$$

Our goal will be to state conditions on the non-stationary random environment $\{(f(\tilde{\varrho}_{t+1}), g(\tilde{\varrho}_{t+1}))\}_{t\in\mathbb{N}}$ which ensures that the price process converges in law as $t \to \infty$.

For that purpose, we analyze the long run behaviour of a stochastic sequence $\{P_t\}_{t\in\mathbb{N}}$ which is defined recursively by the linear relation

$$P_{t+1} = A_t P_t + B_t \qquad (t \in \mathbb{N}) \tag{4.4}$$

in a random environment. The environment is described by the non-stationary stochastic process $\{(A_t, B_t)\}_{t\in\mathbb{N}}$. Conditions on the driving sequence $\{(A_t, B_t)\}_{t\in\mathbb{N}}$ which guarantee that the process $\{P_t\}_{t\in\mathbb{N}}$ converges in distribution as $t \to \infty$ are stated in Theorems 4.9 and 4.12.

Since a large part of mathematical finance is based on models with continuous-time security trading, it seems natural to study a diffusion approximation for the discrete-time price process analyzed in Chapter 4.1. In Section 4.2.3, we state conditions on the mood of the market which guarantee that the price process $\{p_t\}_{t\in\mathbb{N}}$ defined by (4.3) can be approximated in law by a diffusion process.

To this end, we will first analyze a stochastic sequence $\{\hat{P}_t\}_{t\in\mathbb{N}}$ defined by

$$\hat{P}_{t+1} - \hat{P}_t = \hat{A}_t \hat{P}_t + \hat{B}_t \qquad (t \in \mathbb{N})$$

in the random environment $\{(\hat{A}_t, \hat{B}_t)\}_{t\in\mathbb{N}}$. In Section 4.2.1, we consider a stationary reference model. Following an approach proposed by Föllmer and Schweizer (1993), we formulate conditions on the driving sequence $\{(\hat{A}_t, \hat{B}_t)\}_{t\in\mathbb{N}}$ which allow us to obtain a diffusion approximation for the sequence $\{\hat{P}_t\}_{t\in\mathbb{N}}$. In Section 4.2.2, we extend the Föllmer-Schweizer-approach from stationary to the non-stationary setting. We obtain a diffusion approximation for the process $\{\hat{P}_t\}_{t\in\mathbb{N}}$ in a situation where the environment is out of equilibrium but becomes stationary in the long run.

Section 4.3 is devoted to some numerical simulations. For our financial market model, we have sufficient conditions which ensure that the mood of the market becomes stationary in the long run. Nevertheless, the sequence $\{\varrho(x_t)\}_{t\in\mathbb{N}}$ may be subject to large and sudden fluctuations. These fluctuations do not necessarily reflect rational adjustments to new economic fundamentals but may be due to a distinct herd behaviour.

4.1 Discrete-Time Models

4.1.1 Equilibrium Prices in a Stationary Environment

This section is devoted to the analysis of the long run behaviour of our price process in an ergodic reference model. We study the asymptotics of the sequence of temporary price equilibria $\{p_t\}_{t\in\mathbb{N}}$ defined recursively by (4.1) under the assumption that the driving sequence $\{\tilde{\varrho}_t\}_{t\in\mathbb{N}}$ is stationary.

Consider, for example, a mean–field type model or a model with linear individual transition dynamics like (2.78) or (3.71). In such a situation, we have sufficient conditions which guarantee the existence of a random field μ on $(S, \mathcal{S})$ such that the environment $\{\tilde{\varrho}_t\}_{t\in\mathbb{N}}$ for the evolution of the stock price process is ergodic under the law $\mathbb{P}_\mu$. In more general models with locally and globally interacting agents there does not necessarily exist an initial distribution such that the microscopic process generates a stationary driving sequence $\{\tilde{\varrho}_t\}_{t\in\mathbb{N}}$. However, if the stochastic kernel $\tilde{Q}$ on $\mathcal{M}(C)$ satisfies a uniform Lipschitz condition, then the environment $\{\tilde{\varrho}_t\}_{t\in\mathbb{N}}$ for the evolution of the price process can be approximated in law by an ergodic process; cf. (2.98) or (3.76). In this case, an ergodicity assumption on the environment may serve as an approximation whenever the sequence of temporary price equilibria $\{p_t\}_{t\in\mathbb{N}}$ depends continuously on the driving sequence $\{\tilde{\varrho}_t\}_{t\in\mathbb{N}}$.

Some of the most general convergence and stability theorems for recursive sequences in a random environment defined by the (non-linear) relation (4.1) provided in, e.g., Borovkov (1998), use the concept of so-called renovation events. For our financial market model, however, this condition is too strong or too hard to verify.

Other ergodicity conditions are stated in terms of certain analytical properties of the function F. In the sequel, we follow an approach which uses a *mean contraction property* of the transformation F.

We denote by p the initial price at time $t = 0$, put $\tilde{\varrho}_n^0 := (\tilde{\varrho}_1, \ldots, \tilde{\varrho}_n)$ and assume that the following conditions concerning the iterates

$$F(\tilde{\varrho}_n^0, p) := F(\tilde{\varrho}_n, \cdot) \circ \cdots \circ F(\tilde{\varrho}_2, \cdot) \circ F(\tilde{\varrho}_1, p) \qquad (n \in \mathbb{N}).$$

are satisfied; see also Borovkov (1998), Chapter 2, Section 8.

Assumption 4.1 *(i) For some $p_0 \in \mathbb{R}$ and for each $\delta > 0$, there exists $N = N(\delta)$ such that, for all $n \geq 1$, we have*

$$\mathbb{P}[|p_0 - F(\tilde{\varrho}_n^0, p_0)| > N] < \delta.$$

Thus, the sequence $\{p_t\}_{t \in \mathbb{N}}$ is assumed to be bounded in probability.

(ii) The function $F = F(\tilde{\varrho}, p)$ is continuous in p and there exists an integer $r \geq 1$, a number $\beta > 0$, and a measurable function $c : \mathbb{R}^r \to \mathbb{R}_+$ such that

$$|F(\tilde{\varrho}_r^0, p_1) - F(\tilde{\varrho}_r^0, p_2)| \leq c(\tilde{\varrho}_r^0)|p_1 - p_2| \qquad (p_1, p_2 \in \mathbb{R}) \tag{4.5}$$

$$\frac{1}{r}\mathbb{E} \log c(\tilde{\varrho}_r^0) \leq -\beta, \tag{4.6}$$

where $\mathbb{E}$ denotes the expectation with respect to the measure $\mathbb{P}$.

(iii) The sequence $\{\log c(\tilde{\varrho}_{jr}, \ldots, \tilde{\varrho}_{jr+r})\}_{j \in \mathbb{N}}$ satisfies the strong law of large numbers.

Note that our condition (4.5) together with (4.6) may be viewed as a mean contraction condition for the sequence $\{p_t\}_{t \in \mathbb{N}}$ governed by (4.1).

The next theorem follows immediately from Theorem 12.2 in Borovkov (1998). In the case of a linear transformation F, it reduces to Theorem 1 in Brandt (1986); see also Theorem 4.7 below. The case of a log-linear price dynamics is analyzed in greater detail in the next section.

Theorem 4.2 *Suppose that Assumption 4.1 is satisfied. Then there exists a stationary process $\{P_t^*\}_{t \in \mathbb{N}}$ defined on the same probability space $(\Omega, \mathcal{F}, \mathbb{P})$ as the sequence $\{p_t\}_{t \in \mathbb{N}}$ such that, for any starting point p of the sequence $\{p_t\}_{t \in \mathbb{N}}$, we have*

$$\mathbb{P}[\lim_{t \to \infty} |P_t^* - p_t| = 0] = 1. \tag{4.7}$$

If the initial value p has the same distribution as the random variable P_0^*, then the price process $\{p_t\}_{t \in \mathbb{N}}$ is stationary.

For our financial market model, Theorem 4.2 provides a bound for the aggregate effect of interaction between different traders which ensures that the induced price fluctuations are asymptotically stationary. Beyond this bound the price process may become highly transient. A continuous-time analogue of Theorem 4.2 is formulated in Föllmer and Schweizer (1993), where it is shown that the trajectories in a simple log-linear model may either tend to zero or go off to infinity with positive probability if the destabilizing effects of the environment are on average too strong.

Example 4.3 *Consider the log-linear demand structure described by (1.4) together with (1.5) and (1.6). In this case, the market clearing condition implies the log-linear price dynamics of the form*

$$\log p_{t+1} = f(\varrho(x_{t+1})) \log p_t + g(\varrho(x_{t+1})),$$

where the mappings $f, g : \mathcal{M}(C) \to \mathbb{R}$ *are given by (1.16). If the conditions*

$$\mathbb{E} \log |f(\varrho(x_1))| < 0 \qquad \text{and} \qquad \mathbb{E}(\log |g(\varrho(x_1))|)^+ < \infty$$

are satisfied, then the price process converges pathwise to a stationary process in the sense of (4.7). Such a log-linear price dynamics is analyzed in greater detail in Section 4.1.3.

Example 4.4 *(Generalized auto-regression) Suppose that the sequence* $\{p_t\}_{t\in\mathbb{N}}$ *obeys the recurrence relation*

$$p_{t+1} = G(f(\tilde{\varrho}_{t+1})\tilde{G}(p_t) + g(\tilde{\varrho}_{t+1})), \tag{4.8}$$

where $\tilde{G}, G : \mathbb{R} \to \mathbb{R}$ *are Lipschitz continuous functions, i.e.,*

$$|\tilde{G}(p_1) - \tilde{G}(p_2)| \leq \tilde{c}|p_1 - p_2|, \qquad |G(p_1) - G(p_2)| \leq c|p_1 - p_2|.$$

As a result of Theorems 8.4 and 12.2 in Borovkov (1998), the sequence $\{p_t\}_{t\in\mathbb{N}}$ *specified by (4.8) satisfies parts (i) and (ii) of our Assumption 4.1 if*

$$\log |\tilde{c}c| + \mathbb{E} \log |f(\tilde{\varrho}_1)| < 0 \quad \text{and} \quad \mathbb{E}(\log |g(\tilde{\varrho}_1)|)^+ < \infty. \tag{4.9}$$

4.1.2 The Stochastic Equation $P_{t+1} = A_t P_t + B_t$ in a Non-Stationary Environment

Our goal is now to the analysis the asymptotic behaviour of the security price process under the assumption that the mood of the market is out of equilibrium but settles down in the long run. More precisely, we shall assume that the sequence $\{p_t\}_{t\in\mathbb{N}}$ takes a log-linear form and replace the stationarity assumption on the environment $\{\tilde{\varrho}_t\}_{t\in\mathbb{N}}$ by an asymptotic stability condition. Our aim is to formulate conditions which guarantee that the price process converges in distribution as $t \to \infty$.

To this end, we consider a stochastic sequence $\{P_t\}_{t\in\mathbb{N}}$ defined recursively by the linear relation

$$P_{t+1} = A_t P_t + B_t \qquad (t \in \mathbb{N}) \tag{4.10}$$

in a random environment. The environment is described by the stochastic process $\{(A_t, B_t)\}_{t\in\mathbb{N}}$ defined on some probability space $(\Omega, \mathcal{F}, \mathbb{P})$. We state conditions on the driving sequence $\{(A_t, B_t)\}_{t\in\mathbb{N}}$ which guarantee that the solution of (4.10) converges to a stationary regime.

Stochastic sequences of the form (4.10) have been extensively investigated under a mean contraction condition and under the assumption that the driving sequence $\{(A_t, B_t)\}_{t\in\mathbb{N}}$ is *stationary.* For example, Vervaat (1979) considers the case where the environment consists of i.i.d. random variables. Brandt (1986) assumes that the driving sequence is stationary and ergodic under the law $\mathbb{P}$; see also Borovkov (1998). But in our financial market model, the driving sequence is generated by the evolution of the "mood" of the market, and so it seems natural to consider the case where the environment is given by a *non-stationary* sequence $\{(A_t, B_t)\}_{t\in\mathbb{N}}$. However, given that the "mood" is out of equilibrium but settles down in the long run, it is desirable to have sufficient conditions which ensure that the price process is driven into equilibrium.

In this section, we formulate conditions on the non-stationary driving sequence $\{(A_t, B_t)\}_{t\in\mathbb{N}}$ which guarantee that the solution of (4.10) converges in law as $t \to \infty$. In a first step, we will analyze the dynamics of the process $\{P_t\}_{t\in\mathbb{N}}$ governed by (4.10) under the assumption that the driving sequence has a "nice" tail structure. More precisely, we shall assume that there exists a probability measure $\mathbb{P}^*$ on $(\Omega, \mathcal{F})$ such that the driving sequence is stationary and ergodic under $\mathbb{P}^*$ and which coincides with the original measure $\mathbb{P}$ on the tail-field $\mathcal{T}$ generated by the process $\{(A_t, B_t)\}_{t\in\mathbb{N}}$. In this case, we establish a global convergence result under the measure $\mathbb{P}$, namely convergence in law of the shifted sequence $\{P_{t+T}\}_{t\in\mathbb{N}}$ to the uniquely determined stationary solution of (4.10) under the measure $\mathbb{P}^*$ as $T \to \infty$. The results of Brandt (1986) correspond to the case $\mathbb{P} = \mathbb{P}^*$, and in this case one can prove almost sure convergence.

In a second step, we will weaken the regularity condition that the measures $\mathbb{P}^*$

and $\mathbb{P}$ coincide on the tail-field $\mathcal{T}$. Instead, we shall assume that the environment can be approximated in law by a sequence of "nice" processes. In this case, we establish weak convergence of the finite-dimensional distributions of the process $\{P_{t+T}\}_{t\in\mathbb{N}}$ under $\mathbb{P}$ to those of the uniquely determined stationary solution of (4.10) under $\mathbb{P}^*$ as $T \to \infty$, i.e., a local version of the convergence result.

Assumptions and the Main Results

Let $\psi := \{(A_t, B_t)\}_{t\in\mathbb{N}}$ be a sequence of $\mathbb{R}^2$-valued random variables defined on some probability space $(\Omega, \mathcal{F}, \mathbb{P})$, and let $\{P_t\}_{t\in\mathbb{N}}$ be the sequence in (4.10) driven by the "input" ψ. In this section, we will formulate conditions on the driving sequence ψ which ensure that the finite-dimensional distributions of the shifted process $\{P_{t+T}\}_{t\in\mathbb{N}}$ converge weakly to the finite-dimensional distributions of a uniquely determined stationary process as $T \to \infty$. In a first step, we shall assume that the environment ψ is stationary and ergodic under some law $\mathbb{P}^*$ and that the asymptotic behaviour of the driving sequence ψ is the same under the original measure $\mathbb{P}$ and under the law $\mathbb{P}^*$. In order to make this more precise, we introduce the σ-fields

$$\hat{\mathcal{F}}_{t,l} := \sigma\left(\{(A_t, B_t)\}_{t\leq s\leq l}\right) \qquad \text{and} \qquad \hat{\mathcal{F}}_t := \sigma\left(\{(A_t, B_t)\}_{s\geq t}\right), \tag{4.11}$$

where $0 \leq t \leq l \in \mathbb{N}$ and denote by

$$\mathcal{T}_\psi := \bigcap_{t\in\mathbb{N}} \hat{\mathcal{F}}_t \tag{4.12}$$

the tail-σ-algebra generated by the sequence ψ. We denote by $\mathbb{E}$ and $\mathbb{E}^*$ the expectation with respect to the measure $\mathbb{P}$ and $\mathbb{P}^*$, respectively.

Definition 4.5 *We say that a driving sequence ψ has a "nice" tail structure if there exists a probability measure $\mathbb{P}^*$ on $(\Omega, \mathcal{F})$ with the following properties:*

(i) ψ is stationary and ergodic under $\mathbb{P}^*$.

(ii) The asymptotic behaviour of ψ is the same under $\mathbb{P}$ and $\mathbb{P}^*$, i.e.,

$$\mathbb{P} = \mathbb{P}^* \quad \textit{on} \quad \mathcal{T}_\psi. \tag{4.13}$$

The environment ψ is called "nice" if, moreover, one of the conditions

$$-\infty \leq \mathbb{E}^* \log|A_0| < 0 \quad \textit{and} \quad \mathbb{E}^*(\log|B_0|)^+ < \infty \tag{4.14}$$

$$\mathbb{P}^*[A_0 = 0] > 0. \tag{4.15}$$

is satisfied.

Below, we shall consider some case studies where the assumption that the driving sequence has a "nice" tail structure can indeed be verified.

Remark 4.6 *(i) Our first integrability condition in (4.14) may be viewed as a mean contraction condition for the dynamics defined by (4.10). Such a contraction condition has also been imposed by, e.g., Vervaat (1979).*

(ii) In the sequel, we denote by $\|\cdot\|_{\mathcal{E}}$ the total variation of a signed measure on a measurable space $(E, \mathcal{E})$. Since

$$\lim_{t\to\infty} \|\mathbb{P} - \mathbb{P}^*\|_{\hat{\mathcal{F}}_t} = \|\mathbb{P} - \mathbb{P}^*\|_{\mathcal{T}_\psi}, \tag{4.16}$$

a driving sequence ψ satisfies (4.13) if and only if it becomes stationary in the long run. This is equivalent to the existence of a sequence $\{c_t\}_{t\in\mathbb{N}}$ satisfying $\lim_{t\to\infty} c_t = 0$ and

$$\sup_{l\geq t} ||\mathbb{P} - \mathbb{P}^*||_{\hat{\mathcal{F}}_{t,l}} \leq c_t. \tag{4.17}$$

Here, both (4.16) and (4.17) follow from the continuity of the total variation distance along increasing and decreasing σ-algebras; a simple martingale proof can be found in, e.g., Föllmer (1979b), Remark 2.1.

Let us now turn to the solution $\{P_t\}_{t\in\mathbb{N}}$ of (4.10). For a fixed environment ψ and for any initial value $P_0 = p \in \mathbb{R}$, we have the explicit representation

$$P_t = p_t(p, \psi) := \sum_{j=0}^{t-1} \left(\prod_{i=t-j}^{t-1} A_i \right) B_{t-j-1} + \left(\prod_{i=0}^{t-1} A_i \right) p \qquad (t \in \mathbb{N}). \tag{4.18}$$

If the driving sequence is already in equilibrium, i.e., if $\mathbb{P} = \mathbb{P}^*$ then we may as well assume that the environment ψ is defined for all $t \in \mathbb{Z}$, due to Kolmogorov's extension theorem. For notational convenience, we shall assume that the probability space $(\Omega, \mathcal{F}, \mathbb{P}^*)$ is rich enough to carry the sequence $\{(A_t, B_t)\}_{t\in\mathbb{Z}}$.

The case $\mathbb{P} = \mathbb{P}^*$ is analyzed in Brandt (1986). In the stationary setting, our assumptions (4.14) and (4.15) coincide with conditions (0.4) and (0.5), respectively, in Brandt (1986). In this case, there exists a unique stationary solution $\{P_t^*\}_{t\in\mathbb{N}}$ of (4.10) driven by ψ. More precisely, we have the following result which appears as Theorem 1 in Brandt (1986).

Theorem 4.7 *In the stationary situation, i.e., under the measure $\mathbb{P}^*$, the following holds true as soon as one of the assumptions in Definition 4.5 are satisfied.*

(i) There exists a unique stationary solution of (4.10) for the input ψ, i.e., there exists a unique stationary process $\{P_t^*\}_{t\in\mathbb{Z}}$ which obeys the relation $P_{t+1}^* = A_t P_t^* + B_t$ for all $t \in \mathbb{Z}$. The random variable P_t^* takes the form

$$P_t^* = \sum_{j=0}^{\infty} \left(\prod_{i=t-j}^{t-1} A_i \right) B_{t-j-1} \qquad (t \in \mathbb{Z}).$$

(ii) For any starting point $p \in \mathbb{R}$, the process $\{p_t(p,\psi)\}_{t\in\mathbb{N}}$ converges almost surely to the stationary solution. More precisely, $\lim_{t\to\infty} |p_t(p,\psi) - P_t^*| = 0$ $\mathbb{P}^*$-a.s.

(iii) In particular, under the measure $\mathbb{P}^*$ the sequence $\{p_t(p,\psi)\}_{t\in\mathbb{N}}$ converges in distribution to the almost surely finite random variable P_0^* as $t \to \infty$.

Let us consider a simple application of linear stochastic sequences in economics.

Example 4.8 *In economics, one often assumes that a price process $\{p_t\}_{t\in\mathbb{N}}$ takes the form*

$$p_{t+1} = (1+r_t)p_t = p_0 \prod_{i=0}^{t} (1+r_i) \qquad (t \in \mathbb{N}),$$

where $\{r_t\}_{t\in\mathbb{N}}$ denotes a stationary and ergodic sequence of returns. In such a situation, the stability condition (4.14) amounts to

$$\lim_{n\to\infty} \frac{1}{n} \sum_{t=0}^{n-1} \log(1+r_t) := m < 0,$$

and in this case, we have that

$$\lim_{t\to\infty} p_t = \lim_{t\to\infty} \exp\left(\frac{1}{t} \sum_{i=0}^{t-1} \log(1+r_i) + \frac{p_0}{t} \right)^t = 0 \qquad \mathbb{P}\text{-a.s.}$$

Hence, the long run dynamics of the process $\{p_t\}_{t\in\mathbb{N}}$ is trivial.

Let us now denote by B_t the expected price increment in period t, so that $\frac{B_t}{p_t}$ is the expected return at date t. Suppose that the real returns $\{r_t\}_{t\in\mathbb{N}}$ fluctuate around the expected returns and let these fluctuations be described by a sequence of random variables $\{\hat{A}_t\}_{t\in\mathbb{N}}$. In this case, the price process is defined recursively by the relation

$$p_{t+1} = (1+r_r)p_t = \left(1 + \hat{A}_t + \frac{B_t}{p_t}\right) p_t = (1+\hat{A}_t)p_t + B_t =: A_t p_t + B_t. \qquad (4.19)$$

Thus, if our mean contraction condition (4.14) *holds, then the sequence* $\{p_t\}_{t\in\mathbb{N}}$ *governed by (4.19) converges almost surely to a uniquely determined stationary process* $\{P_t^*\}_{t\in\mathbb{N}}$ *in the sense described above.*

In the sequel, it will be convenient to use the following notation. We denote by ν the law of the process $\{P_t^*\}_{t\in\mathbb{N}}$ under $\mathbb{P}^*$, and for any $0 \leq t_1 < t_2 < \cdots < t_m \in \mathbb{N}$, we let $\nu_{t_1,\dots,t_m}$ be the distribution of the vector $(P_{t_1}^*, \dots, P_{t_m}^*)$, i.e.,

$$\nu := \text{Law}(\{P_t^*\}_{t\in\mathbb{N}}, \mathbb{P}^*) \quad \text{and} \quad \nu_{t_1,\dots,t_m} := \text{Law}((P_{t_1}^*, \dots, P_{t_m}^*), \mathbb{P}^*). \tag{4.20}$$

We are now going to formulate a convergence result for the process $\{P_t\}_{t\in\mathbb{N}}$ in a situation where the driving sequence ψ is out of equilibrium but "nice" in the sense of Definition 4.5.

Theorem 4.9 *Suppose that* ψ *is "nice" in the sense of Definition 4.5. Then the process* $\{p_t(p,\psi)\}_{t\in\mathbb{N}}$ *converges in law to the uniquely determined stationary solution* $\{P_t^*\}_{t\in\mathbb{N}}$ *of (4.10) defined on* $(\Omega, \mathcal{F}, \mathbb{P}^*)$*, i.e., for any initial value* $p \in \mathbb{R}$*, we have*

$$\text{Law}(\{p_{t+T}(p,\psi)\}_{t\in\mathbb{N}}, \mathbb{P}) \xrightarrow{w} \nu(\cdot) \qquad (T \to \infty). \tag{4.21}$$

Here, "$\xrightarrow{w}$*" denotes weak convergence of probability measures.*

We shall prove this theorem below.

Let us now consider the case where the environment itself does not have a "nice" tail structure. Our Theorem 4.12 below states that the finite-dimensional distributions of the process $\{p_t(p,\psi)\}_{t\in\mathbb{N}}$ under the measure $\mathbb{P}$ converge weakly to the finite-dimensional distributions of the unique stationary solution of (4.10) under $\mathbb{P}^*$ as soon as the driving sequence ψ can be approximated in law by a suitable sequence of "nice" processes $\{\psi^n\}_{n\in\mathbb{N}}$. The approximating sequence $\{\psi^n\}_{n\in\mathbb{N}}$, $\psi^n = \{(A_t^n, B_t^n)\}_{t\in\mathbb{N}}$, is defined as follows. Let $\{\epsilon_t\}_{t\in\mathbb{N}}$ and $\{\eta_t\}_{t\in\mathbb{N}}$ be sequences of bounded random variables defined on $(\Omega, \mathcal{F})$. Under the law $\mathbb{P}$ these random variables are independent, identically distributed and independent of all (A_t, B_t) $(t \in \mathbb{N})$. We put

$$A_t^n := A_t + \sigma_n \epsilon_t \quad \text{and} \quad B_t^n := B_t + \sigma_n \eta_t, \tag{4.22}$$

where σ_n is of the form $\sigma_n = \frac{c}{n}$. Note that we can chose $c > 0$ such that

$$\mathbb{E}^* \log[|A_0| + c|\epsilon_0|] < 0 \quad \text{and} \quad \mathbb{E}^*[\log(|B_0| + c|\eta_0|)]^+ < \infty \tag{4.23}$$

whenever our condition (4.14) is satisfied. Observe moreover that the sequence of processes $\{\psi^n\}_{n\in\mathbb{N}}$ converges in distribution to ψ both under $\mathbb{P}$ and under $\mathbb{P}^*$, i.e., both in the stationary and in the non-stationary setting. Finally, we introduce a driving sequence

$$\widetilde{\psi} := \{\widetilde{\psi}_t\}_{t\in\mathbb{N}}. \tag{4.24}$$

by the relation

$$\widetilde{\psi}_t := (|A_t| + c|\epsilon_t|, |B_t| + c|\eta_t|) \qquad (t \in \mathbb{N}). \tag{4.25}$$

Assumption 4.10 *The sequences $\widetilde{\psi}, \psi^1, \psi^2, \ldots$ are stationary and ergodic under the law $\mathbb{P}^*$, are "nice" in the sense of Definition 4.5 and satisfy the following regularity conditions:*

$$\mathbb{E}^*(\log|A_0^n|)^+ \to \mathbb{E}^*(\log|A_0|)^+, \quad \mathbb{E}^*(\log|B_0^n|)^+ \to \mathbb{E}^*(\log|B_0|)^+ \quad (n\to\infty) \tag{4.26}$$

$$-\infty < \mathbb{E}^*\log|A_0^n| \to \mathbb{E}^*\log|A_0|, \quad \mathbb{E}^*\log|B_0^n| \to \mathbb{E}^*\log|B_0| \quad (n\to\infty). \tag{4.27}$$

Below, we will consider a Markovian case study where the assumption that the environment ψ can be approximated in law by a sequence of "nice" processes can indeed be verified.

Remark 4.11 *(i) Note that the driving sequences $\psi^n = \{(A_t^n, B_t^n)\}_{t\in\mathbb{N}}$ $(n \in \mathbb{N})$ are stationary and ergodic under the law $\mathbb{P}^*$ whenever the random variables $\{\epsilon_t\}_{t\in\mathbb{N}}$ and $\{\eta_t\}_{t\in\mathbb{N}}$ are independent, identically distributed and independent of all (A_t, B_t) $(t \in \mathbb{N})$ not only under $\mathbb{P}$, but also under $\mathbb{P}^*$.*

(ii) According to (4.26) and (4.27), we may assume that

$$\sup_n \mathbb{E}^*\log|A_0^n| < 0 \qquad \text{and} \qquad \sup_n \mathbb{E}^*(\log|B_0^n|^+) < \infty. \tag{4.28}$$

(iii) In the stationary situation, i.e., for $\mathbb{P} = \mathbb{P}^*$, our assumptions (4.26) and (4.27) coincide with conditions (0.11) and (0.10), respectively, in Brandt (1986).

Let us now state our main theorem.

Theorem 4.12 *Suppose that our Assumption 4.10 is satisfied. Then the finite dimensional distributions of the process $\{p_t(p,\psi)\}_{t\in\mathbb{N}}$ $(p \in \mathbb{R})$ under the law $\mathbb{P}$ converge weakly to the finite dimensional distributions of the unique stationary solution*

$\{P_t^*\}_{t\in\mathbb{N}}$ of (4.10) under $\mathbb{P}^*$. More precisely, for any $m \in \mathbb{N}$ and for all $t_1 < \ldots < t_m$, we have

$$\mathrm{Law}((p_{t_1+T}(p,\psi),\ldots,p_{t_m+T}(p,\psi)),\mathbb{P}) \xrightarrow{w} \nu_{t_1,\ldots,t_m}(\cdot) \qquad (T\to\infty)$$

The proof of this theorem is given below.

Our results should be compared to Theorem 1 in Brandt (1986) or to Theorem 12.2 in Borovkov (1998). If the driving sequence $\{(A_t, B_t)\}_{t\in\mathbb{N}}$ is stationary and ergodic, then the process $\{p_t(p,\psi)\}_{t\in\mathbb{N}}$ governed by the input ψ converges pathwise to the unique stationary solution $\{P_t^*\}_{t\in\mathbb{N}}$ of (4.10) under $\mathbb{P}^*$.

Our Theorem 4.9 shows that in the case of non-stationary but "nice" driving sequences, we can still establish a global convergence result, namely convergence in distribution of the process $\{p_t(p,\psi)\}_{t\in\mathbb{N}}$ to the unique stationary solution of (4.10) under the measure $\mathbb{P}^*$ instead of almost sure convergence. Furthermore, if the governing sequence ψ can be approximated in law by "nice" processes, then we can prove a local version of the convergence result, i.e., convergence of the finite-dimensional distributions of the sequence $\{p_t(p,\psi)\}_{t\in\mathbb{N}}$ under $\mathbb{P}$.

Linear Stochastic Sequences Driven by "Nice" Processes

This subsection is devoted to the proof of Theorem 4.9, and so we will assume that the driving sequence ψ is "nice" in the sense of Definition 4.5. In a first step, we shall demonstrate that the asymptotic distribution as $t\to\infty$ of the process $\{p_t(p,\psi)\}_{t\in\mathbb{N}}$ is the same under $\mathbb{P}$ and $\mathbb{P}^*$, i.e., we are going to show that

$$\mathrm{Law}(p_t(p,\psi),\mathbb{P}) \xrightarrow{w} \nu_0 = \mathrm{Law}(P_0^*,\mathbb{P}^*) \qquad (t\to\infty).$$

In a second step, we will then establish our global convergence theorem. We start with the following preliminary result.

Lemma 4.13 *For any $l \in \mathbb{N}$, we have that*

$$\lim_{t\to\infty}\prod_{i=l}^{t}|A_i| = 0 \qquad \mathbb{P}\text{- and } \mathbb{P}^*\text{- a.s.}$$

Proof: Observe that

$$\prod_{i=l}^{t}|A_i| = \left\{\exp\left(\frac{1}{t-l}\sum_{i=l}^{t-1}\log|A_i|\right)\right\}^{t-l}.$$

Thus, we have

$$\left\{\lim_{t\to\infty}\prod_{i=l}^{t}|A_i|=0\right\}\supseteqq\bigcup_{i=l}^{\infty}\{A_i=0\}\cup D,$$

where

$$D:=\bigcap_n\bigcup_{m\geq n}\left\{\limsup_{t\to\infty}\frac{1}{t-m}\sum_{i=m}^{t-1}\log|A_i|<0\right\}.$$

It is therefore enough to verify

$$\mathbb{P}\left[\bigcup_{i=l}^{\infty}\{A_i=0\}\cup D\right]=\mathbb{P}^*\left[\bigcup_{i=l}^{\infty}\{A_i=0\}\cup D\right]=1.$$

Let us first assume that $\mathbb{P}^*[A_0=0]>0$. Since ψ is stationary under $\mathbb{P}^*$ and because the event $\{A_t=0 \text{ infinitely often}\}$ is a tail-event, it follows from (4.13) and from Theorem A.1.1.2 in Brandt, Franken, and Lisek (1990) that

$$\mathbb{P}[A_t=0 \text{ infinitely often}]=\mathbb{P}^*[A_t=0 \text{ infinitely often}]=1.$$

This yields $\mathbb{P}\left[\bigcup_{i=l}^{\infty}\{A_i=0\}\right]=\mathbb{P}^*\left[\bigcup_{i=l}^{\infty}\{A_i=0\}\right]=1$.

Suppose now that $\mathbb{P}^*[A_0=0]=0$. In this case, we deduce form (4.14) and (4.13) that $\mathbb{P}[D]=\mathbb{P}^*[D]=1$ because $D\in\mathcal{T}_\psi$ and because ψ is stationary and ergodic under $\mathbb{P}^*$. □

The set of all bounded real-valued Lipschitz continuous functions f on $\mathbb{R}$ is dense in the class of uniformly continuous functions $f:\mathbb{R}\to\mathbb{R}$; cf. Lemma 8 in Dudley (1966). In particular, any continuous function f on $\mathbb{R}$ with compact support can be uniformly approximated by a Lipschitz continuous function F with compact support. Thus, in order to show weak convergence of a sequence of probability measure $\{\mu_t\}_{t\in\mathbb{N}}$ on $\mathbb{R}$ to a probability measure μ^*, it is enough to show that

$$\lim_{n\to\infty}\mu_n(F)=\mu^*(F)$$

for any Lipschitz continuous function $F:\mathbb{R}\to\mathbb{R}$ having compact support.

We are now ready to establish weak convergence of the one-dimensional distributions of the process $\{p_t(p,\psi)\}_{t\in\mathbb{N}}$ defined in (4.18) and driven by a non-stationary but "nice" sequence ψ.

Theorem 4.14 *For each starting point $p\in\mathbb{R}$ of the sequence $\{p_t(p,\psi)\}_{t\in\mathbb{N}}$ governed by (4.10), we have that*

$$\mathrm{Law}(p_t(p,\psi),\mathbb{P})\xrightarrow{w}\nu_0=\mathrm{Law}(P_0^*,\mathbb{P}^*)\qquad(t\to\infty).\tag{4.29}$$

Proof: In order to verify (4.29) it is enough to show that

$$\lim_{t\to\infty}\int F(p_t(p,\psi))d\mathbb{P}=\int F(P_0^*)d\mathbb{P}^* \tag{4.30}$$

for any for any Lipschitz continuous function $F:\mathbb{R}\to\mathbb{R}$ with compact support. To this end, we will first approximate the random variable $p_t(p,\psi)$ by an $\hat{\mathcal{F}}_l$-measurable random variable $p_t^l(p,\psi)$ and show that

$$\left|\lim_{t\to\infty}\int F(p_t^l(p,\psi))\mathbb{P}-\int F(P_0^*)d\mathbb{P}^*\right|<\epsilon$$

for all $l\in\mathbb{N}$ large enough. This estimate will then be extended to the case $l=0$. We proceed in several steps.

1. For each $l\in\mathbb{N}$ and for all $t\geq l$, let us consider the random variable $p_t^l(p,\psi)$ given by

$$p_t^l(p,\psi):=\sum_{j=0}^{t-1-l}\left(\prod_{i=t-j}^{t-1}A_i\right)B_{t-j-1}+\left(\prod_{i=l}^{t-1}A_i\right)p. \tag{4.31}$$

Note that, $p_t^l(p,\psi)$ can be interpreted as the state at time $t\geq l$ of a stochastic process governed by (4.10) and by the "input" ψ if it starts at time l at the state p. In particular, $p_t^l(p,\psi)$ does not depend on the random variables $\{A_0,B_0,\ldots,A_{l-1},B_{l-1}\}$. We have that

$$\begin{aligned}|p_t(p,\psi)-p_t^l(p,\psi)| &\leq \left|\sum_{j=t-l}^{t-1}\left(\prod_{i=t-j}^{t-1}A_i\right)B_{t-j-1}+p\prod_{i=0}^{t-1}A_i-p\prod_{i=l}^{t-1}A_i\right|\\ &\leq \sum_{j=1}^{l}\left(\prod_{i=j}^{t-1}|A_i|\right)|B_{j-1}|+|p|\prod_{i=0}^{t-1}|A_i|+|p|\prod_{i=l}^{t-1}|A_i|,\end{aligned}$$

and so it follows from Lemma 4.13 that

$$\lim_{t\to\infty}\left|p_t(p,\psi)-p_t^l(p,\psi)\right|=0 \qquad \mathbb{P}\text{- and }\mathbb{P}^*\text{-a.s.} \tag{4.32}$$

2. Let us fix $\epsilon>0$. Due to Theorem 4.7 (iii), there exists a constant $T_1=T_1(\epsilon)\in\mathbb{N}$ such that

$$\left|\int F(p_t(p,\psi))d\mathbb{P}^*-\int F d\nu_0\right|<\frac{\epsilon}{4} \qquad (t\geq T_1). \tag{4.33}$$

Our aim is now to show that (4.33) holds true with $\mathbb{P}^*$ replaced by $\mathbb{P}$. To this end, we will first show that (4.33) holds true with $\mathbb{P}^*$ replaced by $\mathbb{P}$ and with $p_t(p,\psi)$ replaced by $p_t^l(p,\psi)$ for a large enough $l\in\mathbb{N}$.

3. The event $\{p_t^l(p,\psi) \in B\}$ $(B \in \mathcal{B}(\mathbb{R}))$ belongs to the σ-algebra $\hat{\mathcal{F}}_l$ defined in (4.11). Since our driving sequence ψ is "nice", it follows from (4.17) that there exist a sequence $\{c_l\}_{l\in\mathbb{N}}$ satisfying $\lim_{l\to\infty} c_l = 0$ and

$$\begin{aligned} \sup_{B,t} \left| \mathbb{P}[p_t^l(p,\psi) \in B] - \mathbb{P}^*[p_t^l(p,\psi) \in B] \right| &\leq \|\text{Law}(\psi,\mathbb{P}) - \text{Law}(\psi,\mathbb{P}^*)\|_{\hat{\mathcal{F}}_l} \\ &\leq c_l. \end{aligned}$$

In particular, we can chose a large enough $l \in \mathbb{N}$ such that

$$\sup_t \left| \int F(p_t^l(p,\psi))\,(d\mathbb{P} - d\mathbb{P}^*) \right| \leq \frac{\epsilon}{4}. \tag{4.34}$$

4. For the rest of the proof we fix $l \in \mathbb{N}$ such that (4.34) holds true.

With no loss of generality we may assume that the mapping F is Lipschitz continuous with Lipschitz constant 1. In this case, $|F(x) - F(y)| \leq |x-y|$ and $|F(x)| \leq L^* := \text{diam}(\text{supp}\ (F))$. Since $F(y) = 0$ for all $y \notin \text{supp}(F)$, we have

$$|F(x) - F(y)| \leq \min\{L^*, |x-y|\}. \tag{4.35}$$

Thus, it follows from (4.32) that there exists a constant $T_2 = T_2(l) \in \mathbb{N}$ such that the following estimate holds:

$$\left| \int \left\{ F(p_t^l(p,\psi)) - F(p_t(p,\psi)) \right\} d\mathbb{P} \right| \leq \frac{\epsilon}{4} \qquad (t \geq T_2). \tag{4.36}$$

Indeed, we have that

$$\begin{aligned} &\left| \int \left\{ F(p_t^l(p,\psi)) - F(p_t(p,\psi)) \right\} d\mathbb{P} \right| \\ \leq\ & \int L^* \wedge \left| p_t^l(p,\psi) - p_t(p,\psi) \right| \ d\mathbb{P} \\ \leq\ & \frac{\epsilon}{8} \cdot \mathbb{P}[|p_t^l(p,\psi) - p_t(p,\psi)| \leq \epsilon/8] + L^* \cdot \mathbb{P}[|p_t^l(p,\psi) - p_t(p,\psi)| > \epsilon/8]. \end{aligned}$$

This yields (4.36) whenever T_2 is large enough. By analogy with the above computations we can chose T_2 such that

$$\left| \int \left\{ F(p_t^l(p,\psi)) - F(p_t(p,\psi)) \right\} d\mathbb{P}^* \right| \leq \frac{\epsilon}{4} \qquad (t \geq T_2). \tag{4.37}$$

Thus, due to (4.36), (4.34), (4.37) and due to (4.33), the following inequality holds true for all $t \geq \max\{T_1, T_2\}$:

$$\begin{aligned}
&\left| \int F(p_t(p,\psi))d\mathbb{P} - \int F d\nu_0 \right| \\
\leq\ & \left| \int \left\{ F(p_t(p,\psi)) - F(p_t^l(p,\psi)) \right\} d\mathbb{P} \right| + \left| \int F(p_t^l(p,\psi)) \{d\mathbb{P} - d\mathbb{P}^*\} \right| \\
&+ \left| \int \left\{ F(p_t^l(p,\psi)) - F(p_t(p,\psi)) \right\} d\mathbb{P}^* \right| + \left| \int F(p_t(p,\psi))d\mathbb{P}^* - \int F d\nu_0 \right| \\
\leq\ & \epsilon.
\end{aligned}$$

This shows vague convergence of the sequence $\{\mathrm{Law}(p_t(p,\psi), \mathbb{P})\}_{t\in\mathbb{N}}$ to the probability measure ν_0 on $\mathbb{R}$. Thus, we also have weak convergence. □

We are now ready to prove our global convergence result.

Proof of Theorem 4.9:

From the proof of Theorem 4.14 we deduce that the finite dimensional distributions of the shifted process $\{p_{t+T}(p,\psi)\}_{t\in\mathbb{N}}$ under the measure $\mathbb{P}$ converge weakly to the finite dimensional distributions of the unique stationary solution $\{P_t^*\}_{t\in\mathbb{N}}$ of (4.10) under the law $\mathbb{P}^*$ as $T \to \infty$. Indeed, let $m \in \mathbb{N}$ and $t_1 < t_2 < \cdots < t_m \in \mathbb{N}$ be given. For $t_1 \geq l$, we put

$$p_{t_1,\cdots,t_m}(p,\psi) := (p_{t_1}(p,\psi), \ldots, p_{t_m}(p,\psi)),$$

and

$$p^l_{t_1,\cdots,t_m}(p,\psi) := (p^l_{t_1}(p,\psi), \ldots, p^l_{t_m}(p,\psi)).$$

As in the proof of Theorem 4.14 we have that

$$\lim_{t_1\to\infty} \left| p_{t_1,\cdots,t_m}(p,\psi) - p^l_{t_1,\cdots,t_m}(p,\psi) \right| = 0 \qquad \mathbb{P}\text{- and } \mathbb{P}^*\text{-a.s.},$$

where $|\cdot|$ denotes the Euclidean distance.

Since, for any $B \in \mathcal{B}(\mathbb{R}^m)$, the event $\{p^l_{t_1,\cdots,t_m}(p,\psi) \in B\}$ belongs to the σ-algebra $\hat{\mathcal{F}}_l$, we can use the same arguments as in the proof of Theorem 4.14 in order to verify weak convergence of the finite-dimensional distributions.

Thus, it remains to show that the family of random variables $(\{p_{t+T}(p,\psi)\}_{t\in\mathbb{N}})_{T\in\mathbb{N}}$ – viewed as a family of random variables taking values in the space $\mathbb{R}^{\mathbb{N}}$ – is tight. For this, we have to prove that, for any $\epsilon > 0$ and for all $t \in \mathbb{N}$, there exists a compact set $K_t \subset \mathbb{R}$ such that

$$\sup_T \mathbb{P}[p_{t+T}(p, \psi) \in K_t] \geq 1 - \epsilon;$$

see, e.g., Ethier and Kurtz (1986), Theorem 3.7.2.

To this end, we fix $\epsilon > 0$. Since the random variable P_0^* is $\mathbb{P}^*$-a.s. finite there exists $k \in \mathbb{R}$ satisfying

$$\mathbb{P}^*[|P_0^*| \leq k] > 1 - \frac{\epsilon}{4}.$$

In order verify our assertion, let us now fix $t \in \mathbb{N}$ and proceed as follows.

1. Due to (4.32), there exists $T_0 = T_0(\epsilon, k)$ such that

$$\mathbb{P}[|p_{t+T}(p, \psi)| \leq k + 2\epsilon] \geq \mathbb{P}[|p^l_{t+T}(p, \psi)| \leq k + \epsilon] - \frac{\epsilon}{4} \qquad (T \geq T_0).$$

2. Since the driving sequence ψ is "nice", there exists a constant $l \in \mathbb{N}$ which satisfies

$$\sup_{B,T} \left| \mathbb{P}[p^l_{t+T}(p, \psi) \in B] - \mathbb{P}^*[p^l_{t+T}(p, \psi) \in B] \right| < \frac{\epsilon}{4}.$$

3. Due to Theorem 4.7 and (4.32), the process $\{p^l_{t+T}(p, \psi)\}_{T \in \mathbb{N}}$ converges $\mathbb{P}^*$-a.s. to the stationary sequence $\{P^*_{t+T}\}_{T \in \mathbb{N}}$. This yields

$$\mathbb{P}^*[|p^l_{t+T}(p, \psi)| \leq k + \epsilon] \geq \mathbb{P}^*[|P^*_{t+T}| \leq k] - \frac{\epsilon}{4} = \mathbb{P}^*[|P_0^*| \leq k] - \frac{\epsilon}{4} \qquad (4.38)$$

for all $T \geq T_0 = T_0(\epsilon, k)$.

Thus, we have that

$$\begin{aligned} \sup_{t \geq T_0} \mathbb{P}[|p_{t+T}(p, \psi)| \leq k + 2\epsilon] &\geq \sup_{t \geq T_0} \mathbb{P}[|p^l_{t+T}(p, \psi)| \leq k + \epsilon] - \frac{\epsilon}{4} \\ &\geq \sup_{t \geq T_0} \mathbb{P}^*[|p^l_{t+T}(p, \psi)| \leq k + \epsilon] - \frac{\epsilon}{2} \\ &\geq 1 - \epsilon, \end{aligned}$$

and so we can choose a compact set $K_t = K_t(\epsilon) \subset \mathbb{R}$ which satisfies

$$\sup_T \mathbb{P}[p_{t+T}(p, \psi) \in K_t] \geq 1 - 2\epsilon.$$

This proves the theorem. □

Some Case Studies

We will now consider some case studies where our assumption that the driving sequence has a "nice" asymptotic behaviour can indeed be verified.

Example 4.15 *Let us first analyze a situation where the random environment ψ is generated by an underlying Markov process. We denote by $(\{\xi_t\}_{t\in\mathbb{N}}, (\mathbb{P}_\xi)_{\xi\in M})$ a Markov chain on $(\Omega, \mathcal{F})$ with state space M and with transition operator U. We assume that the process $\{\xi_t\}_{t\in\mathbb{N}}$ has the Feller property and that the sequence $\{\mathrm{Law}(\xi_t, \mathbb{P}_\xi)\}_{t\in\mathbb{N}}$ converges in the total variation norm to a unique stationary measure μ^* as $t \to \infty$. We consider an environment of the form*

$$\psi := \{(f(\xi_t), g(\xi_t))\}_{t\in\mathbb{N}}, \tag{4.39}$$

where $f, g : M_1 \to \mathbb{R}$ are measurable functions. Uniqueness of the stationary probability measure implies that the driving sequence ψ is stationary and ergodic under the law

$$\mathbb{P}^*(\cdot) := \int_M \mathbb{P}_\xi(\cdot)\mu^*(d\xi).$$

For $t \in \mathbb{N}$, we denote by U^t the t-fold iteration of the transition operator U. Since the sequence $\{\mathrm{Law}(\xi_t, \mathbb{P}_\xi)\}_{t\in\mathbb{N}}$ converges in the total variation norm to μ^* we have

$$\sup_{\hat{\xi},l} \|\mathbb{P}_{\hat{\xi}} - \mathbb{P}^*\|_{\hat{\mathcal{F}}_{t,l}} \leq \sup_{F\in B(M), |F|_\infty \leq 1} |U^t F - \mu^*(F)|_\infty \to 0 \qquad (t \to \infty). \tag{4.40}$$

Thus, (4.17) holds true for any initial distribution μ of the Markov chain $\{\xi_t\}_{t\in\mathbb{N}}$, and so the environment $\{(f(\xi_t), g(\xi_t))\}_{t\in\mathbb{N}}$ defined on the probability space $(\Omega, \mathcal{F}, \mathbb{P}_\mu)$ is "nice" in the sense of Definition 4.5 whenever

$$-\infty \leq \int_M \log|f| d\mu^* < 0 \quad \text{and} \quad \int_M (\log|g|)^+ d\mu^* < 0.$$

Next, we consider a situation where the random environment ψ is generated by the signal sequence associated with a random system with complete connections.

Example 4.16 *Let $\{\zeta_t\}_{t\in\mathbb{N}}$ be the signal sequence associated with a distance-diminishing random system with complete connections $\Sigma = ((M_1, d_{M_1}), (M_2, \mathcal{M}_2), Z, v)$ whose associated Markov chain $(\{\xi_t\}_{t\in\mathbb{N}}, (\mathbb{P}_\xi)_{\xi\in M_1})$ converges in law to a unique invariant measure μ^*. If the stochastic kernel Z from M_1 to $\mathcal{M}_2$ satisfies a uniform Lipschitz condition, then the process $\{\zeta_t\}_{t\in\mathbb{N}}$ is stationary and ergodic under the* *law* $\mathbb{P}^*(\cdot) = \int_{M_1} \mathbb{P}_\xi(\cdot)\mu^*(d\xi)$ *and has "nice" tail structure, due to Proposition A.10. Thus, for any two measurable functions* $f, g : M_2 \to \mathbb{R}$ *the environment*

$$\psi := \{(f(\zeta_t), g(\zeta_t))\}_{t\in\mathbb{N}}$$

is "nice" in the sense of our Definition 4.5 as soon as

$$\begin{aligned} -\infty \le \int_{M_2}\int_{M_1} \log|f(\zeta)|Z(\xi;d\zeta)\mu^*(d\xi) &< 0 \\ \int_{M_2}\int_{M_1} (\log|g(\zeta)|)^+ Z(\xi;d\zeta)\mu^*(\xi) &< \infty. \end{aligned}$$

Let us now analyze two examples where the environment ψ takes the form

$$\psi = \{(f(\hat{\varrho}_t), g(\hat{\varrho}_t))\}_{t\in\mathbb{N}} \tag{4.41}$$

for some "smoothed" Markov chain $\{\hat{\varrho}_t\}_{t\in\mathbb{N}}$.

Example 4.17 *Suppose that the dynamics of the sequence* $\{\hat{\varrho}\}_{t\in\mathbb{N}}$ *takes the following form: There exists a deterministic sequence* $\{\xi_t\}_{t\in\mathbb{N}}$ *on a metric state space* (M_1, d_{M_1}) *which is defined recursively by the relation*

$$\xi_{t+1} = u(\xi_t) \qquad (t \in \mathbb{N})$$

for some measurable mapping u *on* M_1 *and which satisfies the contraction condition*

$$d_X(\xi_{t+1}, \xi_t) \le \alpha d_X(\xi_t, \xi_{t-1}) \qquad (t \in \mathbb{N})$$

for some $\alpha < 1$. *Depending on the starting point* ξ, *this sequence converges to* $\xi^* = \xi^*(\xi) = u(\xi^*)$ *The process* $\{\hat{\varrho}\}_{t\in\mathbb{N}}$ *is defined on a probability space* $(\Omega, \mathcal{F}, \mathbb{P}_\xi)$. *The conditional law* $\hat{Q}(\xi_t;\cdot)$ *of the random variable* $\hat{\varrho}_t$ *given* ξ_t, *is described by a stochastic kernel* $\hat{Q}$ *on* M_1. *In particular, the environment is stationary and ergodic under the law* $\mathbb{P}_{\xi^*}$. *If the stochastic kernel* $\hat{Q}$ *satisfies a uniform Lipschitz condition such as (2.94), then the driving sequence* ψ *satisfies (4.16), due to Lemma 2.34.*

The following example is closely related to Example 4.16; see also Remark 3.31.

Example 4.18 *Let us now consider a situation where the dynamics of the process* $\{\hat{\varrho}\}_{t\in\mathbb{N}}$ *take the following form: We denote by* $(\{\xi_t\}_{t\in\mathbb{N}}, (\mathbb{P}_\xi)_{\xi\in M_1})$ *the Markov chain on* $(\Omega, \mathcal{F})$ *with state space* M_1 *which is associated with the distance-diminishing random system with complete connections* $\Sigma = ((M_1, d_{M_1}), (M_2, \mathcal{M}_2), Z, v)$ *and assume* *that the sequence* $\{\xi_t\}_{t\in\mathbb{N}}$ *converges in distribution to a unique invariant measure* μ^* *on* M_1. *The conditional law* $\hat{Q}(\xi_t;\cdot)$ *of the random variable* $\hat{\varrho}_t$ *given* ξ_t, *is described by a stochastic kernel* $\hat{Q}$ *on* M_1. *We assume that the stochastic kernels* Z *and* Q *satisfy a uniform Lipschitz condition. Thus, under the law* $\mathbb{P}^*(\cdot) = \int \mathbb{P}_\xi(\cdot)\mu^*(d\xi)$ *this process is stationary and ergodic, and for any initial value* ξ *of the Markov chain* $\{\xi_t\}_{t\in\mathbb{N}}$, *the driving sequence* ψ *defined on* $(\Omega, \mathcal{F}, \mathbb{P}_\xi)$ *satisfies (4.16), due to Corollary 3.30; see also (3.75).*

Stochastic Sequences Driven by "Almost Nice" Processes

This subsection is devoted to the proof of Theorem 4.12. Let us first sketch the basic idea. In (4.22), we introduced a sequence of "perturbed" random environments ψ^n ($n \in \mathbb{N}$) defined on $(\Omega, \mathcal{F})$ such that $\text{Law}(\psi^n, \mathbb{P}) \xrightarrow{w} \text{Law}(\psi, \mathbb{P})$ as $n \to \infty$. For any $n \in \mathbb{N}$, the sequence ψ^n is "nice", by Assumption 4.10. Thus, due to (4.28), and because of Theorem 4.9 there exists a unique probability measure ν_0^n on $\mathbb{R}$ such that

$$\text{Law}(p_t(p, \psi^n), \mathbb{P}) \xrightarrow{w} \nu_0^n \qquad (t \to \infty). \tag{4.42}$$

Our aim is now to prove that the process $\{p_t(p, \psi)\}_{t\in\mathbb{N}}$ converges in law to the unique weak limit ν_0 of the sequence $\{\nu_0^n\}_{n\in\mathbb{N}}$. To this end, we shall apply a continuity result which follows immediately from Theorem 2 in Brandt (1986).

Lemma 4.19 *Suppose that the Assumptions of Theorem 4.12 are satisfied. In the stationary setting we have the following global stability result:*

$$\text{Law}(\{P_t^n\}_{t\in\mathbb{N}}, \mathbb{P}^*) \xrightarrow{w} \text{Law}(\{P_t^*\}_{t\in\mathbb{N}}, \mathbb{P}^*) \qquad (n \to \infty). \tag{4.43}$$

The next proposition yields a uniform approximation result which will turn out to be the key for the proof of Theorem 4.12.

Proposition 4.20 *For any Lipschitz continuous function* F *on* $\mathbb{R}$ *with compact support, and for each starting point* $p \in \mathbb{R}$ *we have*

$$\lim_{n\to\infty} \sup_t \mathbb{E}|F(p_t(p, \psi)) - F(p_t(p, \psi^n))| = 0. \tag{4.44}$$

Proof: Let F be a Lipschitz continuous function on $\mathbb{R}$ with compact support and with Lipschitz constant $m(F) = 1$. With no loss of generality we may assume that diam(supp F)=1. In this case, we have that

$$|F(x) - F(y)| \le G(|x - y|),$$

where $G(x) := |x| \wedge 1$. It is therefore enough to show that

$$\overline{\lim}_{n\to\infty} \sup_t \mathbb{E}[G(|p_t(p,\psi) - p_t(p,\psi^n)|)] = 0. \tag{4.45}$$

To this end, we proceed as follows. Let us put $\mathcal{I}_j := \{t-j,\dots,t-1\}$ and $\mathcal{I}_0 := \emptyset$. The explicit representation (4.18) of $p_t(p,\psi^n)$ yields

$$\begin{aligned}
&|p_t(p,\psi) - p_t(p,\psi^n)| \\
&\le \sum_{j=1}^{t-1} \sum_{\mathcal{I}\subsetneq\mathcal{I}_j} \left(\prod_{i\in\mathcal{I}} |A_i| \prod_{i\in\mathcal{I}\setminus\mathcal{I}_j} \frac{c}{n}|\epsilon_i| \right) |B_{t-j-1}| \\
&\quad + \sum_{j=0}^{t-1} \sum_{\mathcal{I}\subset\mathcal{I}_j} \left(\prod_{i\in\mathcal{I}} |A_i| \prod_{i\in\mathcal{I}\setminus\mathcal{I}_j} \frac{c}{n}|\epsilon_i| \right) \frac{c}{n}|\eta_{t-j-1}| \\
&\quad + \sum_{\mathcal{I}\subsetneq\mathcal{I}_t} \left(\prod_{i\in\mathcal{I}} |A_i| \prod_{i\in\mathcal{I}_t\setminus\mathcal{I}} \frac{c}{n}|\epsilon_i| \right) |p| \\
&\le \frac{1}{n} \left\{ \sum_{j=0}^{t-1} \sum_{\mathcal{I}\subset\mathcal{I}_j} \left(\prod_{i\in\mathcal{I}} |A_i| \prod_{i\in\mathcal{I}\setminus\mathcal{I}_j} c|\epsilon_i| \right) (|B_{t-j-1}| + c|\eta_{t-j-1}|) \right. \\
&\quad \left. + \sum_{\mathcal{I}\subset\mathcal{I}_t} \left(\prod_{i\in\mathcal{I}} |A_i| \prod_{i\in\mathcal{I}_t\setminus\mathcal{I}} c|\epsilon_i| \right) |p| \right\} \\
&= \frac{1}{n} p_t(|p|,\widetilde{\psi}),
\end{aligned}$$

where $\widetilde{\psi}$ is defined in (4.25). Thus, it suffices to show that

$$\overline{\lim}_{n\to\infty} \sup_t \mathbb{E}\left[G\left(\frac{1}{n} p_t(|p|,\widetilde{\psi}) \right) \right] = 0. \tag{4.46}$$

To this end, we proceed in several steps.

1. Let us first show that (4.46) holds for $\mathbb{P} = \mathbb{P}^*$. In the stationary situation, i.e., under the assumption that $\mathbb{P} = \mathbb{P}^*$, we may with no loss of generality assume that the environment $\widetilde{\psi} = \{\widetilde{\psi}_t\}_{t\in\mathbb{Z}}$ is defined for all integers $t \in \mathbb{Z}$. Due to (4.23), we may apply Theorem 4.7 to the sequence $\widetilde{\psi}$. In particular, there exists a unique stationary solution $\{\widetilde{P}_t\}_{t\in\mathbb{N}}$ of (4.10) driven by the input $\widetilde{\psi}$. The random variable $\widetilde{P}_0$ is $\mathbb{P}^*$-a.s. finite and the process $\{\widetilde{P}_t\}_{t\in\mathbb{N}}$ satisfies

$$\lim_{t\to\infty} \left| p_t(p,\widetilde{\psi}) - \widetilde{P}_t \right| = 0 \qquad \mathbb{P}^*\text{-a.s.} \tag{4.47}$$

In particular, we have that

$$\lim_{n\to\infty}\sup_t \mathbb{E}^*\left[G\left(\frac{1}{n}\widetilde{P}_t\right)\right] = \lim_{n\to\infty}\mathbb{E}^*\left[G\left(\frac{1}{n}\widetilde{P}_0\right)\right] = G(0) = 0$$

by Lebesgue's theorem. This yields

$$\begin{aligned}
&\overline{\lim}_{n\to\infty}\sup_t \mathbb{E}^*\left[G\left(\frac{1}{n}p_t(|p|,\widetilde{\psi})\right)\right]\\
\leq\ &\overline{\lim}_{n\to\infty}\sup_t \mathbb{E}^*\left|G\left(\frac{1}{n}p_t(|p|,\widetilde{\psi})\right) - G\left(\frac{1}{n}\widetilde{P}_t\right)\right| + \lim_{n\to\infty}\sup_t \mathbb{E}^*\left[G\left(\frac{1}{n}\widetilde{P}_t\right)\right]\\
=\ &\overline{\lim}_{n\to\infty}\sup_t \mathbb{E}^*\left|G\left(\frac{1}{n}p_t(|p|,\widetilde{\psi})\right) - G\left(\frac{1}{n}\widetilde{P}_t\right)\right|.
\end{aligned}$$

Let us now fix $\epsilon > 0$. Since the mapping G is bounded and Lipschitz continuous it follows from (4.47) that there exists a constant $T \in \mathbb{N}$ such that, for all $t \geq T$ and for all $n \in \mathbb{N}$, we have

$$\begin{aligned}
&\mathbb{E}^*\left|G\left(\frac{1}{n}p_t(|p|,\widetilde{\psi})\right) - G\left(\frac{1}{n}\widetilde{P}_t\right)\right|\\
\leq\ &\mathbb{E}^*\left[\left|\frac{1}{n}p_t(|p|,\widetilde{\psi}) - \frac{1}{n}\widetilde{P}_t\right| \wedge 1\right]\\
\leq\ &\frac{\epsilon}{2}\cdot\mathbb{P}^*\left[\left|\frac{1}{n}p_t(|p|,\widetilde{\psi}) - \frac{1}{n}\widetilde{P}_t\right| \leq \frac{\epsilon}{2}\right] + \mathbb{P}^*\left[\left|\frac{1}{n}p_t(|p|,\widetilde{\psi}) - \frac{1}{n}\widetilde{P}_t\right| > \frac{\epsilon}{2}\right]\\
\leq\ &\frac{\epsilon}{2} + \mathbb{P}^*\left[\left|p_t(|p|,\widetilde{\psi}) - \widetilde{P}_t\right| > \epsilon/2\right]\\
\leq\ &\epsilon.
\end{aligned}$$

Since $G(0) = 0$, and because the random variables $p_t(|p|,\widetilde{\psi})$ $(t \in \mathbb{N})$ are $\mathbb{P}^*$-a.s. finite, it follows from Lebesgue's Theorem that

$$\begin{aligned}
&\overline{\lim}_{n\to\infty}\sup_t \mathbb{E}^*\left|G\left(\frac{1}{n}p_t(|p|,\widetilde{\psi})\right) - G\left(\frac{1}{n}\widetilde{P}_t\right)\right|\\
\leq\ &\overline{\lim}_{n\to\infty}\sup_{t\geq T} \mathbb{E}^*\left|G\left(\frac{1}{n}p_t(|p|,\widetilde{\psi})\right) - G\left(\frac{1}{n}\widetilde{P}_t\right)\right|\\
&+\overline{\lim}_{n\to\infty}\sum_{t=0}^{T-1}\left\{\mathbb{E}^* G\left(\frac{1}{n}p_t(|p|,\widetilde{\psi})\right) + \mathbb{E}^* G\left(\frac{1}{n}\widetilde{P}_t\right)\right\}\\
\leq\ &\epsilon.
\end{aligned}$$

Since $\epsilon > 0$ is arbitrary, we conclude that

$$\overline{\lim}_{n\to\infty}\sup_t \mathbb{E}^*\left[G\left(\frac{1}{n}p_t(|p|,\widetilde{\psi})\right)\right] = 0. \tag{4.48}$$

2. Let us now define the random variable $p_t^l(|p|, \widetilde{\psi})$ by analogy with (4.31) and fix $\epsilon > 0$. We are going to show that there exists a constant $l \in \mathbb{N}$ such that the following estimate holds true uniformly in $n \in \mathbb{N}$:

$$\sup_t \mathbb{E}\left[G\left(\frac{1}{n}p_t^l(|p|, \widetilde{\psi})\right)\right] \leq \sup_t \mathbb{E}^*\left[G\left(\frac{1}{n}p_t^l(|p|, \widetilde{\psi})\right)\right] + \epsilon. \tag{4.49}$$

Since $\mathbb{P} - \mathbb{P}^*$ is a signed measure on $\mathcal{F}$ with total mass zero, we have that

$$\begin{aligned} &\int G\left(\frac{1}{n}p_t^l(|p|, \widetilde{\psi})\right)(d\mathbb{P} - d\mathbb{P}^*) \\ \leq & \sup_{B \in \mathcal{B}(\mathbb{R}), t} \left|\mathbb{P}[p_t^l(|p|, \widetilde{\psi}) \in B] - \mathbb{P}^*[p_t^l(|p|, \widetilde{\psi}) \in B]\right|. \end{aligned}$$

Observe that the event $\{p_t^l(|p|, \widetilde{\psi}) \in B\}$ $(B \in \mathcal{B}(\mathbb{R}))$ belongs to the σ-field $\hat{\mathcal{G}}_l = \sigma(\{\widetilde{\psi}_s\}_{s \geq l})$. Since the sequence $\widetilde{\psi}$ has a "nice" tail structure, it follows from Remark 4.6 (ii) that there exists a sequence $\{c_l\}_{l \in \mathbb{N}}$ such that $\lim_{l \to \infty} c_l = 0$ and

$$\sup_t \mathbb{E}\left[G\left(\frac{1}{n}p_t^l(|p|, \widetilde{\psi})\right)\right] \leq \sup_t \mathbb{E}^*\left[G\left(\frac{1}{n}p_t^l(|p|, \widetilde{\psi})\right)\right] + c_l$$

holds true. This yields (4.49) for l sufficiently large.

We can use the same arguments as in the proof of Theorem 4.9 in order to show that

$$\lim_{t \to \infty} \left|p_t^l(|p|, \widetilde{\psi}) - p_t(|p|, \widetilde{\psi})\right| = 0 \qquad \mathbb{P}\text{- and } \mathbb{P}^*\text{-a.s.} \qquad (l \in \mathbb{N}). \tag{4.50}$$

In particular, it follows from (4.47) that

$$\lim_{t \to \infty} \left|p_t^l(|p|, \widetilde{\psi}) - \widetilde{P}_t\right| = 0 \qquad \mathbb{P}^*\text{-a.s.} \qquad (l \in \mathbb{N}). \tag{4.51}$$

Thus, by Step 1, there exists a large enough $l \in \mathbb{N}$ such that

$$\begin{aligned} \overline{\lim}_{n \to \infty} \sup_t \mathbb{E}\left[G\left(\frac{1}{n}p_t^l(|p|, \widetilde{\psi})\right)\right] &\leq \epsilon + \overline{\lim}_{n \to \infty} \sup_t \mathbb{E}^*\left[G\left(\frac{1}{n}p_t^l(|p|, \widetilde{\psi})\right)\right] \\ &= \epsilon. \end{aligned} \tag{4.52}$$

In the final step, we are now going to extend this estimate to the case $l = 0$. This will then yield (4.46).

3. Let us fix $\epsilon > 0$ and choose $l \in \mathbb{N}$ such that (4.52) holds true. Using $G(0) = 0$, Lebesgue's theorem and (4.52), we obtain

$$\begin{aligned}
&\overline{\lim}_{n\to\infty} \sup_t \mathbb{E}\left[G\left(\frac{1}{n}p_t(|p|,\widetilde{\psi})\right)\right] \\
\leq\ &\overline{\lim}_{n\to\infty} \sup_{t\geq l} \mathbb{E}\left[G\left(\frac{1}{n}p_t(|p|,\widetilde{\psi})\right)\right] + \overline{\lim}_{n\to\infty} \sum_{t=1}^{l} \mathbb{E}\left[G\left(\frac{1}{n}p_t(|p|,\widetilde{\psi})\right)\right] \\
\leq\ &\overline{\lim}_{n\to\infty} \sup_{t\geq l} \left|\mathbb{E}\left\{G\left(\frac{1}{n}p_t(|p|,\widetilde{\psi})\right) - G\left(\frac{1}{n}p_t^l(|p|,\widetilde{\psi})\right)\right\}\right| + \epsilon.
\end{aligned}$$

Due to (4.50), we can proceed as in Step 2 and choose $T = T(\epsilon, l)$ such that

$$\sup_{t\geq T} \left|\mathbb{E}\left\{G\left(\frac{1}{n}p_t(|p|,\widetilde{\psi})\right) - G\left(\frac{1}{n}p_t^l(|p|,\widetilde{\psi})\right)\right\}\right| < \epsilon.$$

Since $G(0) = 0$ it follows by analogy with Step 2 that

$$\overline{\lim}_{n\to\infty} \sup_t \mathbb{E}\left[G\left(\frac{1}{n}p_t(|p|,\widetilde{\psi})\right)\right] < 2\epsilon.$$

Thus, we have shown (4.46) as $\epsilon > 0$ is arbitrary.

This proves our assertion. □

Corollary 4.21 *Let $m \in \mathbb{N}$ be given. For any Lipschitz continuous function F on $\mathbb{R}^m$ with compact support we have that*

$$\lim_{n\to\infty} \sup_{t_1,\ldots,t_m} \mathbb{E}|F(p_{t_1}(p,\psi^n),\ldots,p_{t_m}(p,\psi^n)) - F(p_{t_1}(p,\psi),\ldots,p_{t_m}(p,\psi))| = 0.$$

Proof: Without loss of generality we may again assume that $m(F) = 1$ and that diam(supp F)=1. Thus, there exists a constant $c \in \mathbb{R}_+$ such that

$$\begin{aligned}
&\mathbb{E}|F(p_{t_1}(p,\psi^n),\ldots,p_{t_m}(p,\psi^n)) - F(p_{t_1}(p,\psi),\ldots,p_{t_m}(p,\psi))| \\
\leq\ & c\sum_{i=1}^{m} \mathbb{E}[|p_{t_i}(p,\psi^n) - p_{t_i}(p,\psi)| \wedge 1] \\
\leq\ & c \cdot m \cdot \sup_t \mathbb{E}\left[G(|p_t(p,\psi^n) - p_t(p,\psi)|)\right],
\end{aligned}$$

and so the assertion follows as in the proof of Proposition 4.20. □

Using Proposition 4.20 and Theorem 4.14, we are now ready to establish weak convergence of the finite dimensional distributions of the process $\{p_t(p,\psi)\}_{t\in\mathbb{N}}$ under

$\mathbb{P}$ to the finite-dimensional distributions of the unique stationary solution of (4.10) under the measure $\mathbb{P}^*$.

Proof of Theorem 4.12:

Let us first establish convergence of the one-dimensional distributions, i.e., let us show that

$$\mathrm{Law}(p_t(p,\psi),\mathbb{P}) \xrightarrow{w} \nu_0 = \mathrm{Law}(P_0^*,\mathbb{P}^*) \qquad (t\to\infty).$$

To this end, it is enough to show

$$\lim_{t\to\infty}\int F(p_t(p,\psi)d\mathbb{P} = \int F d\nu_0$$

for any real-valued Lipschitz continuous function F on $\mathbb{R}$ with compact support.

For any $n\in\mathbb{N}$, the driving sequence ψ^n is "nice" in the sense of Definition 4.5. Thus, under the law $\mathbb{P}^*$, there exists a unique stationary solution $\{P_t^n\}_{t\in\mathbb{N}}$ of (4.10) which is driven by the "input" ψ^n. We put $\nu_0^n := \mathrm{Law}(P_0^n,\mathbb{P}^*)$. This yields

$$\begin{aligned}\left|\int F(p_t(p,\psi))d\mathbb{P} - \int F d\nu_0\right| \;\le\; & \left|\int \{F(p_t(p,\psi)) - F(p_t(p,\psi^n))\}\, d\mathbb{P}\right| \\ & + \left|\int F(p_t(p,\psi^n))d\mathbb{P} - \int F d\nu_0^n\right| \\ & + \left|\int F d\nu_0^n - \int F d\nu_0\right|.\end{aligned}$$

According to Proposition 4.20 there exists a constant $N_1 = N_1(\epsilon)\in\mathbb{N}$ such that

$$\left|\int \{F(p_t(p,\psi)) - F(p_t(p,\psi^n))\}\, d\mathbb{P}\right| \le \frac{\epsilon}{3} \qquad (n\ge N_1, t\in\mathbb{N}).$$

Moreover, we can choose $N_2 = N_2(\epsilon)\in\mathbb{N}$ satisfying

$$\left|\int F d\nu_0^n - \int F d\nu_0\right| \le \frac{\epsilon}{3} \qquad (n\ge N_2),$$

due to Lemma 4.19.

Let us now fix $n_0 \ge \max\{N_1, N_2\}$. Since the environment ψ^{n_0} is "nice", it follows from Theorem 4.9 that there exists a constant $T(n_0)$ such that

$$\left|\int F(p_t(p,\psi^{n_0}))d\mathbb{P} - \int F d\nu_0^{n_0}\right| < \frac{\epsilon}{3} \qquad (4.53)$$

for all $t \geq T(n_0)$. In particular, we get

$$\left| \int F(p_t(p, \psi)) d\mathbb{P} - \int F d\nu_0 \right| \leq \epsilon \tag{4.54}$$

for all $t \geq T(n_0)$. This shows weak convergence of the sequence $\{\text{Law}(p_t(p, \psi), \mathbb{P})\}_{t \in \mathbb{N}}$ to the probability measure ν_0. Convergence of the finite-dimensional distributions follows by analogy with the proof of Theorem 4.9. □

A Markovian Case Study

In this section, we study a class of Markovian models where our Assumption 4.10 that the driving process ψ can be approximated in law by a sequence of "nice" processes $\{\psi^n\}_{n \in \mathbb{N}}$ can indeed be verified.

To this end, we fix Lipschitz continuous functions $f, g : M_1 \to \mathbb{R}$ and consider an environment of the form

$$\psi := \{(f(\xi_t), g(\xi_t))\}_{t \in \mathbb{N}}. \tag{4.55}$$

Here, $(\{\xi_t\}_{t \in \mathbb{N}}, (\mathbb{P}_\xi)_{x \in M_1})$ denotes a Markov chain on $(\Omega, \mathcal{F})$ with metric state space (M_1, d_{M_1}) which is associated with a distance-diminishing random system with complete connections $\Sigma = ((M_1, d_{M_1}), (M_2, \mathcal{M}_2), Z, v)$. We assume that the following conditions are satisfied.

Assumption 4.22 *(i) For any starting point $\xi \in M_1$, the sequence $\{\xi_t\}_{t \in \mathbb{N}}$ converges in law to a unique stationary distribution μ^* on M_1 as $t \to \infty$.*

(ii) The stochastic kernel Z from M_1 to $\mathcal{M}_2$ satisfies a uniform Lipschitz condition in the sense of Definition 2.32 so that the Markov chain $\{\xi_t\}_{t \in \mathbb{N}}$ has the Feller property.

Our Assumption 4.22 implies that driving sequence ψ is stationary and ergodic under the law

$$\mathbb{P}^*(\cdot) := \int_{M_1} \mathbb{P}_\xi(\cdot) \mu^*(d\xi), \tag{4.56}$$

but the environment ψ does not necessarily have a "nice" tail-structure. However, the driving sequence can be approximated in law by a sequence of "nice" processes $\{\psi^n\}_{n \in \mathbb{N}}$, $\psi^n = \{(A_t^n, B_t^n)\}_{t \in \mathbb{N}}$. The approximating sequence may be constructed as follows:

Let $\{\epsilon_t\}_{t\in\mathbb{N}}$ and $\{\eta_t\}_{t\in\mathbb{N}}$ be sequences of random variables defined on $(\Omega, \mathcal{F})$. For each $\xi \in M_1$, these random variables are independent and identically distributed under the law $\mathbb{P}_\xi$. Moreover, they are $\mathbb{P}_\xi$-independent of all ξ_t $(t \in \mathbb{N})$ and satisfy

$$\text{Law}((\epsilon_0, \eta_0), \mathbb{P}_\xi) = \text{Law}((\epsilon_0, \eta_0), \mathbb{P}_{\hat{\xi}})) \qquad (\xi, \hat{\xi} \in M_1).$$

We consider a situation where the probability measure $\text{Law}((\epsilon_0, \eta_0), \mathbb{P}_\xi)$ on $\mathbb{R}^2$ has a bounded Lipschitz continuous density $q : \mathbb{R}^2 \to \mathbb{R}$ with respect to the 2-dimensional Lebesgue measure λ^2 on $\mathbb{R}^2$. For simplicity, we assume that $q = 0$ on $\mathbb{R}^2_-$.

Armed with our Lemma 3.29 we are able to verify that the sequences $\widetilde{\psi}$ and ψ^n $(n \in \mathbb{N})$ have a "nice" asymptotic behaviour. To this end, we introduce a family of stochastic kernels $\widetilde{Q}$, $Q^1, Q^2, \ldots$ form M_1 to $\mathcal{B}(\mathbb{R}^2)$ by the relation

$$Q^n(\xi; B) := \frac{1}{\sigma_n} \int_B q\left(\frac{1}{\sigma_n} y - \frac{1}{\sigma_n}(f(\xi), g(\xi))\right) \lambda^2(dy)$$

and

$$\widetilde{Q}(\xi; B) := \frac{1}{\sigma_1} \int_B q\left(\frac{1}{\sigma_1} y - \frac{1}{\sigma_1}(|f(\xi)|, |g(\xi)|)\right) \lambda^2(dy)$$

Observe that

$$\mathbb{P}_\xi[\psi_t^n \in \cdot | \xi_t, \ldots, \xi_0, \psi_{t-1}^n, \ldots, \psi_0^n] = Q^n(\xi_t; \cdot) \qquad (n \in \mathbb{N})$$

and that

$$\mathbb{P}_\xi[\widetilde{\psi}_t \in \cdot | \xi_t, \ldots, \xi_0, \widetilde{\psi}_{t-1}, \ldots, \widetilde{\psi}_0] = \widetilde{Q}(\xi_t; \cdot).$$

Here, the last equality holds true as $q = 0$ on $\mathbb{R}^2_-$.

Since $f, g : M_1 \to \mathbb{R}$ and $q : \mathbb{R}^2 \to \mathbb{R}$ are Lipschitz continuous functions, there exists constants $L_n < \infty$ $(n \in \mathbb{N})$ which do not depend on $B \in \mathcal{B}(\mathbb{R}^2)$ such that

$$\left| Q^n(\xi; B) - Q^n(\hat{\xi}; B) \right| \leq L_n d_{M_1}(\xi, \hat{\xi}) \qquad (n \in \mathbb{N})$$

and such that

$$\left| \widetilde{Q}(\xi; B) - \widetilde{Q}(\hat{\xi}; B) \right| \leq L_1 d_{M_1}(\xi, \hat{\xi});$$

cf. Lemma A.4. Thus, the stochastic kernels $\widetilde{Q}, Q^1, Q^2, \ldots$ satisfy a uniform Lipschitz condition, and so we can easily establish the following result.

Proposition 4.23 *Under the above assumptions the approximating sequences* ψ^n $(n \in \mathbb{N})$ *and* $\widetilde{\psi}$ *have a "nice" asymptotic behaviour.*

Proof: Since the Markov chain $\{\xi_t\}_{t \in \mathbb{N}}$ converges in law to a unique invariant measure μ^* on M_1, each of the sequences $\widetilde{\psi}$ and ψ^n $(n \in \mathbb{N})$ is stationary and ergodic under the law $\mathbb{P}^*(\cdot)$ defined in (4.56). Thus, the assertion follows from Corollary 3.30 and from (4.16). □

In the sequel, we shall call the measure μ^* on M_1 **stable**, if there exists sequences of i.i.d. random variables $\{\epsilon_t\}_{t \in \mathbb{N}}$ and $\{\eta_t\}_{t \in \mathbb{N}}$ whose laws have bounded Lipschitz continuous densities with respect to the Lebesgue measure on $\mathbb{R}$ such that the sequences ψ^n $(n \in \mathbb{N})$ satisfy the stability conditions (4.26) and (4.27). Note that these regularity conditions involve the measure μ^* via the law $\mathbb{P}^*$. Of course, μ^* is stable whenever f and g are bounded away from zero.

In our present Markovian setting, Theorem 4.12 yields the following result.

Theorem 4.24 *Let* $(\{\xi_t\}_{t \in \mathbb{N}}, (\mathbb{P}_\xi)_{x \in M_1})$ *be a Markov chain on* $(\Omega, \mathcal{F})$ *with state space* M_1 *which is associated with a distance-diminishing random system with complete connections* $\Sigma = ((M_1, d_{M_1}), (M_2, \mathcal{M}_2), Z, v)$. *Assume that the sequence* $\{\xi_t\}_{t \in \mathbb{N}}$ *converges in law to a unique stationary measure* μ^* *and that the stochastic kernel* Z *from* M_1 *to* $\mathcal{M}_2$ *satisfies a uniform Lipschitz condition in the sense of Definition 2.32. Let* $f, g : M_1 \to \mathbb{R}$ *be Lipschitz continuous functions, and consider the environment*

$$\psi = \{(f(\xi_t)), g(\xi_t))\}_{t \in \mathbb{N}}.$$

If the unique invariant distribution μ^* *of the sequence* $\{\xi_t\}_{t \in \mathbb{N}}$ *is stable and satisfies*

$$-\infty \leq \int \log |f(\xi)| \mu^*(d\xi) < 0 \quad \text{and} \quad \int (\log |g(\xi)|)^+ \mu^*(d\xi) < \infty$$

then the finite dimensional distributions of the sequence $\{p_t(p, \psi)\}_{t \in \mathbb{N}}$ *under the measure* $\mathbb{P}_\xi$ $(\xi \in M_1)$ *converge weakly to the finite dimensional distributions of the unique stationary solution of (4.10) under the law* $\mathbb{P}^*(\cdot) = \int \mathbb{P}_\xi(\cdot)\mu^*(d\xi)$.

Proof: The assertion follows from Theorem 4.12 and form Proposition 4.23. □

4.1.3 Equilibrium Prices in a Non-Stationary Environment

We are now going to apply our results about the long run behaviour of linear recursive sequences in a "nice" environment in order to study the asymptotic behaviour of the stock price process in a financial market model with interacting agent.

Asymptotic Dynamics of Asset Prices driven by "Nice" Processes

In this subsection, we are going to analyze the long run behaviour of the asset price process in a financial market model with locally and globally interacting agents under the assumption that the sequence of temporary price equilibria $\{p_t\}_{t\in\mathbb{N}}$ obeys the log-linear relation

$$\log p_{t+1} = f(\tilde{\varrho}_{t+1}) \log p_t + g(\tilde{\varrho}_{t+1}) \qquad (t \in \mathbb{N}). \tag{4.57}$$

Here $f, g : \mathcal{M}(C) \to \mathbb{R}$ are measurable functions. Thus, the logarithmic price process $\{\log p_t\}_{t\in\mathbb{N}}$ may be viewed as a linear recursive sequence the random environment $\{(f(\tilde{\varrho}_{t+1}), g(\tilde{\varrho}_{t+1}))\}_{t\in\mathbb{N}}$; see Example 1.1 and Example 1.3.

Our aim is to state conditions which guarantee that the shifted sequence of temporary price equilibria $\{p_{T+t}\}_{t\in\mathbb{N}}$ converges in law to uniquely determined stationary process as $T \to \infty$. For this purpose, we assume that the following condition holds true.

Assumption 4.25 *The conditional law $\tilde{Q}(\varrho(x_t); \cdot)$ of the random variable $\tilde{\varrho}_t$ given the mood of the market $\varrho(x_t)$ at date t, is described by a stochastic kernel $\tilde{Q}$ on $\mathcal{M}(C)$ which satisfies a uniform Lipschitz condition in the sense of Definition 2.32.*

Remark 4.26 *In terms of the projection mapping $\mathrm{Pr} : \mathcal{M}_s(S) \to \mathbb{R}$ which assigns to a stationary random field μ on $(S, \mathcal{S})$ its marginal distribution at site 0, the conditional law of $\tilde{\varrho}_t$ takes the form $\tilde{Q}(\mathrm{Pr}(R(x_t)); \cdot)$.*

Theorem 4.27 *We assume that our Assumption 4.25 holds true.*

(i) Consider the financial market model with interacting agents in a deterministic environment analyzed in Chapter 2. If the macroscopic process $\{R(x_t)\}_{t\in\mathbb{N}}$ converges in the weak topology to a random field $\mu^* \in \mathcal{M}_s(S)$ and if the integrability conditions

$$\int \log |f(\varrho)| \tilde{Q}(\mathrm{Pr}(\mu^*); d\varrho) < 0 \quad \text{and} \quad \int (\log |g(\varrho)|)^+ \tilde{Q}(\mathrm{Pr}(\mu^*); d\varrho) < \infty$$

are satisfied, then the logarithmic price process $\{\log p_{t+T}\}_{t\in\mathbb{N}}$ converges in law to a uniquely determined stationary process $\{P^*_t\}_{t\in\mathbb{N}}$ as $T \to \infty$.

(ii) Consider the financial market model with interacting agents in a random environment analyzed in Chapter 3.1 and assume that the signal kernel Q from

$\mathcal{M}_s(S)$ to $\mathcal{E}$ satisfies a uniform Lipschitz condition. If the macroscopic process $\{R(x_t)\}_{t\in\mathbb{N}}$ converges in law to a unique probability measure μ^* on $\mathcal{M}_s(S)$ and if the integrability conditions

$$\int_{\mathcal{M}_s(S)} \int_{\mathcal{M}(C)} \log |f(\varrho)| \tilde{Q}(\Pr(\nu); d\varrho)\mu^*(d\nu) < 0,$$

and

$$\int_{\mathcal{M}_s(S)} \int_{\mathcal{M}(C)} (\log |g(\varrho)|)^+ \tilde{Q}(\Pr(\nu); d\varrho)\mu^*(d\nu) < \infty,$$

are satisfied, then the logarithmic price process $\{\log p_{t+T}\}_{t\in\mathbb{N}}$ converges in law to a uniquely determined stationary process $\{P_t^*\}_{t\in\mathbb{N}}$ as $T \to \infty$.

Proof:

(i) This assertion follows immediately from our strong law of large numbers for empirical fields established in Proposition 2.8 and from Lemma 2.34 as in Example 4.17.

(ii) Let $x \in S_0$, and let $\{\xi_t\}_{t\in\mathbb{N}}$ be the Markov chain defined on $(\Omega, \mathcal{F}, \mathbb{P}_{R(x)})$ with initial state $R(x)$ which is associated with the random system with complete connections Σ^* introduced in (3.19).

Consider the environment

$$\hat{\psi} = \{(f(\hat{\varrho}_{t+1}), g(\hat{\varrho}_{t+1}))\}_{t\in\mathbb{N}},$$

where $\{\hat{\varrho}_t\}_{t\in\mathbb{N}}$ is a stochastic process taking values in $\mathcal{M}(C)$.

For a fixed ξ_t, the law of the random variable $\hat{\varrho}_t$ is given by the probability measure $\hat{Q}(\xi_t; \cdot) := \tilde{Q}(\Pr(\xi_t); \cdot)$ on $\mathcal{M}(C)$. Since the process $\{\xi_t\}_{t\in\mathbb{N}}$ has the Feller property and converges in distribution to a unique stationary measure μ^* on $\mathcal{M}_s(S)$, the environment $\hat{\psi}$ is stationary and ergodic under the law

$$\mathbb{P}^*(\cdot) := \int_{\mathcal{M}_s(S)} \mathbb{P}_\xi(\cdot)\mu^*(d\xi).$$

Due to (2.99), the stochastic kernel $\hat{Q}$ from $\mathcal{M}_s(S)$ to $\mathcal{M}(C)$ satisfies a uniform Lipschitz condition, and so the environment $\hat{\psi}$ has a "nice" tail structure, due to Corollary 3.30. Thus, it follows from Theorem 4.9 that there exists a uniquely determined stationary process $\{P_t^*\}_{t\in\mathbb{N}}$ defined on $(\Omega, \mathcal{F}, \mathbb{P}^*)$ such that

$$\lim_{T\to\infty} \mathrm{Law}(\{p_{t+T}(p, \hat{\psi})\}_{t\in\mathbb{N}}, \mathbb{P}_{R(x)}) = \mathrm{Law}(\{P_t^*\}_{t\in\mathbb{N}}, \mathbb{P}^*). \tag{4.58}$$

Due to our Proposition 3.5, we have that

$$\text{Law}(\{(f(\tilde{\varrho}_{t+1}), g(\tilde{\varrho}_{t+1}))\}_{t\in\mathbb{N}}, \mathbb{P}_x) = \text{Law}(\{(f(\hat{\varrho}_{t+1}), g(\hat{\varrho}_{t+1}))\}_{t\in\mathbb{N}}, \mathbb{P}_{R(x)}).$$

This yields

$$\text{Law}(\{p_t(p,\psi)\}_{t\in\mathbb{N}}, \mathbb{P}_x) = \text{Law}(\{p_t(p,\hat{\psi})\}_{t\in\mathbb{N}}, \mathbb{P}_{R(x)}),$$

and so our assertion follows form (4.58).

□

Our Theorem 4.27 states conditions which ensure that the mood of the market drives the price process into a stationary regime as $t \to \infty$. Observe, however, that a uniform Lipschitz condition on the transition kernel $\tilde{Q}$ excludes the case $\tilde{Q}(\varrho;\cdot) = \delta_\varrho(\cdot)$. Without this additional smoothing effect, the random environment for the evolution of our price process does not necessarily have a "nice" tail structure.

In the next subsection, we will consider a situation where the agents have complete information about the average situation throughout the whole infinite system of all traders, i.e., we will analyze the case $\tilde{Q}(\varrho;\cdot) = \delta_\varrho(\cdot)$. We are going to formulate conditions which guarantee that the driving sequence $\{(f(\varrho(x_{t+1})), g(\varrho(x_{t+1})))\}_{t\in\mathbb{N}}$ can be approximated in law a sequence of "nice" processes. In this case, we are able to establish a local version of the convergence result, namely convergence of the finite-dimensional distributions of the process $\{p_t\}_{t\in\mathbb{N}}$.

Asymptotic Dynamics of Asset Prices Driven by "Almost Nice" Processes

In this subsection, we consider the model with locally and globally interacting agents in a random environment analyzed in Chapter 3.1. We assume that the stock price dynamics obey the log-linear equation

$$\log p_{t+1} = f(\varrho(x_{t+1}))\log p_t + g(\varrho(x_{t+1})) \qquad (t\in\mathbb{N}), \tag{4.59}$$

where $f, g : \mathcal{M}(C) \to \mathbb{R}$ are Lipschitz continuous functions. Thus, the logarithmic price process $\{\log p_t\}_{t\in\mathbb{N}}$ may be viewed as a linear recursive sequence the random environment $\{(f(\varrho(x_{t+1})), g(\varrho(x_{t+1})))\}_{t\in\mathbb{N}}$.

Our aim is to state conditions on the environment which guarantee that the finite dimensional distributions of the sequence of temporary price equilibria $\{p_t\}_{t\in\mathbb{N}}$ defined recursively by (4.59) converges weakly to the finite dimensional distributions of a uniquely determined stationary process.

To this end, we denote by $(\{\xi_t\}_{t\in\mathbb{N}}, (\mathbb{P}_\xi)_{\xi\in\mathcal{M}_s(S)})$ the Markov chain on $(\Omega, \mathcal{F})$ which is associated with the random system with complete connections Σ^* defined in (3.19) and introduce the environment

$$\hat{\psi} := \{(f(\Pr(\xi_{t+1})), g(\Pr(\xi_{t+1})))\}_{t\in\mathbb{N}}. \tag{4.60}$$

Here, the Lipschitz continuous projection mapping $\Pr : \mathcal{M}_s(S) \to \mathcal{M}(C)$ is defined in (1.31). For any $x \in S_0$, we have

$$\mathrm{Law}(\psi, \mathbb{P}_x) = \mathrm{Law}(\hat{\psi}, \mathbb{P}_{R(x)}), \tag{4.61}$$

due to our Proposition 3.5, and so

$$\mathrm{Law}(\{p_t(p,\psi)\}_{t\in\mathbb{N}}, \mathbb{P}_x) = \mathrm{Law}(\{p_t(p,\hat{\psi})\}_{t\in\mathbb{N}}, \mathbb{P}_{R(x)}). \tag{4.62}$$

The next result follows immediately from our Theorem 4.24.

Theorem 4.28 *Suppose that the Markov process $\{\xi_t\}_{t\in\mathbb{N}}$ on $\mathcal{M}_s(S)$ associated with the random system with complete connections Σ^* given by (3.19) converges in law to a unique measure μ^* on $\mathcal{M}_s(S)$ and that the integrability conditions*

$$\int_{\mathcal{M}_s(S)} \log|f(\Pr(\nu))|\mu^*(d\nu) < 0 \quad \text{and} \quad \int_{\mathcal{M}_s(S)} (\log|g(\Pr(\nu))|)^+\mu^*(d\nu) < \infty \tag{4.63}$$

hold true. If the "signal kernel" Q from $\mathcal{M}(S)$ to $\mathcal{E}$ satisfies a uniform Lipschitz condition and if the functions $f, g : \mathcal{M}(C) \to \mathbb{R}$ are Lipschitz continuous, then the environment $\{(f(\varrho(x_{t+1})), g(\varrho(x_{t+1})))\}_{t\in\mathbb{N}}$ can be approximated in law by a sequence $\{\psi^n\}_{n\in\mathbb{N}}$ of "nice" processes. If the stability conditions (4.26) and (4.27) are satisfied, then the finite dimensional distributions of our logarithmic security price process $\{\log p_{T+t}\}_{t\in\mathbb{N}}$ under the law $\mathbb{P}_x$ $(x \in S_0)$ converge weakly to the finite dimensional distributions of a uniquely determined stationary process as $T \to \infty$.

Example 4.29 *Consider the log-linear demand structure described by (1.4) together with (1.5) and (1.6), and let us analyze the long run dynamics of the price process induced by the interaction between fundamentalists and chartists under the assumption that the mood of the market is out-of equilibrium. The logarithmic price process is of the form (4.59) with*

$$f(\varrho(x_t)) := \frac{1 - c_f(\varrho_t^+ - \varrho_t^-) - c_c\varrho_t^0}{1 - c_n\varrho_t^0} \quad \text{and} \quad g(\varrho(x_t)) := \frac{c_f(\log L + \varrho_t^+ - \varrho_t^-)}{1 - c_n\varrho_t^0},$$

where ϱ_t^+, ϱ_t^- and ϱ_t^0 denotes the fraction of optimistic and pessimistic fundamentalists and of chartists, respectively, among all traders who are active on the market at date t. If $c_n < 1$, then the functions f and g depend in a Lipschitz continuous manner on the mood of the market. If, in addition, $c_f < 1$ and $|\log L| > 1$, then both f and g are bounded away from zero. Thus, if the macroscopic process $\{R(x_t)\}_{t\in\mathbb{N}}$ converges in law to a unique equilibrium, then the asset price process converges to a stationary regime whenever the destabilizing effects of the environment are on average not too strong.

4.2 Continuous-Time Models

A large part of mathematical finance is based on models with continuous-time security trading. Thus, it seems natural to study a diffusion approximation for the discrete-time price dynamics analyzed in Chapter 4.1. In this section, we will obtain a continuous-time asset price process $\{S_t\}_{t\geq 0}$ by passage to the limit from the discrete-time equilibrium price process $\{p_t\}$ defined recursively by

$$\log p_{t+1} - \log p_t = f(\tilde{\varrho}_{t+1}) \log p_t + g(\tilde{\varrho}_{t+1}) \qquad (t = 0, 1, 2, \ldots). \tag{4.64}$$

The convergence concept we use is weak convergence on the Skorohood space $\mathbb{D}^d$ of all $\mathbb{R}^d$-valued right-continuous functions with left limits on $[0, \infty)$, endowed with the weak topology.

In order to achieve our goal, we shall first consider a stochastic sequence $\{P_t\}_{t\in\mathbb{N}}$ defined recursively by the linear relation

$$P_{t+1} - P_t = A_t P_t + B_t \qquad (t = 0, 1, 2, \ldots) \tag{4.65}$$

in a random environment $\{(A_t, B_t)\}_{t\in\mathbb{N}}$. We analyze some case studies where, after suitable rescaling, the random environment $\{(A_t, B_t)\}_{t\in\mathbb{N}}$ for the evolution of process $\{P_t\}_{t\in\mathbb{N}}$ converges in law to a continuous diffusion process Z with deterministic drift vector B and with deterministic volatility matrix V. Assuming a certain "goodness" condition will allow us to derive a continuous-time limit $\{P_t\}_{t\geq 0}$ for the process $\{P_t\}_{t\in\mathbb{N}}$. Given that the environment is on average not too destabilizing, the process $\{P_t\}_{t\geq 0}$ becomes stationary in the long run, and its invariant measure can be computed explicitly.

In the Section 4.2.1, we concentrate on an ergodic reference model, i.e., we concentrate on a situation where the sequence $\{P_t\}_{t\in\mathbb{N}}$ evolves in a stationary and ergodic random environment thereby following an approach proposed by Föllmer and Schweizer (1993). In Section 4.2.2, we replace the stationarity assumption by an asymptotic stability condition on the random environment. We establish a functional central limit theorem for the process $\{P_t\}_{t\in\mathbb{N}}$ driven by a non-stationary sequence $\{(A_t, B_t)\}_{t\in\mathbb{N}}$ which has a "nice" tail structure. Armed with our results established in Sections 4.2.1 and 4.2.2, we derive in Section 4.2.3 a Black-Scholes type approximation for the asset price process defined by (4.64). In contrast to the model analyzed in Föllmer and Schweizer (1993), we study a sequence of temporary price equilibria which is driven by *endogenously* generated fluctuations in the mood of the market.

4.2.1 Continuous-Time Models in a Stationary Environment

In this section, we denote by $\psi = \{(A_t, B_t)\}_{t\in\mathbb{N}}$ an $\mathbb{R}^2$-valued *stationary and ergodic* sequence of random variables defined on some probability space $(\Omega, \mathcal{F}, \mathbb{P}^*)$. Our goal is to establish a diffusion approximation for the sequence $\{P_t\}_{t\in\mathbb{N}}$ defined recursively by the linear equation

$$P_{t+1} - P_t = A_t P_t + B_t \qquad (t \in \mathbb{N}) \tag{4.66}$$

in the random environment $\{(A_t, B_t)\}_{t\in\mathbb{N}}$. Below, we will use our results in order to show how the discrete-time price process governed by (4.64) may be approximated in law by a Black-Scholes type diffusion with deterministic volatility if the mood of the market is already in equilibrium.

Let us first introduce some notation. We denote by $\mathbb{E}^*$ the expectation with respect to the law $\mathbb{P}^*$ and put

$$\mu_A := \mathbb{E}^* A_0 \quad \text{and} \quad \mu_B := \mathbb{E}^* B_0.$$

For a given $n \in \mathbb{N}$, we introduce the continuous-time processes $\{A_t^n\}_{t\geq 0}$ and $\{B_t^n\}_{t\geq 0}$ by the relation

$$A_t^n := \frac{1}{\sqrt{n}} \sum_{k=0}^{[nt]} (A_k - \mu_A) \quad \text{and} \quad B_t^n := \frac{1}{\sqrt{n}} \sum_{k=0}^{[nt]} (B_k - \mu_B). \tag{4.67}$$

Under "standard assumptions" on the stationary and ergodic driving sequence ψ, we can apply an invariance principle to the stochastic processes $\{(A_t^n, B_t^n)\}_{t\geq 0}$ $(n \in \mathbb{N})$ and show that this sequence converges in law to a continuous Gaussian martingale:

$$\text{Law}(\{(A_t^n, B_t^n)\}_{t\geq 0}, \mathbb{P}_{\mu^*}) \xrightarrow{w} \text{Law}(V \cdot W, \mathbb{P}_{\mu^*}) \qquad (n \to \infty). \tag{4.68}$$

Here, $W = (W_1, W_2)$ is a 2-dimensional standard Brownian motion under $\mathbb{P}^*$. The dispersion matrix $V = (v_{i,j})_{i,j=1,2}$ takes the form

$$v_{1,1}^2 := \mathbb{E}^*[(A_0 - \mu_A)^2] + 2\sum_{t\geq 1} \mathbb{E}^*[(A_0 - \mu_A)(A_t - \mu_A)], \tag{4.69}$$

$$v_{2,2}^2 := \mathbb{E}^*[(B_0 - \mu_B)^2] + 2\sum_{t\geq 1} \mathbb{E}^*[(B_0 - \mu_B)(B_t - \mu_B)], \tag{4.70}$$

$$v_{1,2}^2 = v_{2,1}^2 := \mathbb{E}^*[(A_0 - \mu_A)(B_0 - \mu_B)] + \sum_{t\geq 1} \mathbb{E}^*[(A_t - \mu_A)(B_0 - \mu_B) + (B_t - \mu_B)(A_0 - \mu_A)]. \tag{4.71}$$

We refer to Billingsley (1968), Chapter 20 or to Jacod and Shiryayev (1987), Chapter VIII, Section 3, for a detailed discussion of the "standard assumptions" which guarantee convergence in distribution of the processes $\{(A_t^n, A_t^n)\}_{t\geq 0}$ $(n \in \mathbb{N})$. Below, we will consider two case studies where some of these assumptions can be verified.

Let us now introduce a drift vector B, so that, in the continuous-time limit, the dynamics of the random environment can be described by a diffusion process with deterministic drift vector B and with deterministic volatility matrix V. The canonical drift vector is $B := (\mu_A, \mu_B)$. For $n \in \mathbb{N}$, we define continuous-time processes $X^n = \{X_t^n\}_{t\geq 0}$ and $Y^n = \{Y_t^n\}_{t\geq 0}$ by the relation

$$X_t^n := \frac{1}{\sqrt{n}} \sum_{k=0}^{[nt]} \left\{ A_k - \mu_A + \frac{\mu_A}{\sqrt{n}} \right\}, \quad Y_t^n := \frac{1}{\sqrt{n}} \sum_{k=0}^{[nt]} \left\{ B_k - \mu_B + \frac{\mu_B}{\sqrt{n}} \right\} \tag{4.72}$$

and put $Z^n := (X^n, Y^n)$.

Theorem 4.30 *Under "standard assumptions" on the stationary and ergodic random environment* $\{(A_t, B_t)\}_{t\in\mathbb{N}}$ *we have that*

$$Law(Z^n, \mathbb{P}_{\mu^*}) \xrightarrow{w} Law(Z, \mathbb{P}_{\mu^*}). \tag{4.73}$$

Here, Z is a diffusion process which solves the stochastic differential equation

$$dZ_t = Bdt + VdW_t. \tag{4.74}$$

Proof: See, e.g., Chapter VIII in Jacod and Shiryayev (1987). □

Let us now consider two Markovian case studies where some these "standard assumptions" on the driving sequence ψ can indeed be verified.

Case Study I: "Lipschitz Continuous Environments"

Let $(\{\xi_t\}_{t\in\mathbb{N}}, (\mathbb{P}_\xi)_{\xi\in M})$ be the Markov chain on the compact state space M with transition operator U which is associated with a random system with complete connections. We consider an environment ψ of the form

$$\psi = \{(f(\xi_t), g(\xi_t))\}_{t\in\mathbb{N}},$$

where $f, g : M \to \mathbb{R}$ are Lipschitz continuous functions. We assume that the process $\{\xi_t\}_{t\in\mathbb{N}}$ has the Feller property and converges in law to a unique invariant measure μ^* as $t \to \infty$. Thus, the environment ψ is stationary and ergodic under the law

$$\mathbb{P}^*(\cdot) = \int \mathbb{P}_\xi(\cdot)\mu^*(d\xi).$$

For simplicity, we restrict our attention to the case $\mu_A = \mu_B = 0$.

In such a situation, we can apply Proposition A.9: There exists constants $L < \infty$ and $\alpha < 1$ such that

$$|\mathbb{E}^*[f(\xi_t)|\xi_0]| = |(U^t f)(\xi_0)| = |(U^t f)(\xi_0) - \mu_A| \leq L\alpha^t \qquad \mathbb{P}^*\text{-a.s.} \tag{4.75}$$

Here, U^t denotes the t-fold iteration of the transition operator U. Of course, the same relation holds true if we replace f by g, and so the series in (4.69)-(4.71) are almost surely absolutely convergent. Thus, (4.73) follows from Theorem VIII 3.79 in Jacod and Shiryayev (1987).

Case Study II: "Mixing Environments"

Let us now concentrate on a situation where the random environment ψ is generated by some underlying φ-mixing sequence $\{\hat{\varrho}_t\}_{t\in\mathbb{N}}$.

Definition 4.31 *Let $(X, \mathcal{X})$ be a measurable space and let $\zeta = \{\zeta_t\}_{t\in\mathbb{Z}}$ be a doubly infinite sequence of X-valued random variables defined on some probability space $(\Omega, \mathcal{F}, \mathbb{P})$. The sequence ζ is called **φ-mixing**, if $\lim_{n\to\infty}\varphi(n) = 0$. Here, the mixing coefficients $\varphi(n)$ are defined by*

$$\varphi(n) := \sup_{l\in\mathbb{Z}} \sup_{B\in\mathcal{G}_l, \hat{B}\in\hat{\mathcal{G}}_{l+n}} |\mathbb{P}(\hat{B}|B) - \mathbb{P}(\hat{B})|.$$

and $\mathcal{G}_l := \sigma(\{\zeta_i : i \leq l\})$, $\hat{\mathcal{G}}_l := \sigma(\{\zeta_i : i \geq l\})$.

More precisely, we consider an environment ψ which takes the form

$$\psi = \{(f(\hat{\varrho}), g(\hat{\varrho}))\}_{t\in\mathbb{N}},$$

Here, $f, g : M \to \mathbb{R}$ are measurable functions and $\{\hat{\varrho}\}_{t\in\mathbb{N}}$ denotes the smoothed Markov chain introduced in Example 4.18.

Our aim is now to show that the sequence $\{\hat{\varrho}_t\}_{t\in\mathbb{N}}$ is φ-mixing and that the environment ψ satisfies one of the "standard assumptions". The proof of the following lemma is a modification of an argument given in the proof of Proposition 2.2.11 in Iosefescu and Theodorescu (1968).

Lemma 4.32 *The sequence $\{\hat{\varrho}_t\}_{t\in\mathbb{N}}$ is φ-mixing both under $\mathbb{P}_\xi$ ($\xi \in M$) and under*

$$\mathbb{P}^*(\cdot) := \int \mathbb{P}_\xi(\cdot)\mu^*(d\xi).$$

There exists constants $L < \infty$ and $\alpha < 1$ such that the mixing coefficients satisfy the relation

$$\varphi(n) \le L\alpha^n \qquad (n \in \mathbb{N}). \tag{4.76}$$

Proof: For $l, n \in \mathbb{N}$, let us denote by $\text{Law}((\{\hat{\varrho}_t\}_{t\ge l+n}, \mathbb{P}_\xi)|\hat{\varrho}_1, \hat{\varrho}_2, \ldots, \hat{\varrho}_l)$ the conditional distribution of the sequence $\{\hat{\varrho}_t\}_{t\ge l+n}$ with respect to the measure $\mathbb{P}_\xi$, given the random variables $(\hat{\varrho}_1, \hat{\varrho}_2, \ldots, \hat{\varrho}_l)$. Due to the law of iterated conditional expectations, we have that

$$\text{Law}((\{\hat{\varrho}_t\}_{t\ge l+n}, \mathbb{P}_\xi)|\hat{\varrho}_1, \hat{\varrho}_2, \ldots, \hat{\varrho}_l) = \text{Law}(\{\hat{\varrho}_t\}_{t\ge n}, \mathbb{P}_{\xi_l}).$$

In particular, it follows from Lemma 3.29 and from Proposition A.9 that there exists a constant $\alpha < 1$ and some $L < \infty$ such that

$$\begin{aligned}
& \|\text{Law}((\{\hat{\varrho}_t\}_{t\ge n+l}, \mathbb{P}_\xi)|\hat{\varrho}_1, \hat{\varrho}_2, \ldots, \hat{\varrho}_l) - \text{Law}(\{\hat{\varrho}_t\}_{t\ge n+l}, \mathbb{P}_\xi)\| \\
= \ & \sup_B \left|(U^n\mathbb{P}_\bullet[\{\hat{\varrho}_t\}_{t\in\mathbb{N}} \in B])(\xi_l) - (U^{n+l}\mathbb{P}_\bullet[\{\hat{\varrho}_t\}_{t\in\mathbb{N}} \in B])(\xi)\right| \\
\le \ & L\alpha^n \qquad \mathbb{P}_\xi\text{-a.s.}
\end{aligned}$$

From this it is easily seen that

$$|\mathbb{P}_\xi(\hat{B}|B) - \mathbb{P}_\xi(\hat{B})| \le L\alpha^n \tag{4.77}$$

for all $\hat{B} \in \sigma(\{\hat{\varrho}_i : i \ge l+n\})$ and all $B \in \sigma(\{\hat{\varrho}_i : i \le l\})$ satisfying $\mathbb{P}_\xi(B) > 0$. This establishes $\varphi(n) \le L\alpha^n$ in the non-stationary situation. The mixing property under the law $\mathbb{P}^*$ follows from (4.77) and from the definition of $\mathbb{P}^*$. □

Corollary 4.33 *If the random variables $f(\hat{\varrho}_0)$ and $g(\hat{\varrho}_0)$ have finite variance under the law $\mathbb{P}^*$, then the convergence result (4.73) holds true.*

Proof: The assertion follows from our Lemma 4.76 and form (2.58) and (2.59) in Billingsley (1968). □

A Continuous-Time Approximation for the Process $\{P_t\}_{t\in\mathbb{N}}$

We are now going to demonstrate how one may obtain a continuous-time approximation for the linear recursive equation $\{P_t\}_{t\in\mathbb{N}}$ governed by (4.66) in the random environment $\{(A_t, B_t)\}_{t\in\mathbb{N}}$. To this end, we follow an approach proposed by Föllmer and Schweizer (1993). For any $n \in \mathbb{N}$, we consider the discrete-time process $\{P_k^n\}_{k\in\mathbb{N}}$ given by

$$P_{k+1}^n - P_k^n = \frac{1}{\sqrt{n}}\left(A_k - \mu_A + \frac{\mu_A}{\sqrt{n}}\right) P_k^n + \frac{1}{\sqrt{n}}\left(B_k - \mu_B + \frac{\mu_B}{\sqrt{n}}\right). \tag{4.78}$$

We identify the discrete-time process $\{P_k^n\}_{k\in\mathbb{N}}$ with the continuous-time process $\{P_t^n\}_{t\geq 0}$, $P_t^n := P_{[nt]}^n$ $(0 \leq t < \infty)$. In terms the quantities X^n and Y^n defined in (4.72) our relation (4.78) is equivalent to the stochastic differential equation

$$dP_t^n = P_{t-}^n dX_t^n + dY_t^n. \tag{4.79}$$

Our goal is now to obtain a convergence result for the processes $\{P^n\}_{n\in\mathbb{N}}$. This will be achieved by applying an invariance principle to the processes X^n and Y^n $(n \in \mathbb{N})$ and under the assumption that the sequence $\{Z^n\}_{n\in\mathbb{N}} = \{(X^n, Y^n)\}_{n\in\mathbb{N}}$ is "good" in the sense of the following definition.

Definition 4.34 *(Duffie and Protter (1992)) A sequence $\{Z^n\}_{n\in\mathbb{N}}$ of semimartingales defined on probability spaces $(\Omega^n, \mathcal{F}^n, \mathbb{P}^n)$ is called* ***"good"*** *if, for any sequence $\{H^n\}_{n\in\mathbb{N}}$ of càdlàg adapted processes, the convergence*

$$\text{Law}((Z^n, H^n), \mathbb{P}^n) \xrightarrow{w} \text{Law}((Z, H), \mathbb{P}) \qquad (n \to \infty)$$

implies the convergence

$$\text{Law}\left(\left(Z^n, H^n, \int H_-^n dZ^n\right), \mathbb{P}^n\right) \xrightarrow{w} \text{Law}\left(\left(Z, H, \int H_- dZ\right), \mathbb{P}\right) \qquad (n \to \infty).$$

The next result appears as Theorems 3.1 and 4.2 in Föllmer and Schweizer (1993).

Theorem 4.35 *Suppose that the sequence of semimartingales $\{(X^n, Y^n)\}_{n\in\mathbb{N}}$ introduced in (4.72) is "good" in the sense of Definition 4.34 and that the process $\{(X^n, Y^n)\}_{n\in\mathbb{N}}$ converges in distribution to the continuous diffusion process Z which solves to stochastic differential equation (4.74).*

(i) The sequence $\{(X^n, Y^n, P^n)\}_{n\in\mathbb{N}}$ converges in law to (X, Y, P). Here, $P = \{P_t\}_{t\geq 0}$ is the unique strong solution of the stochastic differential equation

$$dP_t = P_{t-}dX_t + dY_t. \tag{4.80}$$

The semimartingale $\{(X_t, Y_t)\}_{t\geq 0}$ takes the from $(X_t, Y_t) = Bt + VW_t$ $(t \geq 0)$ with the deterministic drift vector $B = (\mu_A, \mu_B)$ and with the deterministic dispersion matrix V defined by (4.69)-(4.71).

(ii) The process $\{P_t\}_{t\geq 0}$ converges pathwise to a stationary process $\{P_t^*\}_{t\geq 0}$ as $t \to \infty$ if $\mu_f < \frac{1}{2}\sigma_f^2$, i.e., if the random environment Z is on average not too destabilizing.

Remark 4.36 *If the destabilizing effects of the random environment are on average not too strong, then one can give an explicit formulae for the density of the invariant distribution of the continuous-time process $\{P_t\}_{t\geq 0}$; see, e.g., Theorem 5.1 in Föllmer and Schweizer (1993).*

Let us now concentrate on a case study where we can verify that the sequence of semimartingales $\{Z^n\}_{n\in\mathbb{N}} = \{(X^n, Y^n)\}_{n\in\mathbb{N}}$ is indeed "good".

Proposition 4.37 *Let the environment $\psi = \{(f(\hat{\varrho}_{t+1}), g(\hat{\varrho}_{t+1}))\}_{t\in\mathbb{N}}$ be as in Example 4.18. Then the sequence $\{Z^n\}_{n\in\mathbb{N}}$ of semimartingales is "good" in the sense of Duffie and Protter (1992).*

Proof: In order to show that the sequence $\{Z^n\}_{n\in\mathbb{N}}$ is "good", we have to find a suitable semimartingale decomposition of the processes Z^n $(n \in \mathbb{N})$. Without loss of generality we may restrict ourselves to the case $\mu_A = \mu_B = 0$.

Following Ethier and Kurtz (1986) and Duffie and Protter (1992), we introduce the σ-fields

$$\mathcal{G}_t := \sigma\left(\{f(\hat{\varrho}_i), g(\hat{\varrho}_i)\} : 0 \leq i \leq t\right) \qquad (t \in \mathbb{N})$$

and the processes $M = \{M_t\}_{t\in\mathbb{N}}$ and $A = \{A_t\}_{t\in\mathbb{N}}$ given by

$$M_t := \begin{pmatrix} \sum_{k=0}^{t} f(\hat{\varrho}_k) + \sum_{k=0}^{\infty} \mathbb{E}^*\left[f(\hat{\varrho}_{k+t})|\mathcal{G}_t\right] \\ \sum_{k=0}^{t} g(\hat{\varrho}_k) + \sum_{k=0}^{\infty} \mathbb{E}^*\left[g(\hat{\varrho}_{k+t})|\mathcal{G}_t\right] \end{pmatrix} \tag{4.81}$$

and

$$A_t := \begin{pmatrix} \sum_{k=0}^{\infty} \mathbb{E}^* [f(\hat{\varrho}_{k+t})|\mathcal{G}_t] \\ \sum_{k=0}^{\infty} \mathbb{E}^* [g(\hat{\varrho}_{k+t})|\mathcal{G}_t] \end{pmatrix}. \tag{4.82}$$

Since the sequence $\{\hat{\varrho}_t\}_{t\in\mathbb{N}}$ is φ-mixing under the law $\mathbb{P}^*$ and because the mixing coefficients satisfy (4.76), the series in (4.81) and (4.82) are almost surely absolutely convergent; see, e.g., Ethier and Kurtz (1986), p. 351. Furthermore, M is a vector of square integrable martingales with respect to the measure $\mathbb{P}^*$ and the filtration $\{\mathcal{G}_t\}_{t\in\mathbb{N}}$. In terms of the quantities

$$M^n = \{M_{[nt]}\}_{t\geq 0}, \qquad \text{and} \qquad A^n = \{A_{[nt]}\}_{t\geq 0}$$

we consider the following decomposition:

$$Z_t^n \;=\; \frac{1}{\sqrt{n}} M_t^n - \frac{1}{\sqrt{n}} A_t^n \qquad (t \geq 0). \tag{4.83}$$

According to Theorem 4.3 in Duffie and Protter (1992), the sequence $\{Z^n\}_{n\in\mathbb{N}}$ is "good" as soon as the following condition is satisfied ("Condition B"):

$$\sup_{n\in\mathbb{N}}\{\mathbb{E}^* [\sup_{t\leq T} |\Delta M_t^n|]\} < \infty \qquad \text{and} \qquad \sup_{n\in\mathbb{N}}\{\mathbb{E}^* [|A^n|_T]\} < \infty.$$

Here, $|A_T^n|$ denotes the total variation of the process A^n on the time interval $[0, T]$ and $\Delta M_t^n := M_t^n - M_{t-}^n$. Obviously, the martingale M^n has uniformly bounded expected jumps. Using standard estimates provided in Duffie and Protter (1992), Example 6.3, it follows that

$$\sup_{n\in\mathbb{N}}\{\mathbb{E}^* [|A^n|_T]\} < \infty.$$

Thus, "Condition B" is satisfied, and so the sequence $\{Z^n\}_{n\in\mathbb{N}}$ is "good". □

4.2.2 Continuous-Time Models in a Non-stationary Environment

In the previous subsection, we derived a diffusion approximation for a linear recursive equation $\{P_t\}_{t\in\mathbb{N}}$ governed by (4.66) using a functional central limit theorem for stationary and ergodic processes. In this section, we shall replace this stationarity condition on the environment by an asymptotic stability assumption.

To this end, let $\psi = \{(A_t, B_t)\}_{t\in\mathbb{N}}$ be a sequence of $\mathbb{R}^2$-valued random variables defined on some probability space $(\Omega, \mathcal{F}, \mathbb{P})$. For any $n \in \mathbb{N}$, we consider a discrete-time process $\{P_t^n\}_{t\in\mathbb{N}}$ given by the linear relation

$$P_{t+1}^n - P_t^n = \frac{1}{\sqrt{n}} A_t P_t^n + \frac{1}{\sqrt{n}} B_t \qquad (t \in \mathbb{N}). \tag{4.84}$$

Our goal is to obtain a convergence result for the processes $\{P^n\}_{n\in\mathbb{N}}$ given that the driving sequence ψ is out of equilibrium, i.e., is a non-stationary sequence. Instead, we assume that the environment becomes stationary in the long run.

Assumption 4.38 *(i) The sequence ψ has a "nice" tail structure in the sense of Definition 4.5.*

(ii) We have $\mathbb{E}^* A_0 = \mathbb{E}^* B_0 = 0$, where $\mathbb{E}^*$ denotes the expectation with respect to the law $\mathbb{P}^*$.

(iii) Under the law $\mathbb{P}^*$ an invariance principle can be applied to the processes

$$X_t^n := \frac{1}{\sqrt{n}} \sum_{i=0}^{[nt]} A_i \quad \text{and} \quad Y_t^n := \frac{1}{\sqrt{n}} \sum_{i=0}^{[nt]} B_i \qquad (t \geq 0). \tag{4.85}$$

induced by the two sources of randomness $\{A_t\}_{t\in\mathbb{N}}$ and $\{B_t\}_{t\in\mathbb{N}}$.

The following Theorem shows that an invariance principle can be applied to the non-stationary sequences $\{X^n\}_{n\in\mathbb{N}}$ and $\{Y^n\}_{n\in\mathbb{N}}$ whenever our Assumption 4.38 is satisfied. Thus, we have a convergence result for the processes $\{P^n\}_{n\in\mathbb{N}}$ whenever the sequence $\{(X^n, Y^n)\}_{n\in\mathbb{N}}$ is "good".

Theorem 4.39 *If the driving sequence $\{(A_t, B_t)\}_{t\in\mathbb{N}}$ for the process $\{P_t\}_{t\in\mathbb{N}}$ satisfies Assumption 4.38, then the following holds true:*

(i) The sequence of processes $\{Z^n\}_{n\in\mathbb{N}} = \{(X^n, Y^n)\}_{n\in\mathbb{N}}$ converges in distribution to the Gaussian martingale $(X, Y) = VW$. Here, $W = (W_1, W_2)$ is a 2-dimensional standard Brownian motion under the law $\mathbb{P}^*$ and V is a deterministic volatility matrix defined by analogy with (4.69)-(4.71).

(ii) If the sequence $\{Z^n\}_{n\in\mathbb{N}}$ is "good" in the sense of Duffie and Protter (1992), then the sequence of processes $\{P^n\}_{n\in\mathbb{N}}$ converges in distribution to the unique strong solution of the stochastic differential equation

$$dP_t = P_{t-} dX_t + dY_t.$$

Proof: In order to verify our assertion, we proceed in several steps.

1. Due to our Assumption 4.38, we know that

$$\text{Law}(Z^n, \mathbb{P}^*) \xrightarrow{w} \text{Law}(VW, \mathbb{P}^*) \qquad (n \to \infty).$$

2. We shall now use the "nice" tail structure of the driving sequence $\{(A_t, B_t)\}_{t\in\mathbb{N}}$ and show that the sequences $\{X^n\}_{n\in\mathbb{N}}$ and $\{Y^n\}_{n\in\mathbb{N}}$ satisfy an invariance principle under the original measure $\mathbb{P}$. More precisely, we are going to verify that

$$\text{Law}(Z^n, \mathbb{P}) \xrightarrow{w} \text{Law}(VW, \mathbb{P}^*) \qquad (n \to \infty). \tag{4.86}$$

To this end, let $\{\sigma_n\}_{n\in\mathbb{N}}$ be a sequence of real numbers such that $\sigma_n \uparrow \infty$ and such that $\sigma_n/\sqrt{n} \to 0$ as $n \to \infty$. For a given "time horizon" $T > 0$ and for each $n \in \mathbb{N}$, we introduce the two-dimensional process $\{\widetilde{Z}_t^n\}_{0\leq t\leq T}$ given by

$$\widetilde{Z}_t^n := \begin{cases} \frac{1}{\sqrt{n}} \sum_{i=\sigma_n}^{[nt]} (A_i, B_i) & \text{if } \frac{\sigma_n}{\sqrt{n}} \leq t \leq T \\ 0 & \text{otherwise} \end{cases}$$

and denote by $d_0(\cdot,\cdot)$ the Skorohood metric[1] on the space $\mathbb{D}_{\mathbb{R}^2}[0,T]$. Note that

$$d_0(Z^n, \widetilde{Z}^n) \leq \frac{\sigma_n}{\sqrt{n}} \left| \left(\frac{1}{\sigma_n} \sum_{i=0}^{\sigma_n} |A_i|, \frac{1}{\sigma_n} \sum_{i=0}^{\sigma_n} |B_i| \right) \right|. \tag{4.87}$$

Since $\mathbb{P} = \mathbb{P}^*$ on the tail-field generated by the sequence $\{(A_t, B_t)\}_{t\in\mathbb{N}}$ and because the environment $\{(A_t, B_t)\}_{t\in\mathbb{N}}$ is ergodic under the law $\mathbb{P}^*$, the series

$$\frac{1}{\sigma_n} \sum_{i=0}^{\sigma_n} |A_i| \quad \text{and} \quad \frac{1}{\sigma_n} \sum_{i=0}^{\sigma_n} |B_i|$$

are $\mathbb{P}$- and $\mathbb{P}^*$-almost surely convergent as $n \to \infty$. Since $\lim_{n\to\infty} \frac{\sigma_n}{\sqrt{n}} = 0$ we obtain that

$$\lim_{n\to\infty} d_0(Z^n, \widetilde{Z}^n) = 0 \qquad \mathbb{P}\text{-a.s. and } \mathbb{P}^*\text{-a.s.} \tag{4.88}$$

Observe now that the event $\{\widetilde{Z}^n \in B\}$ $(B \in \mathcal{B}(\mathbb{D}_{\mathbb{R}^2}[0,T]))$ belongs to the σ-algebra $\sigma(\{\psi_i : i \geq \sigma_n\})$. Thus, since the environment has a "nice" tail structure, there exists a sequence $\{c_n\}_{n\in\mathbb{N}}$, $c_n \downarrow 0$ as $n \to \infty$ such that

$$\sup_B \left| \mathbb{P}[\widetilde{Z}^n \in B] - \mathbb{P}^*[\widetilde{Z}^n \in B] \right| \leq c_n. \tag{4.89}$$

3. Let us now denote by Q^* the law of the Gaussian martingale VW under the measure $\mathbb{P}^*$. By Step 1 above we know that

$$\lim_{n\to\infty} \mathbb{P}^*[Z^n \in B] = Q^*[B] \quad \text{for any } Q^*\text{-continuous set } B \in \mathcal{B}(\mathbb{D}_{\mathbb{R}^2}[0,T]).$$

[1] For the definition of d_0 see, e.g., Billingsley (1968), p. 113.

Thus, due to (4.88) and due to Theorem 4.2 in Billingsley (1968), we have that

$$\lim_{n\to\infty} \mathbb{P}^*[\widetilde{Z}^n \in B] = Q^*[B] \quad \text{for any } Q^*\text{-continuous set } B \in \mathcal{B}(\mathbb{D}_{\mathbb{R}^2}[0,T]).$$

Using (4.89) we see that

$$\lim_{n\to\infty} \mathbb{P}[\widetilde{Z}^n \in B] = Q^*[B] \quad \text{for any } Q^*\text{-continuous set } B \in \mathcal{B}(\mathbb{D}_{\mathbb{R}^2}[0,T]).$$

Therefore, (4.88) and Theorem 4.2 in Billingsley (1968) imply that

$$\text{Law}(Z^n, \mathbb{P}) \xrightarrow{w} \text{Law}(VW, \mathbb{P}^*) \qquad (n \to \infty). \tag{4.90}$$

Convergence in distribution of the process $\{P^n\}_{n\in\mathbb{N}}$ follows from "goodness" of the sequence $\{Z^n\}_{n\in\mathbb{N}}$. This proves our assertion. □

Let us now consider our standard Markovian model. In this case, our Assumption 4.38 can be indeed verified.

Example 4.40 *Let us return to the environment*

$$\psi = \{(f(\hat{\varrho}_t), g(\hat{\varrho}_t))\}_{t\in\mathbb{N}}$$

analyzed in Example 4.18 and assume that $\mathbb{E}^* f(\hat{\varrho}_0) = \mathbb{E}^* g(\hat{\varrho}_0) = 0$. *The driving sequence* ψ *has a "nice" tail structure, due to Corollary 3.30, and it follows from Lemma 4.32 that our Assumption 4.38 (iii) is satisfied if the random variables* $f(\hat{\varrho}_0)$ *and* $g(\hat{\varrho}_0)$ *have finite variance under the law* $\mathbb{P}^*$.

We are now going to show that the sequence of semimartingales $\{(X^n, Y^n)\}_{n\in\mathbb{N}}$ *defined on* $(\Omega, \mathcal{F}, \mathbb{P}_\xi)$ *is "good". To this end, we consider the decomposition given by (4.83) with* $\mathbb{E}^*$ *replaced by* $\mathbb{E}_\xi$, *the expectation with respect to the law* $\mathbb{P}_\xi$. *For a given* $n \in \mathbb{N}$, *the total variation of the process* $\frac{1}{\sqrt{n}} A^n$ *on the compact time interval* $[0,T]$ *is bounded above by*

$$\frac{1}{n}\sum_{t=0}^{[nT]} \left| \left(\sum_{k=0}^{\infty} |\mathbb{E}_\xi[f(\hat{\varrho}_{k+[nt]})|\mathcal{F}_{[nt]}]|, \sum_{k=0}^{\infty} |\mathbb{E}_\xi[g(\hat{\varrho}_{k+[nt]})|\mathcal{F}_{[nt]}]| \right) \right|.$$

Due to the mixing properties of the sequences $\{\hat{\varrho}_t\}_{t\in\mathbb{N}}$ *in the non-stationary situation established in Lemma 4.32, we have* $\mathbb{P}_\xi$*-a.s. that*

$$|\mathbb{E}_\xi[f(\hat{\varrho}_{k+t})|\mathcal{F}_t]| \le L\alpha^k \quad \textit{and} \quad |\mathbb{E}_\xi[g(\hat{\varrho}_{k+t})|\mathcal{F}_t]| \le L\alpha^k \qquad (t \in \mathbb{N})$$

for some constants $L < \infty$ *and* $\alpha < 1$. *Thus, the processes* A^n $(n \in \mathbb{N})$ *have uniformly bounded expected total variation on compact time intervals, and so "Condition B" in Duffie and Protter (1992) is satisfied, i.e., the sequence* $\{(X^n, Y^n)\}_{n\in\mathbb{N}}$ *is "good".*

4.2.3 Diffusion Approximation of the Price Process in a Financial Market Model with Interacting Agents – Some Case Studies

Armed with our convergence results established in Theorems 4.35 and 4.39 we are now ready to derive a diffusion approximation for the discrete-time asset price process $\{p_t\}_{t\in\mathbb{N}}$ defined recursively by the log-linear relation (4.64). We consider the financial market model with interacting agents in a random environment analyzed in Chapter 3.1 and let the assumptions of Theorem 3.7 be satisfied. Thus, we assume that the interaction between different agents is not too strong and that the "signal kernel" Q from $\mathcal{M}_s(S)$ to $\mathcal{E}$ satisfies a uniform Lipschitz and a Doeblin-type condition. In this case, our macroscopic process $\{R(x_t)\}_{t\in\mathbb{N}}$ converges in law to a unique equilibrium μ^* on $\mathcal{M}_s(S)$, due to Theorem 3.10.

Diffusion Approximation in a Stationary Environment

In this subsection, we analyze a stationary reference model. If the measure μ^* is concentrated on the set $\mathcal{M}_0(S)$, then there exists a random field $\tilde{\mu}$ on $(S, \mathcal{S})$ such that both the microscopic and the macroscopic process are stationary under the law $\mathbb{P}_{\tilde{\mu}}$; cf. Theorem 3.17. In such a situation, the sequence $\{x_t\}_{t\in\mathbb{N}}$ generates a stationary environment for the evolution of the price process.

Let us first assume that $f, g : \mathcal{M}(C) \to \mathbb{R}$ are Lipschitz continuous functions and consider a driving sequence ψ of the form

$$\psi = \{(f(\varrho(x_{t+1})), g(\varrho(x_{t+1})))\}_{t\in\mathbb{N}}.$$

In terms of the projection mapping $\Pr : \mathcal{M}_s(S) \to \mathcal{M}(C)$ which assigns to a stationary random field μ on S its marginal distribution at site 0, we can rewrite this as

$$\psi = \{(f(\Pr(R(x_{t+1}))), g(\Pr(R(x_{t+1}))))\}_{t\in\mathbb{N}}.$$

Since our macroscopic process $\{R(x_t)\}_{t\in\mathbb{N}}$ may be viewed as the Markov chain associated with the random system with complete connections Σ^* defined in (3.19) and because the projection mapping Pr from $\mathcal{M}_s(S)$ to $\mathcal{M}(C)$ is Lipschitz continuous, we can apply an invariance principle to the processes X^n and Y^n ($n \in \mathbb{N}$) given by

$$X_t^n = \frac{1}{\sqrt{n}} \sum_{i=1}^{[nt]} f(\varrho(x_i)) \quad \text{and} \quad Y_t^n = \frac{1}{\sqrt{n}} \sum_{i=1}^{[nt]} g(\varrho(x_i)).$$

If the sequence $\{(X^n, Y^n)\}_{n\in\mathbb{N}}$ is "good" in the sense of Duffie and Protter (1992), then we can apply Theorem 4.35. In this case, we obtain a convergence result for the sequence of continuous-time processes $\{P^n\}_{n\in\mathbb{N}}$ defined by analogy with (4.79). Our discrete-time stock price process $\{p_t\}_{t\in\mathbb{N}}$ can then be approximated in law by a diffusion process $\{S_t\}_{t\geq 0}$. The price process $\{S_t\}_{t\geq 0}$ takes the form

$$S_t = S_0 \exp(P_t - P_0),$$

where $\{P_t\}_{t\geq 0}$ solves the stochastic differential equation

$$dP_t = P_{t-} dX_t + dY_t. \tag{4.91}$$

Here, the continuous-time process $(X, Y) = \{(X_t, Y_t)\}_{t\geq 0}$ is of the from $(X_t, Y_t) = Bt + VW_t$ with the deterministic volatility matrix V defined by analogy with (4.69)-(4.71) and with a 2-dimensional standard Brownian motion $W = (W_t)_{t\geq 0}$.

Let us now consider a situation where our price process obeys the log-linear relation

$$\log p_{t+1} - \log p_t = f(\tilde{\varrho}_{t+1}) \log p_t + g(\tilde{\varrho}_{t+1}) \tag{4.92}$$

for arbitrary measurable functions $f, g : \mathcal{M}(C) \to \mathbb{R}$ which are not necessarily Lipschitz continuous. We assume that the following condition holds true.

Assumption 4.41 *(i) The conditional law $\tilde{Q}(\varrho(x_t); \cdot)$ of the random variable $\tilde{\varrho}_t$ given the present mood of the market $\varrho(x_t)$, is described by a stochastic kernel $\tilde{Q}$ on $\mathcal{M}(C)$ which satisfies a uniform Lipschitz condition.*

(ii) The random variables $f(\tilde{\varrho}_1)$ and $g(\tilde{\varrho}_1)$ have finite variance.

Under our Assumption 4.41 the sequence $\{\tilde{\varrho}_t\}_{t\in\mathbb{N}}$ is φ-mixing both in the stationary and in the non-stationary situation, due to Lemma 4.32 and Proposition 3.4. Thus, we can apply and invariance principle to the processes

$$X_t^n = \frac{1}{\sqrt{n}} \sum_{i=1}^{[nt]} f(\tilde{\varrho}_i) \quad \text{and} \quad Y_t^n = \frac{1}{\sqrt{n}} \sum_{i=1}^{[nt]} g(\tilde{\varrho}_i). \tag{4.93}$$

Moreover, the semimartingale $\{(X^n, Y^n)\}$ is "good" in the sense of Duffie and Protter (1992), due to Proposition 4.37. Thus, the sequence of temporary price equilibria $\{p_t\}_{t\in\mathbb{N}}$ defined by the log-linear relation (4.92) can be approximated in law by the diffusion process $\{S_t\}_{t\geq 0}$ for arbitrary measurable functions $f, g : \mathcal{M}(C) \to \mathbb{R}$.

Diffusion Approximation in a Non-Stationary Environment

Let us now weaken the regularity assumption that the microscopic process generates a stationary environment for the evolution of the stock price process. To this end, we assume that our asset price process $\{p_t\}_{t\in\mathbb{N}}$ obeys the log-linear relation (4.92) and that Assumption 4.41 is satisfied.

In this case, the environment $\psi = \{(f(\tilde{\varrho}_{t+1}), g(\tilde{\varrho}_{t+1}))\}_{t\in\mathbb{N}}$ has a "nice" asymptotic behaviour, and so an invariance principle can be applied to the processes X^n and Y^n ($n \in \mathbb{N}$) defined in (4.93) also in the non-stationary situation, due to Theorem 4.39. For any starting point $x \in S_0$ of our microscopic process $\{x_t\}_{t\in\mathbb{N}}$, it follows from Proposition 4.37 that the sequence of semimartingales $\{(X^n, Y^n)\}$ is "good". Thus, our logarithmic price process can again be approximated in law by a continuous diffusion process of the form (4.91).

4.3 Numerical Simulations

Let us now consider some numerical simulations of aggregate behaviour in a financial market model with interacting agents in a random environment. For our financial market model, we have sufficient conditions which ensure that the mood of the market becomes stationary in the long run. Nevertheless, our simulations show that the sequence of empirical distributions $\{\varrho(x_t)\}_{t\in\mathbb{N}}$ may exhibit large and sudden fluctuations. These fluctuations do not necessarily reflect rational adjustments to new economic fundamentals. They may be due to a distinct herd behaviour. Small changes in the external economic conditions may have a lasting effect on the present mood of the market and may therefore lead to large and sudden price overreactions, i.e., to bubbles or crashes.

We assume that only optimistic and pessimistic information traders are active on the market and consider the log-linear demand structure described by (1.4) together with (1.5). In this case, the mood of the market at date t is uniquely determined by the fraction ϱ_t^+ of optimistic information traders who are involved in the formation of equilibrium prices. The empirical average $m_t = m(x_t)$ induced by the configuration $x_t \in S_0$ is of the form $m_t = 2\varrho_t^+ - 1$. Thus, the logarithmic equilibrium price $\log p_t$ at time t is given by

$$\log p_t = \log p_{t-1} + c_f(L + m_t + \log p_{t-1}).$$

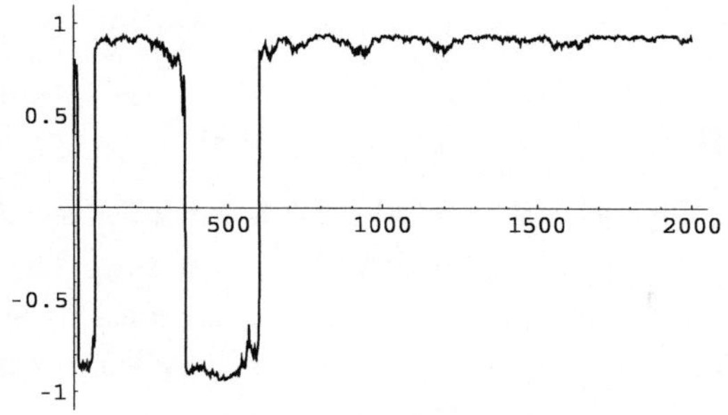

Figure 4.1: Evolution of the Empirical Average; Less Volatile External Field.

The dynamics of the signal sequence $\{e_t\}_{t\in\mathbb{N}}$ takes the form

$$e_{t+1} = m_t + \epsilon_t,$$

and the dynamics of the external conditions $\{h_t\}_{t\in\mathbb{N}}$ is modeled by a random walk:

$$h_{t+1} = h_t + \eta_t.$$

Here, $\{\epsilon_t\}_{t\in\mathbb{N}}$ and $\{\eta_t\}_{t\in\mathbb{N}}$ are sequences of independent and normally distributed random variables with zero mean.

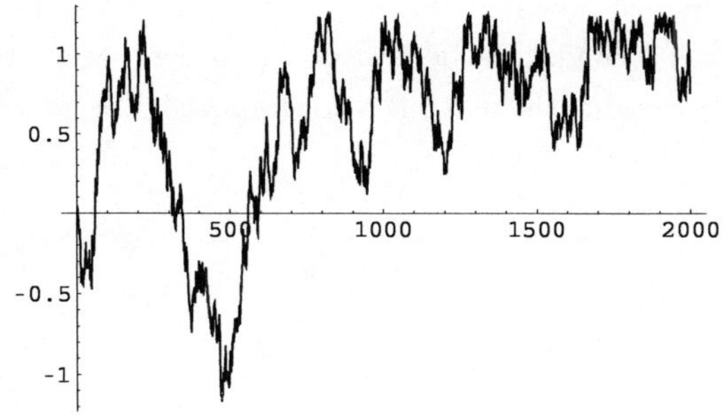

Figure 4.2: Dynamics of Economic Fundamentals.

We consider a simple mean-field model and specify the conditional choice probabilities as

$$\pi^a_{e,h}(x;\pm 1) = \frac{\exp\{\pm\frac{3}{4}(e + \frac{1}{4}x^a + \frac{1}{4}h)\}}{2\cosh\{\pm\frac{3}{4}(e + \frac{1}{4}x^a + \frac{1}{4}h)\}}.$$

In this case, the sequence $\{\varrho_t^+\}_{t\in\mathbb{N}}$ follows almost surely the deterministic dynamics

$$\varrho_{t+1}^+ \;=\; \varrho_t^+ \frac{\exp\{\frac{3}{4}(e+\frac{1}{4}+\frac{1}{4}h)\}}{2\cosh\{\frac{3}{4}(e+\frac{1}{4}+\frac{1}{4}h)\}} + (1-\varrho_t^+)\frac{\exp\{\frac{3}{4}(e-\frac{1}{4}+\frac{1}{4}h)\}}{2\cosh\{\frac{3}{4}(e-\frac{1}{4}+\frac{1}{4}h)\}}.$$

Figures 4.1 and 4.4 show the evolution of the empirical average if the volatility of the external conditions is small and large, respectively. The mood of the market is subject to large and sudden fluctuations. Of course, these fluctuations are transferred to the asset price process, and so a sudden shift in the sentiment of investors may lead to a stock market crash. If the market is sufficiently enthusiastic,

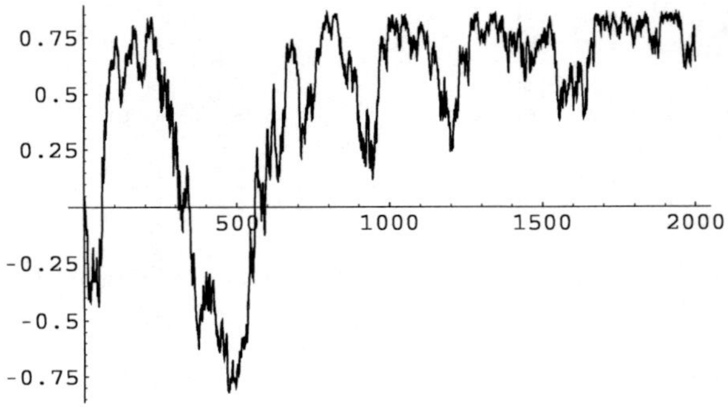

Figure 4.3: Evolution of the Empirical Average without Interaction.

then negative economic fundamentals are neglected. A sudden price overreaction occurs if the external conditions become too negative. Moreover, due to "wrong signals" about the mood of the market, a crash may also occur without any changes in economic fundamentals.

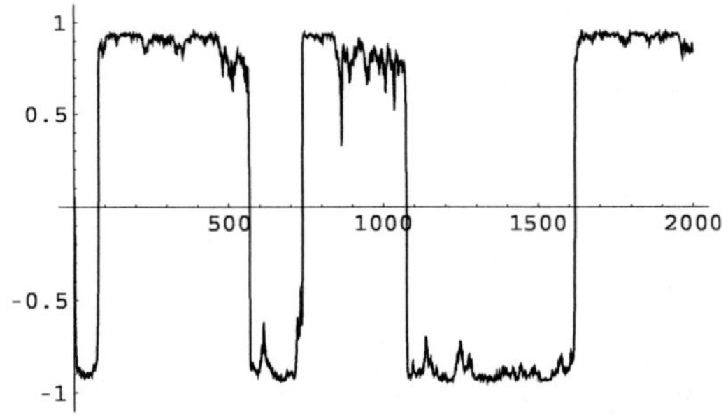

Figure 4.4: Evolution of the Empirical Average; Highly Volatile External Field.

Appendix A

Random Systems with Complete Connections

In this appendix, we summarize the main results about distance-diminishing random systems with complete connections whose associated Markov process takes values in a **compact** metric space. For a detailed discussion of random systems with complete connections, we refer to the books of Iosefescu and Theodorescu (1968), Norman (1972) and Iosefescu and Gregorescu (1993).

Definition A.1 *Let (M_1, d_{M_1}) be a metric space and $(M_2, \mathcal{M}_2)$ be a measurable space. Let Z denote a stochastic kernel from M_1 to $\mathcal{M}_2$ and let $v : M_1 \times M_2 \to M_1$ be a measurable mapping.*

(i) Following Iosefescu and Theodorescu (1968), we call the quadruple

$$\Sigma := ((M_1, d_{M_1}), (M_2, \mathcal{M}_2), Z, v) \tag{A.1}$$

***a homogeneous random system with complete connections** (RSCC).*

(ii) Given an initial value $\xi \in M_1$, a RSCC induces two stochastic processes $\{\xi_t\}_{t=0,1,2,..}$ and $\{\zeta_t\}_{t=0,1,2,...}$ on the canonical probability space $(\Omega, \mathcal{F}, \mathbb{P}_\xi)$ taking values in M_1 and in M_2, respectively, by

$$\xi_{t+1} = v(\xi_t, \zeta_t) \qquad (\xi_0 = \xi \qquad \mathbb{P}_\xi\text{-}a.s.) \tag{A.2}$$

and by

$$\mathbb{P}_\xi(\zeta_t \in \cdot | \xi_t, \zeta_{t-1}, \xi_{t-1}, \zeta_{t-2}, \ldots) = Z(\xi_t; \cdot). \tag{A.3}$$

These processes are called the ***associated Markov process*** *and the* ***signal sequence****, respectively.*

(iii) We call a random system with complete connections a ***distance-diminishing model****, if the transformation v satisfies the* ***contraction property***

$$d_{M_1}(v(\xi,\zeta),v(\hat{\xi},\zeta)) \leq \theta d_{M_1}(\xi,\hat{\xi}) \qquad (\theta < 1) \tag{A.4}$$

uniformly in $\zeta \in M_2$ $(\xi, \hat{\xi} \in M_1)$.

(iv) We call the signal sequence $\{\zeta_t\}_{t\in\mathbb{N}}$ ***uniformly ergodic in the strong sense*** *if, for any $t \in \mathbb{N}$, there exists a measure Z_t^* on $\mathcal{M}_2^{(t)} := \otimes_{i=0}^t \mathcal{M}_2$ such that*

$$\lim_{T\to\infty} \sup_{t,\xi} \|Z_t^T(\xi;\cdot) - Z_t^*(\cdot)\| = 0. \tag{A.5}$$

Here, $Z_t^T(\xi;\cdot) := \mathrm{Law}(\{\zeta_T,\ldots,\zeta_{T+t}\},\mathbb{P}_\xi)$.

The Associated Markov Process

Let us now introduce the class $L(M_1)$ of all real-valued Lipschitz continuous functions f on M_1. We denote by

$$m(f) := \sup_{\xi\neq\hat{\xi}} \frac{|f(\xi) - f(\hat{\xi})|}{d_{M_1}(\xi,\hat{\xi})} \quad \text{and} \quad \|f\|_{Lip} := m(f) + |f|_\infty \tag{A.6}$$

the Lipschitz constant and the Lipschitz norm, respectively, of the function f. Note that $L(M_1)$ is a normed linear space with respect to both the maximum norm $|\cdot|_\infty$ and the Lipschitz norm $\|\cdot\|_{Lip}$.

Definition A.2 *(i) A Markov process $\{\xi_t\}_{t\in\mathbb{N}}$ with state space M_1 and transition operator U is called* ***orderly****, if there exists a bounded linear operator U^* on $L(M_1)$ such that*

$$\lim_{n\to\infty} \left\| \frac{1}{n}\sum_{t=1}^{n} U^n - U^* \right\|_{Lip} = 0. \tag{A.7}$$

Here, U^n denotes the n-fold iteration of the operator U.

(ii) A Markov process $\{\xi_t\}_{t\in\mathbb{N}}$ with transition operator U which takes values in M_1 is called ***aperiodic*** *on $L(M_1)$, if there exists a bounded linear operator U^* on $L(M_1)$ such that*

$$\lim_{n\to\infty} \|U^n - U^*\|_{Lip} = 0. \tag{A.8}$$

*(iii) The Markov process $\{\xi_t\}_{t\in\mathbb{N}}$ is called **regular**, if U is orderly and aperiodic and if, in addition, $U^*(L(M_1))$ is one dimensional.*

In the sequel, we shall assume that (M_1, d_{M_1}) is a compact metric space and impose the following uniform Lipschitz condition on the stochastic kernel Z from M_1 to $\mathcal{M}_2$.

Assumption A.3 *There exists a constant $C > 0$ such that*

$$\sup_{B\in\mathcal{M}_2}\sup_{\xi_1\neq\xi_2}\frac{|Z(\xi_1;B)-Z(\xi_2;B)|}{d_{M_1}(\xi_1,\xi_2)}\leq C<\infty. \tag{A.9}$$

This assumption holds true if, for example, the measures $Z(\xi;\cdot)$ $(\xi \in M_1)$ have a density which is uniformly Lipschitz continuous. More precisely, we have the following result.

Lemma A.4 *Suppose that the measures $Z(\xi;\cdot)$ $(\xi \in M_1)$ have a density $z(\xi,\cdot)$ with respect to some measure ν on $(M_2, \mathcal{M}_2)$ which is uniformly Lipschitz continuous in the first argument, i.e., assume that there exists a constant $C_0 < \infty$ such that*

$$\sup_{\zeta}|z(\xi_1,\zeta)-z(\xi_2,\zeta)|\leq C_0 d_{M_1}(\xi_1,\xi_2).$$

Then the stochastic kernel Z satisfies Assumption A.3 with constant $C = C_0$.

Proof: Obviously, we have, for any $B \in \mathcal{M}_2$, that

$$|Z(\xi_1;B)-Z(\xi_2;B)|\leq\sup_{\zeta}|z(\xi_1,\zeta)-z(\xi_2,\zeta)|\nu(B)\leq C_0 d_{M_1}(\xi_1,\xi_2)\nu(B).$$

This proves our assertion. □

Under Assumption A.3 the Markov chain $\{\xi_t\}_{t\in\mathbb{N}}$ is a compact Markov process in the sense of Definition 3.3.1 in Norman (1972) and, therefore, the process $\{\xi_t\}_{t\in\mathbb{N}}$ is orderly, due to Theorem 3.3.1 in Norman (1972). In this case, the operator U admits the following representation: There exists finitely many functions $g_1, \ldots, g_k$: $M_1 \to \mathbb{R}$ and finitely many probability measures $\mu_1, \ldots, \mu_k$ on M_1 such that

$$U^*f(\xi)=\sum_{i=1}^{k}g_i(\xi)\mu_i(f)\qquad(f\in\mathcal{C}(M_1)); \tag{A.10}$$

cf. Theorems 3.3.2 and 3.4.2 in Norman (1972). The set $\{\mu_1, \mu_2, \ldots, \mu_k\}$ is a basis for the set of all invariant measures for the Markov chain $\{\xi_t\}_{t\in\mathbb{N}}$. In particular, we have the following result.

Proposition A.5 *Under Assumption A.3 the Markov chain $\{\xi_t\}_{t\in\mathbb{N}}$ associated with the random system Σ admits an invariant measure.*

Suppose now that the transition operator U of the Markov chain $\{\xi_t\}_{t\in\mathbb{N}}$ on M_1 associated with a distance-diminishing random system with complete connections is regular. In such a situation, there exists a unique probability measure μ^* on M_1 such that

$$U^* f(\cdot) = \mu^*(f) \qquad (f \in \mathcal{C}(M_1));$$

see (A.10). Let us denote by μ_t^ξ the law of the random variable ξ_t under the measure $\mathbb{P}_\xi$. For any $f \in L(M_1)$ with $\|f\|_{Lip} \leq 1$ and for all $t \in \mathbb{N}$, we have that $U^t f(\xi) = \int f(\eta)\mu_t^\xi(d\eta)$, and so

$$\left| \int f(\eta)(\mu_t^\xi(d\eta) - \mu^*(d\eta)) \right| \leq \|U^t - U^*\|_{Lip} \to 0$$

as $t \to \infty$. Thus, we have shown:

Lemma A.6 *If the operator U of the Markov chain $\{\xi_t\}_{t\in\mathbb{N}}$ is regular, then the process $\{\xi_t\}_{t\in\mathbb{N}}$ converges in law to a unique invariant measure μ^* on M_1.*

In order the ensure convergence in law of the Markov process associated with a distance-diminishing random system with complete connections to a unique equilibrium, we could impose an additional Doeblin-type condition on the kernel Z.

Assumption A.7 *There exists a measure ν on $(M_2, \mathcal{M}_2)$ and a constant $\lambda > 0$ such that*

$$Z(\xi; B) \geq \lambda\nu(B) \qquad (B \in \mathcal{M}_2). \tag{A.11}$$

The following result appears as Theorem 4.1.1 in Norman (1972); see also Barnsley, Demko, Elton, and Geronimo (1988)

Proposition A.8 *Under Assumptions A.3 and A.7, the transition operator U of the Markov process $\{\xi_t\}_{t\in\mathbb{N}}$ associated with a distance-diminishing random system with complete connections is regular. In particular, the sequence $\{\xi_t\}_{t\in\mathbb{N}}$ converges in law to a unique stationary distribution μ^*.*

Due to Theorem 2.1.57 in Iosefescu and Theodorescu (1968), we have the following important estimate.

Proposition A.9 *Suppose that the Markov chain $\{\xi_t\}_{t\in\mathbb{N}}$ associated with the random system Σ is regular and that Assumption A.3 is satisfied. Then there exist constants $L(f) > 0$ and $\alpha < 1$ such that*

$$|U^t f - \mu^*(f)|_\infty \leq L(f)\alpha^t \tag{A.12}$$

for any Lipschitz continuous function $f : M_1 \to \mathbb{R}$. The constant $L(f)$ depends on f only through its Lipschitz constant $m(f)$ and through its global maximum $|f|_\infty$.

The Associated Signal Sequence

Let us now consider the asymptotic behaviour of the signal sequence $\{\zeta_t\}_{t\in\mathbb{N}}$ associated with a distance-diminishing random system with complete connections. The next result follows from Theorems 2.1.65, 2.2.9 and 2.2.12 in Iosefescu and Theodorescu (1968).

Proposition A.10 *Assume that the stochastic kernel Z from M_1 to $\mathcal{M}_2$ satisfies the uniform Lipschitz condition (A.9). Then the following holds true:*

(i) If the Markov chain associated with the random system with complete connections Σ is regular, then the associated signal sequence $\{\zeta_t\}_{t\in\mathbb{N}}$ is uniformly ergodic in the strong sense. The measures Z_l^* $(l \in \mathbb{N})$ take the form

$$Z_l^*(\cdot) = \int_{M_2} Z_l(\xi;\cdot)\mu^*(d\xi).$$

Here, μ^* is the unique stationary measure of the associated Markov process.

(ii) Under the law

$$\mathbb{P}_{\mu^*}(\cdot) := \int \mathbb{P}_\xi(\cdot)\mu^*(d\xi),$$

the signal sequence is stationary and ergodic.

Bibliography

BACHELIER, L. (1900): "Théorie de la Spéculation," *Annales Scientifiques de l'École Normale Supérieur*, 17, 21–86.

BAK, P., K. CHEN, J. SCHEINKMAN, AND M. WOODFORD (1993): "Aggregate fluctuations from independent sectoral shocks: Self-organized criticality in a model of production and inventory dynamics," *Ric. Econ.*, 47 (1), 3–30.

BARNSLEY, M. F., S. G. DEMKO, J. H. ELTON, AND J. S. GERONIMO (1988): "Invariant Measures for Markov Processes Arising from Iterated Function Systems with Place-Dependent Probabilities," *Ann. Inst. Henri Poincare*, 24, 367–394.

BARNSLEY, M. F., AND J. H. ELTON (1988): "A New Class of Markov Processes for Image Encoding," *Adv. Appl. Prob.*, 20, 14–32.

BICK, A. (1987): "On the Consistency of the Black-Scholes Model with a general Equilibrium Framework," *J. Financial Quant. Anal.*, 22, 259–275.

BILLINGSLEY, P. (1968): *Convergence of Probability Measures.* John Wiley & Sons, New York.

BLACK, F. (1986): "Noise," *J. Finance*, XLI, 529–543.

BLACK, F., AND M. SCHOLES (1973): "The Pricing of Options and Corporate Liabilities," *J. Political Economy*, 81, 637–654.

BLUME, L. (1993): "The Statistical Mechanics of Strategic Interaction," *Games and Economic Behaviour*, 5, 387–424.

BOROVKOV, A. A. (1998): *Ergodicity and stability of stochastic processes.* John Wiley & Sons, New York.

BRANDT, A. (1986): "The Stochastic Equation $Y_{n+1} = A_n Y_n + B_n$ with Stationary Coefficients," *Adv. Appl. Probab.*, 18, 211–220.

BRANDT, A., L. FRANKEN, AND B. LISEK (1990): *Stationary Stochastic Models.* John Wiley & Sons, New York.

BROCK, W. A. (1991): "Understanding Macroeconomic Time Series Using Complex SystemTheory," Discussion paper 392, University of Wisconsin-Madison.

BROCK, W. A., AND C. HOMMES (1995): "Rational Routes to Randomness," Discussion paper 9505, SSRI.

DOBRUSHIN, R. L. (1968): "Description of Random Fields by Means of Conditional Probabilities and the Conditions Governing its Regularity," *Theor. Probab. Appl.*, 15, 458–486.

DUDLEY, R. M. (1966): "Convergence of Baire Measures," *Stud. Math.*, 27, 251–268.

DUFFIE, D., AND P. PROTTER (1992): "From Discrete- to Continuous-Time Finance," *Mathematical Finance*, 2, 1–15.

DURLAUF, S. N. (1993): "Nonergodic Economic Growth," *Review of Economic Studies*, 60, 349–366.

ETHIER, S. N., AND T. G. KURTZ (1986): *Markov Processes Characterisation and Convergence.* John Wiley & Sons, New York.

FÖLLMER, H. (1974): "Random Economies with many interacting agents," *Journal of Mathematical Economics*, 1, 51–62.

——— (1979a): "Macroscopic Convergence of Markov Chains on Infinite Product Spaces," in *Colloquium on Random Fields*, pp. 363–371, Esztergom, Ungarn. Math. Soc. Janos Bolyai.

——— (1979b): "Tail Structure of Markov Chains on Infinite Product Spaces," *Z. Wahrscheinlichkeitstheorie Verw. Geb.*, 50, 273–285.

——— (1982): "A Covariance Estimate for Gibbs Measures," *Journal of Functional Analysis*, 46,3, 387–395.

——— (1994): "Stock price fluctuation as a diffusion in a random environment," *Philos. Trans. R. Soc. Lond., Ser. A*, 1684, 471–483.

Föllmer, H., and M. Schweizer (1993): "A Microeconomic Approach to Diffusion Models for Stock Prices," *Mathematical Finance*, 3, 1–23.

Georgii, H. (1989): *Gibbs Measures and Phase Transitions.* Walter de Gruyter, Berlin.

Ioannides, Y. M. (1995): "Evolution of Trading Structures," Discussion paper 9604, SSRI.

Iosefescu, M., and S. Gregorescu (1993): *Dependence With Complete Connections And Its Applications.* Cambridge University Press, Cambridge.

Iosefescu, M., and M. Theodorescu (1968): *Random Processes and Learning.* Springer-Verlag, Berlin.

Jacod, J., and A. Shiryayev (1987): *Limit Theorems for Stochastic Processes.* Springer-Verlag, Berlin.

Kirman, A. (1993): "On Ants, Rationality and Recruitment," *Q. J. Economics*, CVIII, 137–156.

——— (1998): "On the Transitory Nature of Gurus," Working paper, EHESS et Université de Marseille III.

Kreps, D. (1982): *Multipiriod Securities and the efficient allocation of Risk: A Comment on the Black-Schles OptionProcing Model.* In: The economics of uncertainty and information (ed. J.McCall), University of Chicago Press, Chicago.

Lux, T. (1998): "The Socio-Economic Dynamics of Speculative Markets: Interacting Agents, Chaos, and the Fat Tails of Return Distributions," *Journal of Economic Behavior and Organization*, 33, 143–165.

Lux, T., and M. Marchesi (1999): "Scaling and Criticality in a Stochastic Multi-Agent Model of a Financial Market," *Nature*, 370, 498–500.

Norman, F. M. (1972): *Markov Processes and Learning Models.* Academic Press, New York.

SAMUELSON, P. A. (1964): *Rational Theory of Warrant Pricing.* In: The random character of stock market prices (ed. P.H. Cootner), pp. 506-525, MIT Press, Cambrigde, Mass.

SHIRYAEV, A. (1989): *Probability, 2nd edition.* Springer-Verlag, Berlin.

VASSERSTEIN, L. N. (1969): "Markov Processes over Denumerable Product of Spaces Describing large Systems of Automata," *Problemy Peredaci Informacii*, 5, 64–72.

VERVAAT, W. (1979): "On a stochastic difference equation and a representation of non-negative infinitely divisible random variables," *Adv. Appl. Probab.*, 11, 750–783.

Index of Notation

$\mathbb{N} = \{0, 1, 2, \ldots\}$	set of natural numbers
$\mathbb{R}$	set of real numbers
C	finite set of individual states
$\mathbb{A}$	d-dimensional integer lattice; set of agents
$\mathbb{A}_n$	$\mathbb{A} \cap [-n, n]^d$
$\mathcal{A}$	set of all finite subsets of $\mathbb{A}$
$S = C^{\mathbb{A}}$	configuration space
$\mathcal{S}$	Borel σ-field on S
$x = (x^a)_{a \in \mathbb{A}}$	configuration
$S_0 \subset S$	set of configurations which admit the ergodic empirical field $R(x)$; see (1.30)
$R(x)$	empirical field associated with the configuration $x \in S$; see (1.30)
$\varrho(x)$	empirical distribution associated to the configuration $x \in S$; see (1.11)
$\mathcal{M}(C)$	set of probability measures on C
$\mathcal{M}(S)$	set of probability measures on S
$\mathcal{M}_s(S)$	set of stationary probability measures on S
$\mathcal{M}_0(S)$	set of ergodic probability measures on S
$\mathcal{M}(\mathcal{M}_s(S))$	set of probability measures on $\mathcal{M}_s(S)$
$\mathcal{M}(\mathcal{M}_0(S))$	set of probability measures on $\mathcal{M}_0(S)$
d_S	metric on the configuration space S; see (2.1)

d	metric on $\mathcal{M}(S)$; see (2.53)
d_V	Vasserstein distance; see (2.54)
$\lvert \cdot \rvert$	Euclidean distance
$\lVert \cdot \rVert$	total variation norm
$\mathcal{C}(M)$	set of continuous functions on M
$B(M)$	set of bounded measurable functions on M
$\mathcal{L}(S)$	set of local functions on S
$\mathcal{B}(M)$	Borel-σ-field on M
$\Delta(f)$	oscillation of the function f; see (2.11)
$\Delta_a(f)$	oscillation of the function f at site $a \in \mathbb{A}$
$m(f)$	Lipschitz constant of the function f
$\mathbf{1}_B$	indicator function
$\lvert B \rvert$	cardinality of the set B
B^c	complement of the set B
$\mu(f)$	$\int f d\mu$
$\xrightarrow{w}$	weak convergence of probability measures
δ_x	Dirac measure at x
$\mathrm{Law}(X; \mathbb{P})$	law of the random variable X defined on a probability space $(\Omega, \mathcal{F}, \mathbb{P})$